Creaking Door

Alejo Melendez

Creaking Door

© 2017 Alejo Melendez All Rights Reserved
Print ISBN 978-1-941071-77-9
ebook ISBN 978-1-941071-78-6

This book is sold subject to the condition that it shall not, by way of trade or otherwise, be lent, resold, hired out or otherwise circulated without the publisher's prior consent in any form of binding or cover other than that in which it is published and without a similar condition including this condition being imposed on the subsequent purchaser.

This is a work of fiction. Names, characters, businesses, places, events and incidents are either the products of the author's imagination or used in a fictitious manner. Any resemblance to actual persons, living or dead, or actual events, is purely coincidental.

STAIRWAY PRESS—APACHE JUNCTION

Cover Design by Guy D. Corp, www.GrafixCorp.com

STAIRWAY≡PRESS

www.StairwayPress.com
1000 West Apache Trail—Suite 126
Apache Junction, AZ 85120 USA

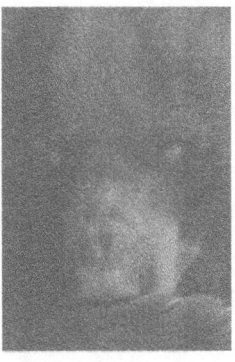

Dedication

To my family, whose nearly unconditional love propped me up when support seemed just a myth.

And, to Ivy, the first in the continuing saga of our next generation.

Special thanks to:

Publisher, Ken Coffman, who ate my homemade chili and heard a vocabulary that made him wonder. I can never repay you.

Editor, Keith Ougden, whose left brain combined with my right hemisphere to make an incomplete brain for our scarecrow, but also a singular knucklehead out of two, thus ridding the world of one more genetic downgrade yet to be passed on.

Seriously, thank you, Eagle Eye, you were my rock in this venture.

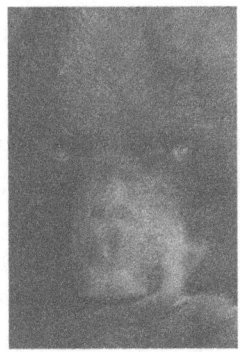

Generally when pronouncing Hawaiian words it is best to sound out no more than two letters at a time. Examples:

Oopu= oh oh poo.

Moiliili= mo ee lee ee lee.

Kaneohe= kah nay oh hay

W's are usually pronounced as V's, there are no R's or long A's

GLOSSARY

For authenticity, some Hawaiian words and slang are included in the text, as follows:

calabash	non-blood related person addressed and treated like family, e.g. adult males as uncles, etc.
camo	short for camouflage
drop	the journey from the top of the wave to the bottom, from crest to trough
five oh	slang for police

goofy footed	surfer whose stance is right foot forward, may also refer to all board riders: snow, skate, etc.
halau	a hula dance troupe in which hula is learned privately and performed publicly.
haole	literal translation meaning "newcomer" that has come to mean any Caucasian since the early 20th century.
hapa haole wahine	hapa: half or partial, haole: Caucasian, wahine: female. Mixed race woman having white blood.
Hawaii nei	nei: Beloved
juice	common slang for energy or power as in electricity
kahuna	tribal medicine man, spiritual advisor, uses both mediums to heal and guide.
kamaaina	aina: the land, kamaaina: One who is of the land, native person, a local.
kanaka	a local, especially of Hawaiian blood
kekoa	warrior
LEO	Law Enforcement Officer
paipo	surfing body board
pakalolo	marijuana. paka: weed, plant; lolo: crazy

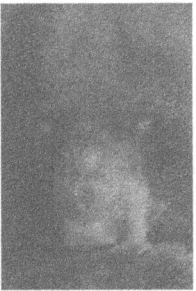

Befall

JIMMY KANOHO, NOTED big-wave rider and a big-game hunter, is shaking violently and as frightened as he has ever been in his entire life. His involuntary tremors make him feel like he is wearing beach clothes in Antarctica. He has just fired his pistol, a Taurus Raging Bull .454 Casull, with an 8.4-inch barrel, a mini cannon. Burning metal and gunpowder scents the damp heavy forest air. Chirps from frightened critters, big and small, eventually return, ring out, and those who are not alerting the others have already hightailed it away from the blast.

The explosion was deafening and the shot managed to peel some bark off of a nearby tree as one of the bullets passed right by his victim. His best friend Mark Tam is dead, a bloody mess atop the acorns, leaves, pine needles, and dirt at the base of a mighty thirty-foot oak and a slightly smaller maple. There are also massive firs and conifers surrounding them. Mark's head is nearly severed from his torso and his entrails are spilled out in grotesque fashion. There is blood everywhere.

Not only is the weapon still in Jimmy's trembling hands, it is still drawn, aiming out into the vast nothingness of this western Alberta forest.

The babbling sounds of a nearby running creek washing its

currents over ancient, smooth river stones can be heard. Chunks of weakened ice break off and flow with it. There is summer moss being scrubbed off the boulders on the banks by the new sheriff in town—the spring snow melt being sent down by the mountain gods on high. The trickle has become something less than a torrent but has enough moxie to let the landscape know who is boss and that the season is turning more or less at her behest.

Every tree shows green-brown shoots sprouting off its tendrils; even the newest, most remote branches are on display. Red Squirrels with great white tufts of ear hair pointing up like devil's horns chase each other across the foliage-speckled loam, dried leaves and twigs crackling underfoot, and the musky smell of thaw and animal emergence is like a powerful but subtle call to arms. It is time for its inhabitants to awaken and reclaim their forest.

Jimmy does not remember using his phone but in seemingly no time at all (within half an hour in real time) he is surrounded by the local authorities. Because of his stupor, they had seemingly descended upon him from out of nowhere.

When Jimmy finally does move he notices his shoe sticks to the hardpan; there is so much blood he can taste the metal. He had not realized how much of Mark's pooled blood had spilled over and congealed onto the area in which he stood and fired the shot.

A member of the Royal Canadian Mounted Police gently takes hold of his arm and guides him toward a police vehicle. The rear door is opened and Jimmy is allowed a seat while being questioned. He has not yet been placed under arrest but at this point Jimmy could care less about legal rights and police procedure; he is deep into a state of shock that will last well into tomorrow. Knowing this, the officers detaining him allow him the time and space needed by asking minimally invasive and basic questions for posterity. Jimmy's emotions are racing and frazzled. His best friend is dead and he was holding the gun. There is certainly guilt, and Jimmy's moral compass is nowhere near true north at this point. The

Creaking Door

tougher questions will come later at a more coherent point in Jimmy's consciousness.

He has fired his weapon, gunpowder residue will be all over his hands, his best friend is not only dead but horribly dismembered, and Jimmy sits in the back of a police vehicle uncuffed and completely ignorant of the troubles that are about to befall him.

Alejo Melendez

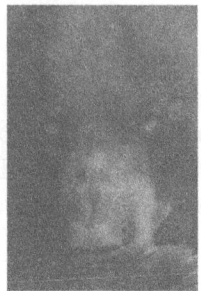

Mystery Woman

THE STURDY OUTDOOR water bottle hangs in its display case in the middle of the third aisle of a busy Honolulu sporting goods store. It is tightly contained in form-fitting, shrink-wrapped plastic and encased in bright black and orange cardboard with even more colorful emblems designed to catch the eye.

The bottle is made of brushed steel. It has a black plastic screw on lid attached via a small chain with fine loops and links like a man's necklace. It is top of the line as far as outdoor gear goes, and it is also priced like it. But it is guaranteed for life and would make any avid outdoorsman happy. And this is precisely the goal of the woman who is about to purchase it.

Her fine delicate fingers take hold of it. She slides it off the small steel rod with its customary open end bent upward to hold the merchandise in place. It is mounted on a peg board along with similar items, but this is the precise unit she wants, the one she knows the gifted individual will appreciate and use.

The other water bottles are made of plastic or cheaper alloys and manufactured in places like Mexico or China, but hers is a steel compound and made in the good old U.S. of A., just outside of steel town, Pittsburgh, to be precise. In television commercials, they show full sized F-10 pickup trucks running over it leaving it

Creaking Door

unscratched and undamaged. How could her ex-lover, an avid hunter and waterman, not cherish it as part of his arsenal?

She takes it to the cashier, a dark-skinned local beach girl of about seventeen, and is careful not to give the overhead security cameras a direct view of her face. The cashier, still in high school, is consumed with her own social situations and pays the woman no mind. The woman is wearing a large-billed fisherman's cap and large sunglasses as an added incognito measure, and she of course pays in cash.

The Muzak is imperceptibly low so as not to be intrusive. She fails to notice the current song, "Killer Queen", on the overhead speakers hidden and mounted flush with the chalky-white speckled drywall ceiling. She would have chuckled at that comically appropriate selection.

The item, singular and easily toted, is not bagged. The woman takes her receipt and the canteen and walks inconspicuously toward the exit, head still down and mindful of the other cameras outdoors. The sporting goods store has two in the parking lot and a nearby intersection has four mounted on each directional traffic light. One of those is facing her.

The smell of saltwater hits and refreshes her nostrils. The locals are immune but her Midwestern nose picks it up every time, even when she is miles from a beach. The sky seems bluer here, a reflection of the thousands of miles of surrounding ocean. The palms sway to the trades in a most clichéd and unassuming manner. She is in love with Hawaii and walks to the bus stop, takes a bench seat next to an elderly woman of Japanese descent, nods her head to be civil, then waits ten minutes until the next bus comes along. They both board the nearly empty bus. The clang of coins from both women can be heard as they each pay their fare. The older lady takes a seat in the front while the other sits in the middle, right next to the rearmost exit doors. She plans on exiting in a few stops to a public park, where she has left her car precisely because there are no video cameras.

Alejo Melendez

She has planned this well. She has taken extra measures to be careful that no one has seen her purchase this non-descript object that any normal person could care less about. But this expensive water bottle will soon be an instrument of death and a key piece of evidence in a murder investigation. Knowing this, she is doing all of these covert things in the most ordinary manner she can execute, and so far her plan to anonymously obtain this soon to be deadly artifact has worked to perfection.

Creaking Door

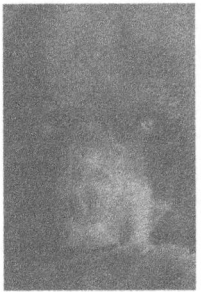

Fifteen Seconds

MARK TAM IS grabbed from behind and taken by absolute surprise. The first thing he notices is the tremendous strength of his as yet unseen attacker. The second is his horrendous foul-smelling breath. He is shaken like a five-ounce rag doll rather than the two-hundred-pound apex predator that he is. He struggles with a previously unknown vigor as he now realizes he is fighting for his very life, but his opponent is far too big and far too strong. He is also vicious.

Time slows, becomes erratic and comes to a virtual standstill really. Random images of his life swirl before him. Twelve seconds left. He sees his grade school teachers chiding him for his rambunctious spirit, the one that made him a successful big-wave rider, and his parents smiling at him as he stands on a makeshift platform when he wins his first surfing competition at the age of twelve, fifty whole dollars from a local AM radio station. It was a lot of money.

At seven seconds, he is the happiest he has ever been as he sees his wife with their only child together for the first time, it had been a difficult labor and when the two emerged healthy and glowing, he'd found the two things missing in his life: a deep, abiding and resounding joy, and something other than his own self to live for.

Alejo Melendez

There is no adrenaline for dulling, and at the five seconds remaining mark he feels the stabbing wounds of teeth and nails slicing through his flesh. Again, the strength of this foe is other-worldly and Mark, a seasoned and well-conditioned specimen himself, finds he is no match for this thug. He begins seeing transgressions, the things in his life he is sorry for, the mistakes, the sins, and the things he knows now he can never take back or correct. There were prostitutes, affairs, his juvenile crimes and the schoolboy beatings of lesser males. He has lied on his business applications in order to obtain his one-man charter fishing company. He has even hit on Kuialoha, Jimmy's mom, who chalked it up as a drunken youth acting the fool, although truthfully she was flattered and angered at the same time.

Four seconds left. For the first time in all of this, the pain exceeds his tremendous threshold for it.

Spurts of red shoot out in all directions, he sees them splat onto nearby tree trunks, and all the while there is that stench of rotting meat and death coming from the ragged grunts and wet exhalations. There are tremendous gashes in his arms, the exposed pink flesh laid bare through his torn sleeves.

Three seconds, he has been turned around and he takes his first direct close-up look at his vicious, unmerciful assailant, another hunter, a magnificent fellow; Mark even looks him squarely in the eye, both reassuring each other that this is God's plan, that this gruesome act is completely natural and that there can be no other way, that, once begun, this was an inescapable fate. This oddly brings Mark a kind of inner peace knowing it is this particular killer rather than a random mugger or thief in some dimly lit urban area.

He is on the Championship golf course at the Awaawa, involved in a big two-on-two money match with Jimmy as his partner. Here there was the joy of loss in self-immersion, the retreat to that safe place when all about you continue to scramble; for footing, for glory, for control, and all the while Mark is

Creaking Door

dreaming of waves, sugar-cane juice, pineapples stolen from the vast fields of Wahiawa, moments with Kelly and Lei, and of Roy Hobbs shattering the stadium lights and rounding the bases amidst a brilliant shower of tumbling sparks.

The reverie was ethereal, a beautiful wisp of perfumed smoke, sticks of incense at attention in a place of reverence. It was like a gentle and persistent mountain stream flowing over smooth ancient stones and happy, lustful, spawning trout, transporting fertilized eggs to their next destinations, the translucent orange orbs speckling the gravelly river bed. The flow was both beautiful in its contrasting fleck and annoyingly disruptful in the way it propagated the always unwelcomed change.

He flowed with it willingly, plunging downhill and inexorably toward Mother Ocean, seeking her body, loving her pull, wanting to join her and become something greater, something deep and blue and infinite. Mark was free to move, to flow, to become one with his clubs and the golf ball. His mind was staggering but unaware. He was gravely injured and wishing no pain, praying to be anesthetized and freed of all agonies, tossed about and bitten at like a kitten-caught mouse, but courageous despite his oblivion, and motivated to meekly fight back with ever diminishing strength.

Whatever propelled him into a last-minute ground hunt was now replaced by an unconscious serenity not unlike his mountain stream flowing toward its fate.

In his final two seconds of life, Mark, ripped to bloody shreds, still has enough life and wherewithal to cry out, whether for help or just plain agony he will never know as the involuntary ear piercing shriek comes so vigorously it could have set the ears of both Angels and Demons on fire.

In that interminable finality he remembers the five-star breakfast he'd been served that morning; he tasted the American-style crispy bacon, the poached salmon and the soft-boiled eggs with rye toast points smeared with rich Wisconsin aerated butter and how easily it spread whereas most other butters needed to be worked onto the bread with several swipes. This was fresh. one-swipe butter, and he appreciated it.

He appreciated, most of all, his friendship with Jimmy Kanoho, and the many adventures they had experienced together, and how he was missing him at this moment, and how, once he realized there was no possible means of escape, he would miss him forever. This unexpected moment of sadness momentarily interrupted the returning wave of panic and terror coursing through him, and a moment later he felt a sharp, stinging vice-like grip exert what had to have been a massive amount of pressure on his fully exposed and vulnerable neck. He saw a final spurt, this one the most energetic, and he lost all muscular control.

The forest is alive, abuzz, small animals sprinting to the next tree or lair. It is chaotic because there are more movements than ever at this year's hunt. They are being led to each destination by God and fear. There is a Pantheon and Mark is ascending it, like jasmine or nightshade he is an evening perfume wafting lazily upward and outward, it catches everyone's attention because it must, it is not a thing one can ignore or turn away from, it is that powerful and commanding unseen force that nature often brings to its most primal acts. The rest of his precious chi is on the moment, his last. It does not worry him. He is lost, his mind wandering amiss on this huge parcel of lush forest vegetation, trekking with indolence, striking at his killer with futile intent, and moving like a man inebriated by his massive loss of blood.

The flash of elapsing time became irrelevant in relation to the pain, which had *almost* (three eternal seconds ago) yielded to the adrenaline, and he actually felt the life flow out of him in his final second. He looked up at the greenish-brown tree canopy mixed with the blue and white radiance of the Canadian sky, and it all seemed so virtuous and pretty as it faded into a blur and eventually into a blackened nothingness, a slow and interminable fifteen second journey into the netherworld, a place of peace initiated with brutality, and a natural violence brought on by a complete absence of malice.

It was fifteen anonymous seconds for its host the forest, fifteen seconds of excruciating helplessness for its victim, and fifteen seconds of glorious, unmitigated, brutality for its perpetrator.

It was pure pain and useless struggle, but in it, he saw his entire life.

The sky shone cool and its high cirrus clouds moved with a deliberate elevated slowness, like feathery tai chi embodiments. The wind whispered its gossamer kisses between the leaves and branches. The forest seemed to sing out its death knell as a processional echoing hymn, the trees seemed to bow in reverence, and the dirt he'd been laid to his final rest upon seemed to weep as the moist spread-pattern of his still warm blood trickled outward in random, mournful fractal splotches.

And then, like a shot, it was over. And almost as if a message from a higher power, none of those fifteen seconds was devoid of pain. He was too busy dying to feel any regret. What seemed a gross unkindness was actually benevolent necessity.

Alejo Melendez

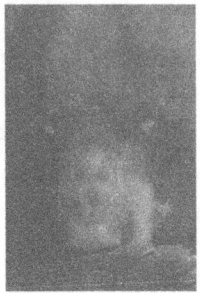

Pauly Boy

HE WAS PERSPIRING heavily as he executed his dry runs. Although it was dusk and he was under a large mango tree, the high humidity and vestigial heat from this hot Hawaiian summer day continued to permeate the air and all things hard and earthen, like the cement walkway nearby, or the cinder block wall that surrounded his property.

And one could not escape the urban trappings of the ubiquitous asphalt. After all, what is modern life without paved roads? But he soldiered on, not because of dedication, the likes of which had faded slowly over the years, but because his physical exam was coming up, and even as lead homicide detective for the Honolulu Police Department, he would be granted no favoritism and would want none. Being a police officer of any rank demanded one be at a better than average level of physical fitness. One's life depended upon it.

So Pauly Boy Magat jumped rope next. He was winded after five grueling minutes, took a break, and continued for another seven. And so it went; he would skip rope for several minutes, take almost equally long breaks, and then resume. He believed, rightly so, that the cumulative effects were worth more than any other callisthenic.

Creaking Door

His knees creaked and groaned as he bent to seat himself on the floor. He had just tucked his toes under a five-foot high, seven-drawer tool chest to do sit-ups when the phone rang.

He hoisted himself up and walked gingerly into the house. The screen door hydraulics had just sighed to a close when he answered. His kitchen was lemon yellow—the walls, the Formica on both the breakfast counter and the island station with a rinse sink. Even the refrigerator was a near perfect lemon yellow match. He leaned on that as he answered the yellow wall-mounted phone with the tangled ten-foot cord.

"Hello, this is Pauly," he spoke as he opened the fridge door and sought out a cooling beverage.

"Pauly Boy," answered the deep baritone of his commanding officer. "It's Captain Kipana. Can you make it down to the Waipahu precinct? We have a bad one, happened about an hour ago. The desk sergeant can fill you in."

"I'm on it cap," came his rapid, no nonsense reply.

His office was fifty miles away in downtown Honolulu but there was a precinct a mile away in his hometown of Waipahu. A lot of the cops there were friends of his from childhood, including the sergeant he was to liaise with, Devon Kamaka.

Weekends in lively Waikiki have a way of breeding trouble. A few of the servicemen on leave, and some let-the-hair-down tourists who behave very differently from the locals, are there to imbibe and let loose. For some Hawaiians there is a deeply felt dislike for these oafish outsiders, and that, combined with alcohol and/or drugs, will often foster the kind of clashes that arise from cultural shock and xenophobia.

And on this night an atypical scenario has sprung forth; an Arab tourist has opened fire on military servicemen in a popular and crowded nightclub; several are dead. The body count is fluid and rising as Pauly and Devon confer on the radio.

Pauly's squad has already been notified. Some are already at the scene. Pauly knows he can delegate and not even show up. His second-in-command is more than qualified to run the crime scene. Suddenly Pauly harkens back a few winters ago.

A big ocean swell had arrived from Japan and was hitting Makaha with major juice. The swell direction was a perfect pure westerly and the winds a soft five miles an hour offshore, just enough to produce elliptical glass chambers on every wave. Blue, the color of proud peacock brilliance, ran deep into the horizon; parabolic swells kept marching onward toward Oahu in perfect synchronization that was not only big, put perfectly rounded and slanted. Every takeoff a breeze, every drop a glide on well-oiled marble floors, and every turn maneuvered with a feathery minimal body shift.

It seemed a mere thought could propel you at the wave's bottom perpendicularly onto its face where a glassy sheen awaited to cascade and shroud you into the eye of its storm. That is what Pauly thought of, what he wanted to do, right now, at this very moment. He was sick of the violence, of the same old bullshit, the hate, the slurs and epithets, the thanklessness, the danger. The crime scene was the next right just off busy Beretania Street. Pauly Boy took a left. The captain might get pissed, but Pauly didn't give a fuck, not at this very moment. It had been building to this crescendo, but he found himself suddenly disgusted at the way his Hawaii nei was transforming into just another American urban tragedy.

He would go to his dojo, a few miles away in Kaimuki. He had trained in Aikido since he was thirteen, and now, at forty-two, was in his twentieth year as a black belt, his seventh as sensei.

The place would be empty of course, but he would lay out a tatami mat and meditate. He was trained to do this when feeling overwhelmed. He found himself getting farther away from this ritual, but it was also like riding a bike. He looked forward to the emptying of his mind and the quiet of his soundproof studio. This regimen also included segmented body stretches to extract stress and unwanted adrenaline from his muscle fibers. He couldn't wait,

Creaking Door

he needed this. Pauly flips on his grill and rear window beacons, lets the siren wail, steps on the gas, then casually weaves through the light traffic on his way to his own special brand of Nirvana. The cold, cruel world and all of its shittiness could wait.

Alejo Melendez

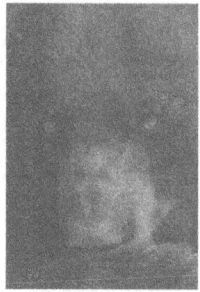

Survivalist

HE TURNS HIS nose up and sniffs. There is something in the wind; food. But he recognizes this odor. It is very similar to his normal diet of wild vegetation and free-range meat, but it is tinged with the taint he has encountered in the past, the taint of those who would do him harm.

He legs it past a tree grove on his massive property, then makes his way to a slight clearing. Here, there are trees, maple, oak, pine, but they are spaced out and not as dense as the section he has emerged from, the section which provides him cover and therefore comfort. He is a hunter, and he is always looking for prey.

Living alone in his domain, it is the only sustainable source of protein. Berries and other plants are plentiful and he can always have his fill of those.

He slows his gait. When the odor becomes stronger he freezes. All he can do is stand stock still and observe; stillness has become his greatest ally and only came with the maturity he obtained about four winters ago. He has seen almost fourteen winters now, and he feels more powerful than ever.

Suddenly, about thirty feet away, he sees his younger sister with a handful of white goop. She is eating hardily and enjoying the ambrosia, *his* ambrosia.

There is yet another movement, one he almost failed to detect because it bears the same colors and patterns of the tree it is next to. This tree trunk-like figure raises up with practiced silence and subtlety.

Big brother takes a few silent steps closer, and now the previously masked smell is unmistakable; it is his enemy. Despite their best efforts to conceal themselves, his senses are far superior, so much so that he can often detect an enemy as of yet unseen. He is the king of his domain and all intruders must be punished, including friends he has known since childhood. The intrusion of friend or foe alike will not be tolerated.

With all the power, might, strength, and speed he can muster he leaps forward and grabs the moving tree trunk. He has it in his clutches and begins savagely attacking it. Blood spews as he carries out his interminable terror. Little sister is startled and without any of his provocation she sprints deep into the woods, dropping her treasured food.

But big brother only slightly notices with relief that she has gone and is safe. He is busy tearing his enemy limb from limb. He is doing what he does best when under duress; he is ruthless.

The meat of his enemy is tough, he tastes nothing. He is enjoying the softer parts at his leisure for a few minutes when he hears a sound. It is another foe, and this one is pointing something at him. He smells the death in his enemy's hand; it is the thing that cracks loud noises and kills. He does not hesitate to turn and run, but it is too late, a stinging, burning sensation is felt in his leg. There were two bursts of thunder but the second one missed.

Injured, more pissed than he has ever felt, he limps off at as full a sprint as he can muster to the safety of the deep cover. He is far bigger and stronger than his enemy but knows he is no match for the weaponry. Discretion is the better part of valor. He will heal and seek out these enemies for the remainder of his natural life. That is a promise and a guarantee bestowed upon him by his almighty Creator. It is murderous, primitive, instinctive, and his birthright.

He does not yet know it but those who will seek him out to kill him will derogatorily nickname him "Limpy."

Creaking Door

Zora's Virgin Sex

NEWLY EIGHTEEN YEARS of age, Zora Vukovich is sweating and panting in the hot, tropical heat and humidity. Her back is sticking to the vinyl bench seat of a late sixties Chevy SS Nova. She is in a great deal of pain but it is tempered by the fact that she is being made love to for the very first time. Her Hawaiian lover, having been told this, is gentle at first, but only selfishly because of his own difficulties.

His penetration is not easy. She is young and has strong muscles from her farm upbringing. Her contractions hinder his progress, and his difficulties are exacerbated by the mild blood flow congealing and becoming adhesive-like as he attempts to glide. She is crying out in mostly pain but she is also taking some pleasure in knowing a man actually desires her, and it is all being drowned out by, strangely enough, an elephant trumpeting, various birds shrieking, and several monkeys howling; probably from the noises of passion disturbing their normally quiet and placid evening and the faint scent of her blood. She and her lover hear none of this and remain thoroughly engaged in their somewhat awkward conjoining.

She is clinging to his sweaty body very tightly and digs her nails involuntarily into his hard back muscles. This pain serves to spur him on and, in time, the going gets easier as she herself becomes more stimulated, acclimated, and moist.

He is a strong boy with a terrific body and even better stamina. For him, it is old hat, and he thrusts away once she is "loosened" up. They are locked in coitus for a good twenty minutes before his climax, and the entire time Zora wants it to both end and never stop. It is a confusing emotion, as is this entirely new experience.

Just before his fateful finish, he pulls out to avoid those annoying unwanted pregnancies and the very messy emotions they impart, but she is still contracting and a few drops of his semen spill inside of her. Nether notices.

He rises up and wipes himself with his T-shirt, then gently wipes himself off of her. They are both smiling and euphoric. She tells him he was fantastic and raises her head to kiss him. He at first moves his head backward, but leans in and lies atop her and reciprocates with a deep, passionate kiss. Zora mistakes it as a loving gesture but he is merely hoping for a second go round.

They rest for a few minutes before Zora complains mildly of the deep throbbing pain in her loins. She asks to be taken home so she can shower and take some aspirin. Spent, he agrees. He himself wishes to wash her now sticky blood off.

He drops her off at her hotel and promises he will call her tomorrow, then heads for the nearby beach, where public outdoor showers are available for both tourists and locals alike. She expectantly pauses a beat before opening the car door; he does not kiss her goodbye.

She walks sullenly into her room. Willa is alone and home early from her date; Kelly has obviously been more successful. Willa looks up from her book and asks Zora how her evening was. Her mouth opens in a gasp as she first sees the strange faraway look in Zora's eyes, then her disheveled appearance, and finally the spots of smudged blood on her thighs peeking beneath her nylon shorts.

Zora practically runs into the bathroom before Willa has a

chance to ask any questions; she has many, but decides discretion is the better part of their friendship right now.

As hot water rains down on her, Zora begins to feel pain in places she didn't know she had places. Her mind is racing. The shower and all its cleansing promises make her feel much better. By the time she is dried off, dons a hotel-furnished Terri cloth robe, and has her wet hair in a twisted towel turban, she exits the bathroom practically chipper. She has also downed three aspirins from their medicine cabinet. Despite the pains, she walks out a refreshed young woman and tells Willa she thinks she is in love.

Even in the dark he can see the reddened water swirl down the grated drain. It is yet another notch on his belt. For Zora this was beyond special. For him, it was sport.

Satisfied, he dries himself off with the damp towel he'd brought and used earlier. The stars twinkle and blink through the softly swaying fronds of the coconut trees. He puts on his slippers and walks back to his car, which is parked nearby.

After he is seated sideways in the driver's seat with his legs sticking out, he removes his slippers and claps them clean of the sand he has tracked onto them. The healthy sound of a tuned Chevy motor soon roars to life, he smiles and makes the long drive home to the other side of the island.

Even though Zora feels the loving warmth of a post-coitus glow, there is something that feels oddly wrong about the whole thing, something she cannot put her finger on just yet. Something about his penis entering her vagina that just felt wrong, like it was all one big mistake. She believes it is buyer's remorse, chalks it up to her lost innocence's hormonal releases, and then goes back to eating the double-decker ham and cheese sandwich she has ordered. She is famished, and Willa has always had the greatest ear to bend in the history of all teenaged girls ever.

She waited to hear from him. The farm boys back home were all either creeps or just downright boring. But this new guy was spectacular. He had a smile that could put the sun out of business and a body that was rock hard, built for adoration, and would make renaissance artists declare it a masterpiece and weep at having witnessed such Godly perfection.

Little did she know the loss of her virginity was but a freak coincidence, the coalescing of her own body's awakening, her sudden need for intimacy, and her vacation-mode loss of inhibition. She was ripe for the taking, and the world was full of charmers who would follow their own anatomical demands to carelessly bed as many girls as possible. Her loins had awakened, his were always ready.

He did not call the next day, nor the next, nor the next. The hurt was imminent. The rage would take years to manifest. When it emerged, it would bloom, expand, and do a world of damage, not the least of which was going to be to Zora Vukovich herself.

Creaking Door

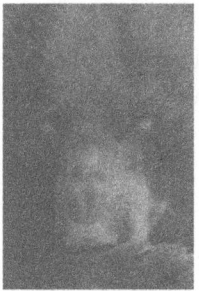

Willa in Hawaii

WILLADEAN JANZEN HAS just met Mister right now. She has had a few cocktails and was dancing at a Waikiki disco with her two besties Zora and Kelly. She has been dancing with a local boy and they have been all over each other. She slides over to Zora, who had been intimate the night before and is also otherwise entangled with her own surfer boy, and tells her she may be leaving soon, without them, and to not worry or wait up.

Willa's dance partner sees her talking to Zora, and he slides his fedora lower and ducks back out of the lighting. For good measure, he turns his back on them and pretends he does not see them talking.

It is dark but for the strobing glitter-ball, and everyone is feeling no pain. They came to Hawaii looking for a good time, three seventeen and eighteen-year-old Nebraska farm girls sprinting into womanhood, hormones ablaze, airline tickets in hand, and now housing the prerequisite loss of inhibitions.

Zora does not get a good look at Willa's consort; Kelly, limber and liquefied at an entirely separate section of the dance club, does not see him at all.

And with that, Willa and Mark Tam make their escape. Mark performs his well-rehearsed routine; a ton of compliments, some well-timed humor and wit, a bite to eat, a torrid make-out session and the inevitable loss of garments in the backseat of his father's car while parked in a local nook that will offer them enough privacy to come to completion.

Mark was brusque and his primary motivation was frequent sexual conquest. His methodology involved a standard routine of deception and charm. Jimmy on the other hand took a more humanitarian approach. He too used charm and humor, but when interested in pursuing intimacy, he would take a genuine interest in getting to know the woman, familiarize himself with her soul and her needs. Not that he intended to fulfill them but as a measure of security; he wanted to know who and what he was dealing with; he had a lot more to lose than Mark Tam. They took decidedly different approaches; Mark wanted as much pussy as he could get. So did Jimmy, but he found the quality of time invested and the frequency of intimate companionship were not mutually exclusive.

Willa, wanting only physical satisfaction, instead receives elation, and her schoolgirl insecurities bubble up to the surface. They cuddle, during which time Mark continuously reassures her he will see her again and take care of her for as long as she needs, for as long as she wants. This comforts her although she was really only out for a fling. But instead Mark never calls her again. It stings a little but is of no great concern to her. It is actually somewhat of a relief. She suffers from the wounded pride but enjoys the otherwise fabulous ocean view from the balcony of the room they are staying in for the next two days.

Creaking Door

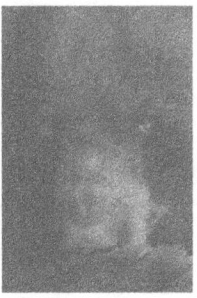

Bully

LITTLE JOHNNY FONSECA is sitting on an unused duck. It is cemented into the ground with a giant flexible spring as its base, the kind that makes the duck wobble for children's enjoyment. There is also a pony, a zebra, a seal, and a beaver.

St. Luke's has a very nice, fully equipped playground. While all the kids run and jump during their first break from class, Johnny sits pensive and enjoying the half apple his mother has wrapped in cellophane. There is also a bag of his favorite cheesy snack chips, which he plans on consuming next. He is hungry from eating less than half of his oatmeal this morning.

A shadow looms from behind and Johnny turns his head to investigate. He is shoved hard from behind and is suddenly on the dirt cowering in fear. Henri Laplatt, big for his age and much larger than Johnny, grabs the bag of chips and laughs. Johnny's lip quivers but Henri's glare tells him to stifle it. Henri opens the chips, tilts the bag up to his mouth and starts munching away. He turns as if nothing has transpired and walks calmly away. It is a manifestation of his sociopathy, born of his abusive, alcoholic father and his weak willed, enabling mother.

For years Henri would continue this pattern, using the anger to make himself into a top-notch football and hockey player. He was never the best stick handler but he was a tremendous goon, an enforcer of unequalled skill who could not be rubbed out and usually was the one left on his skates during on-ice collisions.

When he received a hockey scholarship with his marginal grades, his hockey coach, Pierre Lafont, took him under his wing. Lafont saw him as a very troubled youth and was fearful this bull would contaminate his china shop team with his somewhat uncontrolled emotions.

One day, coach invited Henri to go moose hunting. Henri's own father dared not place a gun in his hand, but Lafont took the chance that the great outdoors would enlighten Henri as to the both gentle and savage ways of the Canadian wilderness. Henri, he felt, did not need taming, he just needed balance. This was also in the interest of keeping his hockey ferocity.

On their first hunt, unknown to the young student, Pierre loaded Henri's rifle with blanks. He instructed Henri to leave his gun un-cocked with the safety on. They spent five hours wandering the woods and just observing. The turning point was when they were able to come within ten yards of a mother moose and her young calf. They'd been sitting quietly in some scrub when the pair wandered into range. Coach's words were gospel to the impressionable Henri, and when coach asked him to freeze, he did so, experiencing a bit of fear at the large, muscular animal. But Henri twitched and the Mother moose saw it. She charged the pair as Henri panicked and fumbled with his useless weapon. As Henri felt the fear of death a loud blast erupted and Henri nearly pissed his camos. The moose buckled down onto its front knees and staggered. Coach put the Henry rifle to its head and fired right between the eyes. It was the first time Henri saw anything die. He felt a wave of nausea sweep through him like snowmelt over the ancient Canadian rivers carved out from subordinating stone, its waters crystalline and pure washing over the rocks smoothened over time. The torrent crumbled the earthen banks, its clods dissolving instantly as they fall into the icy fire, particulate matter

Creaking Door

and granules swirling into muddy, distorted clouds that form and flow and dissipate in one unstoppable motion. Henri feels just like that now, like a singular grain, a speck of dirt, tiny and indistinguishable from all other matter in the universe. He realizes the magnitude of the cosmos at that moment, learns he is part of a greater whole, and that he must find his place in the grand scheme of things, even if it is only to be washed away and transformed. He was a bully so he could feel strong. He now knows there are much stronger things and forces out there that he must make peace with, or perish. Like this comparison, his emotional distress was ancient, needed, and unstoppable. Out in the vastness of the Canadian wilderness, having confronted a being far more muscular and powerful than himself, and having faced his own impugned mortality, he felt something he'd never felt and desperately needed; diminished. The immediate connection with the cosmic life force was planted and realized.

The calf scrambled but soon returned. Coach and Henri waited ten minutes for this, and then coach quietly scooped up the very frightened and confused baby, who refused to leave his mother's side. Coach placed a towel over its eyes and carried it back to the car. They dropped it off at the ranger station. Henri remained in shock for several hours. They were at the station for over an hour filling out paperwork and giving statements. Coach was well known and they were never in any trouble for the unmitigated act of self-defense, but something happened to Henri. He spent whatever free time was given looking at or stroking the calf. It made no sound but trembled continually. Henri's soothing words and gentle touches eventually put the calf at ease.

For the first time in his young thug life Henri exhibited an act of pure kindness and felt genuine remorse. He knew the calf was helpless, just like the smaller kids he had intimidated or beaten up for no good reason. Coach never once said a harsh word and let the moment and the experiences, however unpleasant and traumatic, sink in.

Alejo Melendez

Henri watched and admired the rangers as they exuded calm and authority, basically lording over this most unfortunate situation. Henri decided he wanted this in his life. To protect and serve. But he didn't want to just enforce the woods; he knew the real challenges were in the cities, in the populated areas where people like the boy he used to be continued to wreak havoc on the innocent, just like the innocent trembling calf. Although he never physically saw the calf again, he saw it and its angry mother every day in his mind for the rest of his life. He graduated from Red Deer Community College with honors and instead of pursuing a post-graduate degree, applied to the Edmonton Police Academy instead.

The academy was a place Henri truly felt he belonged. His fellow cadets were mostly all big and burly like him. His personality changed, his rage stifled. He actually became a little nurturing, and he finally knew what it meant to have someone's back. The primary lesson was that if they didn't watch out for each other, they were as good as dead. With that foremost in his mind, and having learned the codes, the regulations, the defense techniques, and the tactical strategies, ten months later Henri graduated to Officer Laplatt.

His size and strength would serve him well in the intervening years, but unbeknownst to his superiors, the raging bully often made an appearance and "willed" his suspects and arrestees into compliance. You could not take the country out of the boy.

He and his superiors endured multiple citizens' complaints of excessive force. Eventually the brass promoted him to detective because he was a *go getter*. He closed out his share of cases and when the commander of his squad retired, he was made lead homicide detective. His superiors had given him the job more to keep him off the beat and away from complainants than on merit alone.

Creaking Door

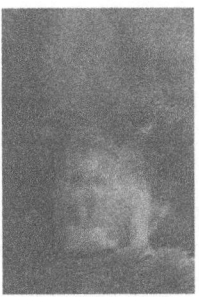

Lovers

HOALOHA AO-SMITH STUCK her head out through the door of her office. She snuck a peek, looked both ways, and made sure the coast was clear. It was high noon and she knew most of her coworkers were out to lunch. She made her way into the women's bathroom bursting with excitement and anticipation. A hunger, a craving that had consumed her all morning was about to be met head on and satiated, as it was every day at about this time when the top floor was empty.

She entered the restroom and stepped toward the large mirror, eight feet long and four feet high, and stared momentarily at her appearance; she looked beautiful, desirable. Every hair in place, lipstick unsmudged, teeth unstained, a spot-on makeup application.

In the mirror's reflection a shadowy figure emerges behind her from one of the stalls. It is her coworker, head researcher, and girl Friday Dawn Novak, basically her chief of staff. Hoaloha has a crew of three to help her with her weekly newspaper column.

They stare at each other for a long three seconds of penetrating silence. Dawn steps toward the bank of wash basins sunken into the tidy gloss black faux marble counter. Her slinky approach makes Hoaloha shudder. Suddenly Hoaloha spins around and grabs Dawn. Their lips lock, their tongues writhe. Hands begin probing, skirts are hiked up.

They have longed for each other since taking separate routes to work this morning. They each have their own offices close to each other but prefer the excitement and voyeuristic thrill of possible exposure. The danger fuels the adrenaline of these midday sessions that, as far as they are aware, no one else knows about. It would be fatally scandalous and ruinous should they ever be caught. But they cannot stop. They cannot keep their hands off each other.

This is how their session starts off; with the tantalizing foolhardy haphazard risk of heavy foreplay in a public place. Dawn takes Hoaloha's hand and pokes her head out the door. When it is safe, she leads Hoaloha into her office and locks the door.

For the next thirty minutes, while their associates eat sushi or plate lunches, they have both transformed back into seven-year-old girls and they have each just received the big box of crayons, the one with sixty-four colors, two tiers, the fold-back box top, and the built-in sharpener in the back. The one every kid wanted. The one every kid would die for. The big rectangular yellow box will not be the only explosion of colors behind Dawn's closed doors today.

Creaking Door

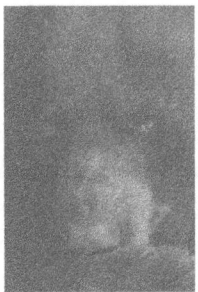

Corduroy

KELLY WAS THE first to arrive. She looked over the scenic landscape from high atop the silo roof ledge she had climbed this morning. It was five stories high but Mount Everest as far as the prairies were concerned. There was still a bit of frost and streaks of splotchy white snow that were strewn about everywhere. It had permeated the fallow fields that stretched out as far as the eye could see. With the sun still low and the snow settling in and favoring the low ridges between the rows, the fields looked like one big, dark-brown striped corduroy swatch being sampled for coverage across the whole of the prairie states.

It was pristine, beautiful, and the reason she had decided to schedule this trek so early in her otherwise busy day. She wanted to reconnect with some of the natural wonder she'd lately become detached from.

The first Müllers had come to Nebraska in 1831, right at the very beginning of Manifest Destiny. Elias Müller had just arrived in New York and used his life's savings to partner up with other German immigrants, purchase several chuck wagons, then head westward out on the dusty trail.

Their wagon train had been attacked by everything from Indians to wild weather and disease. A common cold could be a death sentence in the middle of nowhere. Elias had made it out to an area of large, flat lands with vast oceans of grass and millions of stampeding buffalo.

With his trusty long rifle, he was sure he could make a life here. He would send back for a team of horses, one animal at a time, and work the land.

So he unloaded his belongings and the prairie schooners continued west without him or his bride. He cut huge squares of sod and put together a sturdy enough one-room structure they lived in for over a year. As wagon trains passed through on the trail nearest his homestead, he would barter and trade for goods and services, and ultimately he'd gathered enough logs from the nearest wooded area to construct a cabin less susceptible to inclement weather than his sod home, which continued to stand for fifty more years and was used as a storage unit until a veritable prairie monsoon finally laid it to waste in the winter of 1882.

The Müllers had very deep roots in the prairies, and Kelly yearned to lift her anchor and cast off into the great unknown. Her "known" was farm life in the hot, dry middle of a huge continent. What she really wanted was adventure, maritime adventure, the kind she read about from Melville and Stevenson and Defoe.

She saw this yearning as ephemeral and very much like a fast-moving Boston whaler pursuing angry sperms on the high seas. Because maritime lore was completely absent from her upbringing on the farm, she romanticized such things, and they manifested themselves in her goals and fantasies.

She loved tall ships from centuries past and the varied and storied missions they set sail upon. Such seemingly unreachable visions felt to her like an ambergris-fed fire that burned away at its fuel within a lantern that was not unlike her vanishing youth, and it hung symbolically from a wooden mast and burned bright behind the billowing canvas mainsails of her history, catching the winds of her present and whose gales made unstoppable the prow that sliced hungrily through rolling black aquatic moguls and sailed her inexorably toward the dreams and ambitions of her future. She was frustrated by the limitations of Nebraska. Her powerful seafaring fire was lighting the way across vast eternally deep blue oceans and distant green and fertile tropical archipelagos; it was illuminating her path towards Hawaii, a destination and a place she now saw as possible with the advent of being able to choose a college, the aid of her good grades, and the well-deserved fruit of her academic labors.

Elias Müller had left his tumultuous life by embarking on a large wooden ship not unlike the Mayflower and began his new one content and happy, feeling he was right where he needed to be. Five generations later his female descendant Kelly would also leave her current life, this time out of boredom but also, like Elias, with a thirst for new adventures, by booking passage on board a modern sailing ship, a jumbo jet airliner and, also like her ancestor Elias, she would end up in the place she knew she belonged.

Kelly had been busying herself lately with college entrance preparations, mailing letters, answering questionnaires, studying for her SAT's, and looking over the many campus brochures that had been sent to her. She knew she would leave the farm and be destined for a far different life than that of corn, soy, and livestock. She yearned for the big-city lights, or at least a change of scenery, and Hawaii was about as different from Nebraska as a horse was from a pig, as Timbuktu in July was from Anchorage in January. Little did she know that the country girl inside would never leave her and the rural, gentle ways of Western Oahu would provide a perfect compromise to those teenaged innate longings.

Steam misted out of her pretty little nostrils as the crystalline morning was suddenly interrupted by some familiar voices; it was her best friends Zora and Willadean. She'd been so caught up in her reverie that she failed to hear them ascending the lengthy fifty-foot ladder. Every farm kid grows up scaling silos and these gals were no exception; the danger readily apparent to non-farming outsiders was all but invisible to these young homesteaders. It was second nature to them. Three all-American heartbreakers were congregated on a prairie farm's high point giddy of what lay ahead.

Basketball was a religion in the heartland and Kelly had been named thusly because her father's favorite team was the Kelly-green uniformed Boston Celtics. Willadean had been named after Wilella Sibert Cather, the great Nebraska novelist who detailed frontier life in such glorious eloquence. They were both best known by their nickname Willa. Zora is a female name of Slavic origin. Zora's grandparents had immigrated to America from Croatia over seventy years before. The three young girls were bright, beautiful, and would soon blossom into womanhood. They had agreed to meet here this morning, the day before they would fly off to Hawaii to celebrate their high-school graduation. It would be a memorable trip for all, but exceptionally special, romantic, and literally unforgettable for one of them.

Creaking Door

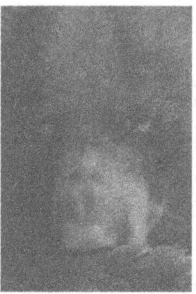

Mark Tam

HE'S ONLY THIRTEEN but has already had his heart broken. The girl he was so in love with, Susan Sonada, was not shy. In fact, she was very gregarious. She spoke easily with him the first time, easing up to him during recess and asking for a bite of his candy bar. With perfectly pink pouty lips and a wondrous look of interest, she thanked him by kissing him on his cheek. She smelled of flower blossoms and chocolate, and this was all it took to make Mark Tam fall in love for the very first time. He was still, sexually, a baby, but the sudden release of hormones had awakened an unstoppable force within, and for the next several weeks he did nothing but think of her. A few nights after the kiss he'd had his nocturnal emission. Young Susan and her burgeoning adolescent breasts had been in the dream, and he woke up even more in love, more confused, and with sticky, moist underwear.

Susan, however, being one of the popular girls, had all but forgotten him. She flowed easily between social circles and cliques, one minute flirting with jocks, the next charming the nerdy boys to do her math homework. She was known to be dating already, and sometimes with the high-school boys.

When Mark could no longer contain his feelings he walked up to Susan in the hallway, where she was congregating with her gang of cool friends next to their lockers, and presented her with a candy bar.

"Hi Susan," he stammered, "I bought this for you." He slowly and awkwardly thrust his arm out with the Snickers gripped with nervous fingers.

She looked at him like he was an alien. "Yuck!" she exclaimed, "why would I want that crap?"

It was said so coldly and with such bile that Mark froze up in terror and surprise. The other girls chuckled. Susan did it to solicit laughter. Rhonda, the not-so-pretty one who acted as their enforcer, snatched the candy bar from his fingers and proclaimed "thanks loser!" all in one fell swoop. She unwrapped it and was about to take a prodigious bite when a two-hundred-page hard cover science textbook slammed into the side of her head.

The Snickers went flying across the speckled white linoleum. Rhonda dropped her books. There was a ringing in her ears. The shock-induced numbness only lasted for a second before the pain came charging like an angry silverback. She'd been hit and was on her knees. Still in shock, she remained shaken and on all fours staring at the ground weaving in and out of focus and at the black-and-white Converse high-top sneakers next to her left hand. She looked up to see Jimmy Kanoho calmly eating an apple and holding Mrs. Ikinaga's fourth period science book.

"You shouldn't eat candy, it's bad for you," he smirked. He then casually kicked at her left arm undoing one of her four support beams. Her face landed with a splat onto the cold linoleum. Jimmy then stared down Susan and told her, "Try fruit, it's better for your looks. And next time you want candy, buy your own, you lowlife bitch."

Rhonda looked up to see Jimmy's and Mark's backs as they calmly walked away. The muffled sounds came into focus as she realized her frenzied friends were yelling and screaming to no one in particular.

One of the girls directed her nasty verbiage at Mark who

calmly turned his head and flipped her the middle finger. He smiled as he did this but did not break stride. In an instant, his anger had turned him from a caring, shy, stammering, and awkward adolescent into an angry, apathetic, and misogynistic sociopath. The beast that would define his treatment and attitude toward women was born.

The love and affection he'd been so consumed with was suddenly gone. He felt cleansed. He did not know it but this was the planting of a seed that would grow within his psyche for the rest of his life. Like a man's orgasm, the passion he had aggressively hungered for was gone the instant the emotional build-up ejaculated from his body. He not only felt sanitized, but cold. He no longer felt a need for that bitch Susan's affections, and he never thought about her again, even though they schooled together for the next five years.

The already strong bond between the two boys was now locked in a screw-tightened iron vice with fully cured barnacle strength epoxy. Through thick or thin, they would henceforth have each other's backs. Mark in particular would never, despite his moral shortcomings, cross the Kanoho family. Jimmy had earned his undying loyalty.

Alejo Melendez

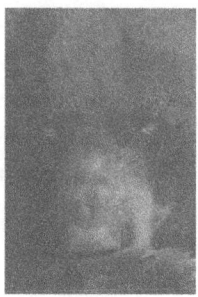

Players

JIMMY KANOHO WOKE up to the smell of homemade pork sausages frying in the kitchen. It was a familiar scent permeating the house and his olfactory senses. When his eyes opened, it was to bright blue-and-white painted walls with a smattering of old surfing posters as scenery. His surfing idols, Gerry Lopez, Larry Bertleman, and Buttons Kaluhiokalani, among other notable Hawaiians, were captured slashing 1970's North Shore waves in four-page wide unfolded Surfer Magazine centerfolds.

There was also a large life-sized poster of Jimi Hendrix on one wall and a few framed autographed photos of famous athletes who'd stayed at his family's hotel, his favorite being of Joe Montana. He intentionally left off celebrity photos thinking most if not all of them were vainglorious blowhards with inflated egos. At least the ones he'd met in person were that way, transparent even with the best efforts to conceal it.

Rather, their photos were kept in the hotel's restaurant, where his mother, who *did* favor such celibridom, could keep an eye on them and show them off to hotel guests who were equally impressed.

He'd slept at his parent's place again after helping around their old wooden beachfront house yesterday. There was a small plywood paipo board made by his father when he was just five mounted high on one of his bedroom walls. It was the first object he had ever ridden a wave with besides his body. He'd put in a hard day as their handyman/carpenter and had slept in his boyhood room again. He always slept well in that room and on that bed. Jimmy awoke completely restored and refreshed.

They lived on the western side of Oahu in the coastal town of Makaha, a small demi-resort town in a lush valley with one of the most famous breaks in the surfing world. During the winter, huge waves descend upon that entire famous Waianae coast, and Makaha Beach, a small scrape smack dab in the middle of that long stretch, gets its fair share of the fabled winter juice.

His dad James Sr. is nearly full-blooded Hawaiian, a rarity these days, and his mom Kuialoha, or Kui, is Hawaiian/Chinese/Filipino American and was born and raised on Oahu, mostly right there in Makaha. Kui's father was an airline executive so she grew up better privileged than most of her friends. James' parents were blue collar and worked hard to put their son through private schools which undoubtedly led to his being a self-made man. The Kanoho family owns the land on the back end of the Makaha Valley, and here James' grandfather constructed the wooden home they live in to this very day. It was the family homestead and those carpentry skills were passed on to all succeeding Kanoho men, James and Jimmy included.

As a typical offspring Jimmy viewed his parents as not that big a deal. But he had been told repeatedly by others both young and old that his parents were still very attractive. His father cuts an impressive muscular, outdoorsy figure, sinewy, square-jawed, and tanned. His mom still looks awesome in a bikini with a nice trim athletic figure, no overt full-figured curves or big fatty breasts, just slim, leggy girl-next-door stunning good looks. But of course to Jimmy they're just Mom and Dad.

The Kanohos owned the Awaawa (every "a" pronounced "ah", like the "o" in otter, ava ava), a beautiful resort hotel set deep in their humble valley. It is far enough from the madding crowds of Honolulu and Waikiki yet still located on Oahu, a critical need for most of their guests. Having access to business-centric Honolulu without requiring airline travel is a huge selling point, although a helipad was constructed a few years ago to combat the horrendous traffic Oahu has since become known for. A helicopter hop still beats an inter-island airplane flight any day of the week.

During his upbringing, he attended a grade school about thirty miles away from their remote coast. For Jimmy and a handful of kids from his parochial school in Aiea it was on to an all boys' private Catholic high school in Kaimuki, a subsection of Honolulu and about sixty miles away from Makaha, further than that if you compare them culturally.

That vaunted high school was set upon a ridge of the Ko'olau Mountains his ancestors called Kalaepohaku. Its large campus was composed of several Spanish missionary style buildings. White multi-storied masonry buildings with red clay-tiled roofs give it a distinct appearance among its modern neighbors. The high school was founded by Marianists in the 1850's, this current campus constructed in the 1920's. It has a long and rich history echoing throughout its halls of academia. During the attack on Pearl Harbor it was converted into a hospital, its faculty and then small student body recruited and transformed into nurses and care givers. The school's faculty included mostly ordained Catholic priests who said Mass and gave last rites when needed. The University of Hawaii, from which Jimmy also graduated with honors, exists in the next valley over, Manoa. He played football for both institutions.

The University, like their hotel, is set back in a recessed, lush, rain-forested valley. One can see rainbows there constantly, certainly daily. The University's team name was the Rainbows, and it had been for decades. It was changed to Rainbow Warriors to accommodate its entry into the national sports theater. It was supposed to sound more fearsome. Truthfully, anything sounded more competitive than the "Rainbows." But they are still lovingly nicknamed the Bows and the locals are fiercely devoted to them. Hawaii, geographically and therefore economically isolated, has never been a prime or even feasible choice for any professional sports franchise. High school and college sports thrive because of that. The "Bows" are it.

Joining Jimmy on this life journey is his very best friend Mark Tam. Mark was considered by many to be misogynous and could often be a cur, but Jimmy loved him like a brother and they *always* had each other's backs. The Kanoho family knew he could be misunderstood, but they all felt he just needed to find the right woman.

Growing up, Mark lived with his parents about a mile from Jimmy in Makaha; they went to the same school until the ninth grade and ended up going to different high schools but both of them ended up playing football for the University. He and Mark had a nice, large circle of friends but those two were thick as thieves, inseparable, and did mostly everything together. Mark is also employed by Jimmy's father and has actually worked at their hotel since he was fifteen, longer than Jimmy who was officially hired after he graduated from high school. As a young adult enrolled in University, Jimmy would need money for incidentals and his father James was not about to just "give" it to him. All grown up now with his own domicile, Mark still lives nearby.

The island of Oahu is comprised of two volcanoes, the Waianae Mountains to the west and the Ko'olau Mountains to the east. Ancient lava flows filled in the space between them to create a connecting plateau. The Makaha Valley is comprised of two vast ridges that connect to and are offshoots of the coastal side of the mighty Waianae Mountain Range. It is therefore not an open-ended valley such as the famous Silicon Valley. The front end, the opening, was decreed state land to be used for public good from the time of British Rule. The back end, the more lush, mountainous, and rain forested section has been Kanoho land since before the time of the last Hawaiian Monarchy, the time of Queen

Liliuokalani. Kanohos have been Alii from time immemorial. Alii were esteemed members of Hawaiian society that were connected to royalty, to the leaders. Alii could be kings, chiefs, nobility and in the case of the Kanoho ancestry, Royal Guards. The British transitioned Hawaii into a model of its own style of monarchy, and elite land owners, most Alii included, were left alone while the imperialist limey douche-bags confiscated everything else to pillage. The family's ancestral land, the Makaha Valley, remote, beautiful and heavily defended by Kanohos and Hawaii's greatest warriors, was thankfully beyond the scope of British exploitation.

Awaawa means valley, and for about a year Jimmy's dad named it Kala Awaawa, which means valley of the sun, but the deep recessed valley they were situated in is more rain forest than outback, and the two mountain ridges that envelope them make for limited exposure to direct sunlight every day. Still, in the tropical heat of the equator and the growing concerns regarding melanoma, their place has developed a solid reputation for service and the benefits of their precise geographic location. The Makaha Valley is nice and cool even on those hot and humid Hawaiian days. A gentle, cooling, mountain mist always seems to flow down from the gods on high to sweetly kiss the valley floor every night. Its coolness sticks around all day while its low-hovering dampness is usually gone by mid-morning.

Before the hotel had even broken ground in the early seventies, friends and investors had disliked his chosen name and pleaded for a more conventional sounding moniker. James, a fiercely proud Hawaiian, resisted. The name was unique, unforgettable, and had actually become fun for the tourists to pronounce. It stuck, and combined with its location, its service, and its amenities, the humble Awaawa became world renowned and sought after by the wide variety of clientele James had targeted from the start.

Three years ago Mark married his college sweetheart Kelly. Theirs was a happy, healthy marriage. She was gainfully employed

Creaking Door

by a chemical research firm on the outskirts of Honolulu, and Mark, who has worked for James Sr. unofficially since before high school, also owns a charter service that offers fishing, diving and surfing excursions. A year after marriage Kelly became pregnant with their daughter Leinaala, or Lei for short. Lei calls both Jimmy and James Sr. uncle, and the Kanohos all fully accept Lei, and of course her parents, as family.

It was nice to get the kind of "refined" exposure the city life imparted upon Jimmy, but he was truly happiest being a country boy living as simple a life as possible. These days, he works for his father, which is of course no surprise, and he spends his free time closely connected to the beach; he surfs when there are waves and he dives when it's flat. He has also been busy building their hotel's website on this newfangled internet and finding other online avenues to get even more people to come and visit them. Their way was to be quiet and discreet. He could draw more attention with the kind of blatant in your face advertising others vainly do, but it is not their way. He and Mark and their families are simple country folk and have the old school belief that the truth will always prevail, meaning they know their product is good and rely on the testimony and kind words of the good, honest people familiar with them.

Jimmy and his father are quite the fisherman both above and beneath the water, and having fresh seafood is never a problem in their household. The waters off their Waianae Coast are bountiful and have been harvested by the same families for millennia. The hotel is stocked with the same fresh seafood bought in bulk by local commercial and individual fishermen. Catch more fish than you need? "Bring it to the Awaawa" is a well-known and well-heeded axiom not just up and down the coast but across the entire island. It ensures the menu is always stocked with fresh product and always appreciated by the hotel's guests.

Jimmy moved out of his parent's house about a year ago but still spends most of his time there. Living independently suits him, but the house he has purchased is more love shack than permanent residence. He is currently only twenty-three and in many ways feels like he's twelve. His mother babied Jimmy much to his chagrin but she also taught Jimmy the rather old fashioned useful household skills delegated to her throughout her life: laundry, cooking, cleaning, etc. He can sew on a button or repair torn fabric as well as remove wine stains from wool blends. His father however, did just the opposite. He continually forced tough assignments upon Jimmy, telling his son repeatedly that real life was far worse and it would be best if he trained early on for those hardships. The elder Kanoho had a favorite saying: "You have to put the steel to the fire before it can become a sword." He was right. He has acquired his mother's sensibilities and his father's resilience, and luckily their good looks.

He majored in computer science and had been recruited by several top Silicon Valley companies. He even flew to San Jose and looked over the various prospects. When one particular startup offered Jimmy oodles of money, he agreed and did some noble research and coding for these people. After three months, Hawaii nei called to him at every waking second. He stove it off for another month but ultimately returned home with a new, grander vision of Hawaii being a technological bridge to Asia. This plan is still developing as he accumulates contacts and information, many gathered from his time in Northern California. Many of his high-tech coworkers dreamed of nothing but settling in Hawaii. This inertia unquestioningly works to his benefit should he ever decide to make use of it.

He'd actually chosen this major based on a television report he saw way back in the late seventies. A noted professor said that in the future the mobile cellular phone would be the controlling device in everyone's personal lives. Jimmy remembers hearing this man say airline and movie theater tickets would be obtained. You would hail a cab or control your house with it. It was so long ago the only thing Jimmy grasped was how cool it was that you could have what could be viewed now as a primitive beeper version of

Creaking Door

Beethoven's fifth when your phone rang (they were not yet called ringtones). The professor was quick to point out the functionality of this. If multiple phones rang in a crowd you would more easily identify your phone. It was all so farfetched but fascinating nonetheless for Jimmy the boy. Now Jimmy the grown man knows there is an app for any such misunderstood concepts.

Alejo Melendez

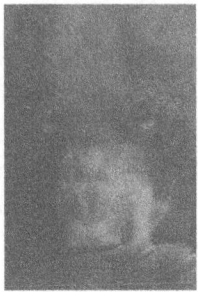

First Hunt

JIMMY AND MARK follow the surf religiously. One winter when they were seventeen they decided to hit up a few spots on Maui. The Kanohos have a sturdy twenty-eight foot fishing boat named after Jimmy's mother but crossing the Molokai Channel is rough at that time of year so they decided to fly. The pair dislike having to check in their fragile surfboards so they have a few "sticks" at Jimmy's uncle's house. Kaimana Kanoho, James' older brother, lives in a town called Kula, about five thousand feet *"up country"*, the local term for Haleakala, the ancient dormant volcano on East Maui that rises a towering 10,023 feet and whose Hawaiian translation is "house of the sun". It is the *kamaaina* or local side of the island. Lahaina is on the other side, the one that accommodates tourists. Between Mark and Jimmy, they have relatives on each island and have surfboards stowed with most of them. This "family" option also gives the boys the added luxury of borrowing boards as well.

During this particular visit to Maui they had something delicious for lunch and Jimmy's uncle mentioned he had recently gone on his first hunt in over a decade. He and Mark were eating the meat he had killed just three days earlier, a male deer. It was different, but it was good. Jimmy was told it was because it was grass fed and not overcooked.

Creaking Door

So Uncle Kaimana said he hunted with a good friend, a seasoned hunter, and asked the boys if they wanted to accompany them on the next hunt. Mark and Jimmy said yes. A few minutes later Jimmy's uncle returned from his phone call and said this hunter friend was going to be indisposed for the next several weeks. His niece was getting married. But he recommended a local outfitter, a family business that had operated for over twenty years and covered all of the islands but were based on Maui. Mark and Jimmy agreed and were actually excited by this prospect.

So they called the gentleman and booked a Maui hunt two days from then. Jimmy's uncle recommended they not surf until after the hunt because tracking wild animals was "grueling". They would also spend that time on gun safety and target practice. Uncle Kaimana had an almost endless backyard being that he lived halfway up the mountain in this rural part of Kula, so firing off ammo would not be a problem. Besides, Uncle needed to shoot the occasional wild pig rutting in his garden. He and Mark laughed but decided to listen to the old coot. So they hung around the next day and watched the foamy white trails along the coasts from high atop this mountain perch. Even from way up here you could tell the surf was pumping. Slow peeling, perfectly arced lines rolling across the azure seascape made them feel regretful. Each of these perfectly arced lines was accompanied by a slow, almost undetectable moving whiteness that was being drawn from left to right in uniform and unbroken segments. These were perfect lefts from a freak swell direction, a once every decade rarity, and because both boys were goofy footed, an unbearable spectacle. It was a dull, throbbing surfer's ache that would soon be replaced by a much greater and grander emotion, one that would invoke greater passions as well.

Jimmy and Mark helped Uncle perform chores around his ancient country house. They mended fences, fixed roof leaks, sealed drafty walls and doors, and cleaned the overgrown parts of the yard. They were starting to feel bamboozled into giving up their surfing safari to become indentured slaves. But they loved this old guy and they did as much as they could. Target practice was fun, the boys were naturals.

The cold beer that night was good, and the food always is. He and Mark ate more of that delicious venison, some fresh fish from the market, vegetables from Kaimana's garden, and of course lots of steamed white rice. One of Jimmy's and Mark's favorite things to do was watch "The Natural", the epic Robert Redford movie, whenever they wanted to pump themselves up; before a big game, big waves, and, now, big hunts. They did so just before dinner. It turns out Uncle Kaimana loved that movie as well.

Exhausted from chores and bellies full from good eats, they retired early because their start time was going to be about 4 am. Despite the excitement of hunter's anticipation, fatigue and beer won out and they slept very well that night.

At 3:30 a.m. they were awoken, had breakfast and lots of good, hot fresh coffee that jolted them awake. Uncle Kaimana drove them the few miles to the outfitter's locale, and there they met, for the first time, Ray Espinoza. He was about fifty, thin but wiry, and possessed of a good firm handshake. Jimmy and Mark spent a few minutes filling out forms, disclaimers and permit applications, which were faxed and almost immediately approved, even at that early hour. The permits office was open early because hunting was also open early. He and Mark watched a safety video that Ray paused a few times to emphasize various points, and then they were on their way.

Hawaii is on the equator, but nine thousand feet up Haleakala and before the sun rises it is freezing cold. Jimmy and Mark were dressed for it and perfectly insulated under their camouflage gear. Ray opened a locked, gated dirt road and drove a few miles in before they parked and exited the vehicle. And then they walked, and walked, and walked some more. He and Mark hiked about six miles going mostly uphill. The clothing and thermals were top notch and breathable so their bodies overheated but were not

Creaking Door

soaked by any kind of perspiration. Using a tiny but powerful flashlight, Ray guided them into a small thicket of bushes, found a miniscule clearing, and promptly sat on the ground. He told the boys to follow suit, and unpacked a few small items, one of which was a small but very powerful pair of binoculars. They were in a natural blind Ray had used many times. It was one of many scattered throughout Haleakala's higher slopes. The sun came up shortly after they were situated, which is precisely the way Ray had timed it. Then they waited. In the interim Mark and Jimmy had cooled off. The morning chill was creeping in and they started to become uncomfortable, but they never said a word. Uncle put in a good word for Ray so they put their complete faith in the man.

After the sun rose, which imparted some warmth and felt good eventually, they still sat around doing nothing but waiting. Jimmy and Mark asked Ray if they could move around to get warm. He promptly vetoed that request. Ray told them the animals were quite possibly aware of them already and they should not give them any further cause for suspicion. He told them they could do pushups if they stayed silent and low to the ground. So they did this several times over the next few hours. Beyond impatient, Jimmy was actually getting angry. But he held his tongue. Looking back, this was Jimmy's first lesson about the most important skill in hunting; not gunmanship, or stealth, or strength or even the conditioning required to hike long distances over rugged terrain, but patience and the ability to sit still for long periods of time.

Jimmy and Mark arrived at their location, that natural hunting blind they currently occupied, at about 6 a.m. It was now 9:30 a.m. and nothing had happened. Even from up here they caught glimpses of the ocean below and the trails of white upon blue that indicated the waves were fantastic. Much to Jimmy's surprise Mark endured this far better than he. Perhaps in gratitude he was being naturally subservient to either Jimmy or Ray or perhaps even both. But for whatever reason Jimmy was amazed at how Mark just sat there and remained alert. This was another first lesson for Jimmy;

that Mark was going to be the ideal hunting partner should they ever attempt this again.

Ray had equipped them with two Remington MODEL 700 CDL SF rifles. Ray had sighted them personally the day before. They sat idle until just after 9:30 am. That's when Ray asked them to carefully check the chambers to make sure they were empty and that there was no ammunition on or in the guns. Ray also told them to pick the rifles up and quietly rub down the stock. He also showed them how to slide the barrel back and forth between their armpits. He and Mark were warming up the equipment, just an extra precaution Ray liked to take. A few minutes later the first deer entered the pasture they had been eyeing. It took a few minutes but another deer entered. Soon there were over a dozen does languishing in the morning light. At about 9:50, the first buck came into view. He was larger than the females and skittish but undoubtedly very protective of his harem. He and Mark watched in anticipation and fascination. Ray told them to keep rubbing down the rifles. He was right; when they first started doing this the rifle's steel and stock were ice cold. He and Mark later asked if this altered its performance and Ray said it was for their comfort; the shock and discomfort of holding a cold rifle can take away from the precision of their focus and aim. "Pit fucking and stock jerking their rifles", the sexually perverted names they gave those maneuvers, became a fixed habit whenever they hunted in cold climes from that point on.

Soon there were five bucks in the area. Ray pointed one out for harvesting. Jimmy would go first, and if another opportunity presented itself that day, Mark would take it. That was more or less lip service; Ray knew there would be no second opportunity. He also knew if the boys bagged a buck, neither would care.

The herd had been up to five hundred yards away but had since moved closer, and the target buck was now about two hundred yards away, hovering on the near edge of that next ridge, but it looked and seemed more like a country mile. It was right on

Creaking Door

the precipice and looked like it was going to venture down into that barranca. It never did and soon turned sideways, presenting a perfect profile to Jimmy. Ray set up a tripod for Jimmy to mount and steady the rifle upon. He got Jimmy into position. Stock backed into Jimmy's right shoulder, eye focused into the scope, Jimmy saw his target through the crosshairs. Ray told Jimmy to take his finger off the trigger. Jimmy complied as he asked in a whisper, "why?"

Ray had already read Jimmy's mind and told him he wasn't ready. Without realizing it he was sort of hyperventilating, so he told Jimmy to focus on relaxing and to breathe. Deep breaths, in and out, steady the nerves; take in some oxygen despite the thin air of this high altitude. He was being shown to NEVER take the shot unless you were one hundred percent ready. Opportunities for a shot are so few and far between that one must never be wasted or taken for granted. And he was right, again. It took about three minutes until Ray thought Jimmy was ready. In the interim the buck had moved a few feet and turned several times while grazing. But now it was in profile again, so Ray told Jimmy to sight the buck again, aim where they had learned from him and the training video, about a foot behind the buck's front shoulder. He told Jimmy to be steady even in the face of the backlash the rifle would produce. He focused. He took his time. He became one with the rifle. It was like being in the tube at Pipeline. All extraneous matters disappeared and suddenly there was just Jimmy timelessly attached to this magnificent creature. He squeezed the trigger. The recoil was tremendous and jolted Jimmy out of his spell.

Because of this powerful kickback he actually never saw the deer go down. The action had shoved Jimmy's eye out of the scope, his head from its forward-facing direction, and his torso back about four inches. With Jimmy's naked eye he could not see the buck through a small cloud of gunpowder smoke, which hung heavy in the cold damp mountain air. He was confused, thinking he had missed and that it had run away. But Mark and Ray were whooping it up and told Jimmy that the buck went down like a sack of bricks; a first timer's lucky kill shot. They needed to wait, they were told by Ray, about thirty minutes to ensure the animal was completely dead but that was also about the length of time needed to hike to their kill and for Jimmy to come back down to earth.

The feeling was indescribable, the rush unlike any he'd ever felt. He was trembling and now fully hyperventilating again. Ray broke out a flask of whiskey in a paper bag. He told Jimmy to take a big swig then told him to breathe into the bag. It helped. Jimmy was a scotch drinker and always disliked whiskey, thinking it vile and unrefined taste-wise, like rubbing alcohol or antiseptic. But Ray's bottle of Jack juice perfumed the air with nothing short of heavenly grace and a perfectly timed opiate induction. It's entry into his taste buds was an explosion of nefarious wheat and rye complexity. It was Papa Hemmingway's magical absinthe, a cleansing medicine on the deep and open wound of his freshly sliced and misplaced hunting virginity. He suckled the whiskey with trembling hands like an abandoned quivering newborn wailing on the firehouse steps swaddled in extra layers on a cold and forever lost morning. Deep liquor store paper bag breaths complete with pulpy woody particulates rasping his taste buds and uvula, tasting like freshly pressed particle board smelled, took fascist control of his once rapid and now dissipating blood flow and pulse rate . The control and tamping down of his blood pressure's revolution would have made Mussolini proud. After a few minutes he regained his semblance of control, but the euphoria and adrenaline was still coursing through his body. Little did he know at the time that it would last for several weeks and in some ways, the rest of his lifetime.

The meadow was on the other side of an impossibly deep barranca. It took them the requisite thirty minutes to traverse the trench's brambles and scrub brush and to skip across the slippery rocks of the brook at the bottom. Once across, it was a sweaty climb up the ridge—it took another twenty minutes to reach the buck. He'd never seen a deer that close. It was scary. He'd set spring–jaw rat traps in a supply cottage they kept on the hotel property. It was separate from the main buildings which are fumigated annually. He would sometimes see very large rats dead in the traps. Even though they were lifeless, it still frightened Jimmy to get near them and to have to dispose of the wretched creatures. The color of the fur, that certain wild shade of gray and white, the black eyes and that long file-like tail were all quite frightening, even to a grown man like himself. But this dead deer was different because of its scale. This deer had the same wild fur, the same black lifeless eyes, and it was huge. One hundred and sixty plus pounds they later estimated.

Jimmy was actually too afraid to touch it. Ray, with Job-like patience, guided and encouraged Jimmy to come and enjoy his handiwork. Ray grabbed the buck's rack and twisted its head into position so Jimmy was forced to face it head on. He looked into the face of that animal and grew even more frightened. It still looked like it could spring up and impale him with its angry and vengeful tines. Eventually, after Mark handled it by its antlers and challenged him, Jimmy relented and let Ray place his hand on its rib area. He stroked it, felt the softness and warmth of its pelt, then rubbed its antlers and felt the coarse, bony ridges and some of its remaining velvet. After what was actually a good long while, Jimmy's reverence remained but the fear and anguish subsided. He grabbed the buck's rack and posed for a classic deer hunter's photo.

The animal was heavy. Ray decided they would process the buck on the spot as part of the ongoing education. Jimmy had skinned and butchered the wild pigs caught near the hotel property before, but that and this were two entirely different things.

When they harvested feral pigs back in Makaha they had animal enclosure traps, large steel cages baited with whatever food their target animal liked. When checked, they would find the captured animal angry and violent, often rushing at them and banging into the black steel bars. Sometimes they were large, sometimes small. Since feral pigs are a nuisance animal they would kill and eat whatever was in the cage, small medium or large, and they only ate them three or four times a year, on special occasions like Christmas, Thanksgiving, birthdays, etc. The traps were always set and they caught about fifteen pigs annually. The other captures were donated to local food banks where they were butchered, sectioned, cooked, and fed or given to less fortunate families throughout the islands.

Once, a cage contained a sow and four of her piglets. The trapped babies had obviously followed her in before she set off the baited spring. She was lying on her side and allowing her young to feed off her swollen conical teats. Two other babies were outside of the bars, crying in fear and hunger. They did not try to run away when the scouting party stumbled upon them, opting instead to remain close to the only thing they knew—their mother's love, protection, and her nourishing milk. A twenty-two Winchester rifle was used at about thirty feet from behind some ten-foot tall sandstone rock croppings. Mother leaped up in protest and anger when the shot was fired but the remaining free piglet stayed put. It was an easy target in that it did not move but a far more difficult one morally. There was something that felt very wrong about shooting a terrified baby so close and yet so far from its mother. The loud panicky squeals of maternal rage were serving to stir up a hornet's nest and confusing the free pig into the uncertainty of fight or flight. The second shot was taken immediately. The moral dilemma was diffused because little pigs grow up to be big gigantic property destroying nuisances, and the boys discovered something their tribal elders had known for quite some time: those little ones are more tender and taste better than the big ones. The four captured babies were kept alive and given to a local friend who owned a piggery down in Ewa Beach, about fifteen miles as the crow flies southeast of Makaha.

Jimmy's father owned a few guns, not many, and one of them was a Mossberg 590 pump-action shotgun. This is what they used to kill the caged pigs. Jimmy and Mark would position a few lassos through the bars, the first being an animal control pole that they placed around its neck, usually from above where the unsuspecting creature had its blind spot. Once this was in place the rest was fairly easy. He and Mark would get it to walk over another lasso on the ground. Once its hind feet were within its circumference they would tighten it up and fully secure the animal. The shotgun was placed either on the back of its head or right between its eyes, depending on the position or the situation afforded them. If they were skilled enough, the shooter would drop the pig like bag of cement off a hungover construction worker's shoulder where it would lay instantly motionless, the beneficiary of an instant and humane killing. Other times the pig would quiver and squeal its haunting and frightening death throes for a minute or two before it was sometimes decided to waste a second bullet on what should have been a single bullet job.

When he was older, fifteen, Dad allowed Jimmy to perform this chore. It was different when Jimmy himself had to pull the trigger and watch the animal die. Regret mixed with adrenaline overcame him, and the memory of that emotion returned with the killing of the deer. But the animal, especially if it was a large boar, needed to be despatched, and you could see in its rage that it was dangerous, so there was also relief at putting it down. Of course, eating it also tended to push those confusing feelings aside.

To accomplish the very difficult task of preparing the animal for consumption, an old industrial sixty-gallon drum filled with water was brought to a rolling boil.

They then placed the entire freshly killed pig into an old junkyard porcelain bathtub. The old bathtub had its drainage hole plugged by an old fashioned heavy duty vulcanized rubber stopper, one that could withstand the high heat. Next the tub was carefully filled with the scalding hot water thereby submersing the animal. Some long two by fours were used to easily scrape the now softened and easily detachable fur. The end result was a pink skinned hairless fleshy pig. And all of it, snout to tail, was edible. It was quite the impressive process.

The entire pig was then either roasted on a spit over keawe, the uniquely flavored Hawaiian wood, or cooked Kalua style, buried in the ground for an entire day with super-hot rocks and banana leaves. And that was the extent of Jimmy's experience killing wild animals. That and of course fishing.

Once in a great while the hog was butchered and partitioned. They used the sectioned meats for the usual uses: legs and shoulders for smoking or curing into hams, loins for oven roasts or the grill, chops for the frying pan, ribs barbecued and slathered with honey teriyaki or some other homemade sauce, belly for bacon, fatback for salt pork, and of course their homemade sausages; cleaned intestines stuffed with the trimmings and pieces too small for anything else. Butchering was tedious; cooking the whole pig meant a party, *and* seemed tastier, so that was the preferred method.

Ray had Jimmy and Mark drag the buck to the nearest sturdy tree, about fifty yards away. It was hard work and the boys had lathered up a good sweat in doing so. The smell of fallen, decaying mountain fruit was pungent and ubiquitous. That same smell wafted down into the Makaha valley from the ridge tops. It was welcome and familiar. Jimmy then realized his kill would taste sweet because of this.

Ray used slim but incredibly strong nylon ropes to fasten each of the animal's hind feet, threw both ends over the strongest low overhanging branch. He hoisted the deer upward to suspend it about a foot off the ground. Ray then spread those hind feet as far apart as they would go before tying it off at the trunk.

Ray then took out a knife no longer than six inches and about as big as one of their restaurant steak knives. The boys watched in amazement as Ray gutted then skinned the animal in less than thirty minutes. One hand wielded the knife, the other hand pulled at the pelt; soon the animal was nothing but naked flesh waiting to be partitioned, not into final, cookable cuts, but rather pieces that would fit and stack efficiently on their backpacks for manual transport down the mountain. It was a special hunting knife with interchangeable blades, and he changed blades every ten minutes or so. The boys had never seen anything like it, or like that knife Ray was using. They used eighteen-inch curved butcher knives and huge cleavers that you could shelter an entire village behind when processing the pigs back home, but Ray's use of a six inch hunting knife to slice flesh, skin fur, and remove organs would have made Christiaan Barnard green with envy.

The butchering took another twenty minutes. They watched Ray expertly navigate the carcass, starting at the bottom, disarticulating joints big and small, severing tendons where needed and sectioning the pieces into manageable chunks that their backpacks could both balance and accommodate. The head, without the antlers and tongue, and the guts, except the heart and liver, were allowed to tumble into a hole situated directly under the carcass. It was dug by Jimmy with a portable folding spade Ray had stowed in his gear. When Ray was done, only the hind ankles, replete with fur, were left hanging on the ropes. These were eventually also placed in the hole. Ray proceeded to use the rest of his cordage to secure three loads wrapped in burlap and divvied up between them upon their backpacks. He left the butchering ropes hanging on the branch.

There was another more important trick of the trade. Sometimes there is a lot of meat to carry. After bundling up the meat onto one's backpack, it is often too heavy to lift and wear. So Ray showed them how to loop some string around the finger loop located atop every backpack, hunting or otherwise, use the same overhanging branch you just used to gut the animal as a kind of block and tackle, and then hoist your pack up onto shoulder height. That kind of leverage makes all the difference. Slipping your arms through the shoulder loops is academic at that point. A very handy trick of the trade they've since used often. There cannot be enough emphasis placed on a great mentor. An as of yet unborn young lady named Leinaala Tam would discover that in the distant future.

Once the loads were secured, he instructed the boys to cover the hole to thoroughly bury the unused parts. He did not want the stench of death spooking the herd for the next couple of days. This task of burial was performed last, he taught them, in case they discovered something else that needed to be covered at the last minute. Each had a thirty-pound load on average. It was very manageable for these tough, strong warriors. The antlers were mounted atop Jimmy's cargo to symbolize it was his kill. Ray even managed to face the antlers away from his head's range of motion lest he poke an eye out. Ray said he had carried loads better than a hundred pounds down many a mountain. The key was packaging your cargo so the weight was distributed evenly and could therefore be balanced, something one could only perfect through trial and error.

The trek down this new ridge was more treacherous and studded with bigger thickets and extensive cat-clawed brambles. The going was slower than Christmas in Libya. They were buoyed by the meat on their backs and the primordial and ancestral dreams of fire and feast ahead. Ray knew these mountains like the back of his hand, and three hours later, having taken a more rugged trail directly down this new ridge, they arrived back at Ray's good old 1973 four-wheel-drive Ford Bronco, an ancient but reliable vehicle. They were parked next to a towering kukui tree, and the guys were thankful for the shade it provided after the long, laborious hike. They unburdened their trophy into the cargo space in the back of the Bronco; all but the antlers was pure edible game meat. After loading the butchered beast Jimmy and Mark naively asked why they hadn't just hiked up to that other ridge and set up for the hunt. Ray smiled and told the boys to get back to work packing up the gear, securing their weapons, and removing their top layer of clothing, which was sweaty, bloody, and dirty and making them overheat as well. There was more water in the

Creaking Door

Bronco and Ray reminded them to hydrate. In all of the excitement they'd forgotten about their need to do so despite not feeling the least bit thirsty.

On the drive back Ray finally explained. Jimmy and Mark would have been not only too close but upwind; the herd would have smelled or sensed them. Because of this the deer never would have entered this meadow or even come close to it. This also would not have been sporting. That open patch was a known feeding area and Ray knew best to set them up far away enough so as to be undetected. The boys offered no arguments. The man was a hunting guru.

In subsequent hunts, he showed them other tasks and tricks. Like how to skin and gut the animal on the ground, and the boys saw it was easier and more efficient to execute Ray's first shown technique; drag the carcass to a tree, string it up by its hind legs spread as far apart as they will go, then gut, skin and butcher it while it hangs. This could all be done, as Ray had shown them, on the ground but was much easier when suspended and allowing gravity to be a big help and do its thing. Of course, Ray showed them this because sometimes there would be no tree.

Another important lesson Ray Espinoza imparted on them was the value of having the very best optics on hand when in the field. Using high powered magnification to scout distant areas is known as glassing, or in the vernacular of them good ole boys "glassin'". Being able to spot prey from far away enough without spooking them is invaluable. This allows the hunter to set a course of complete stealth based on visibility and wind direction. One must always be downwind of the animal and invisible.

They now love both types of hunting; stalking and waiting in a blind. A few years ago, Jimmy spent a pretty penny on a pair of Swarovski EL Range Rangefinding Binoculars. These give you precise distances, like a golfing range finder, but for up to 1500 yards and are accurate to within a yard. It is phenomenal technology.

Alejo Melendez

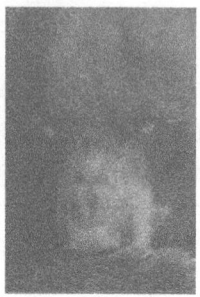

College

THE UNIVERSITY OF Hawaii football team was not very good when Jimmy and Mark were on it. UH Football could not compete with other top programs when it came to the basics, like recruiting, booster support, and hiring top-notch coaches to change the culture and elevate the play and talent. But most of the players, including Jimmy and Mark, had fun despite being perennial losers. Like any footballers, Jimmy and Mark were big men on campus and were invited to all of the good parties and got to "date" all of the prettiest girls.

Jimmy was lean and quick and, at six feet tall, was placed at the wide receiver position. Mark was stocky and quick and placed at the cornerback position. His predatory instincts were evident even back then. Jimmy's evasive skills combined with his speed were enough to land him one of the starting wide-out positions. This complement is also what eventually made them a good team, albeit for different reasons, in sports and in hunting.

Even in college, the two had continued their exciting life of adventure. They were becoming more engrossed in hunting, surfed whenever there were waves and, as two impressive specimens in their sexual and physical prime, enjoyed the occasional jaunt with the ladies.

Creaking Door

They were both considered very handsome. Their lifestyle contributed a great deal to this. Women seemed to gravitate a little more toward Jimmy though; he had inherited his mother's beauty which was then set within his father's masculinity and jaw line. He had James' face offset with Kui's natural good looks and a physique tempered by his coarse interactions with Mother Nature.

Whenever Jimmy and Mark wanted to get laid they'd set out for Waikiki. Lots of tourists, and the mainland gals just seemed more adventurous than the virtuous local wahines. Plus, Jimmy and Mark weren't looking to get married or involved, just a night or two of fun, which these mainlanders were here to do. It was especially beneficial to perform this task at the beach. These pasty white gals and women would ogle at the bronzed, lean beach boys like candy and objects of desire, very much like inanimate objectified surfing machines. It was easy to engage them. And the way Jimmy and Mark saw it, they were helping the Chamber of Commerce by making the visitors feel welcome.

Nor did they age discriminate. Jimmy had on several occasions slept with women at least twice his age. His only requirement was that they fit his superficial profile, slender, small breasted, and sweet smelling. Tellingly, they kind of had to be like his mom. All women smell nice but on a few encounters the women he ended up with seemed to be lacking in feminine hygiene, a malodor that can only be discovered once they had disrobed.

On the beach at Waikiki during Jimmy's freshman year, in a section known as Queen's Surf, he met a beautiful haole wahine who had a fantastic light bronze tan. He complimented her on her skin.

He asked her why she didn't burn like the rest of the tourists. She said her family owns a farm in the Midwest and that she is always out in the sun, working the fields, feeding the animals, and of course, helping with the harvest. She tells him she is the youngest of seven children, six brothers and her, so she had protectors but was here without them but not alone; she and two other friends had barely pooled enough money to treat themselves to a graduation present, this trip to Hawaii. Their parents, who of course were against it, eventually relented and had kicked in the rest of the funding.

Jimmy asked her if she wanted to learn to surf. She said it depended.

"On what?" he asked

"On the cost of the lessons."

He told her it was free and was part of what Jimmy and all Hawaiians called the Aloha Spirit. He also asked if she would agree to have dinner with him that evening in an exchange of interstate good will. She did not answer right away but was smiling. It was 3 p.m. and not so hot anymore. The sun was edging toward the horizon and the indirect rays revealed a few freckles that, for some reason, he found irresistible. She wore a dorky woven hat made of coconut fronds, the kind street vendors hawk all day for quadruple of what they are really worth, like the beer-bellied guy twenty feet away and clamoring like Paul Revere. Jimmy thinks he might have gone to school with that guy's younger brother.

Normally, Jimmy and most locals don't fancy any of that pale, mainland haole stuff; red or blonde hair, green eyes, freckles, skin so white it actually hurt your eyes to stare at it. But he could see she had a beautiful soul, decent soft looking skin, and a killer farm girl body. And she was *very* pretty.

"I assure you, you're going to be starving by the time we're done surfing."

She looked at him semi suspiciously for just the briefest of seconds, then put out her hand and said, "well kanaka, don't just stand there, help me up!"

Jimmy's charm and affability were nuclear armaments, but his thousand-watt smile and sculpted auburn body had leveled her defenses and won out again.

Her use of that word impressed and surprised him. He liked

this gal. She had moxie.

The Waikiki waves were perfect, especially on *that* day; small and gentle with just enough kick to move a surfboard. He showed her how to position herself to catch an oncoming wave, paddle beforehand to gain momentum as it arrived, then let the wave's natural power lift her surfboard and take her for a ride.

She never quite got the hang of it and ended up belly boarding most of her attempts. She came close a few times but the transfer to a standing position was what got her; she always lost her balance or her footing and fell. She was starting to anger. This told him she was competitive, a good thing. More of that moxie. He found it entirely very sexy.

Dinner was just across the street on Kalakaua Avenue at a nice Japanese restaurant in the International Market Place. She'd never eaten any kind of foreign or exotic food so he ordered her the beef teriyaki with rice, simple but he knew she must've eaten beef a million times on the farm. She genuinely loved it and cleaned her plate. She and Jimmy split a second plate, this time chicken katsu; she loved that as well and actually ate most of it, which he was glad to give up. She laughed at how hungry she was and said she thought he was full of it when he told her she would be starving after the lessons.

But it is something Jimmy and most Hawaiians have known all of their lives. There is something sneaky about swimming in the ocean. Like having pleasurable pain-free rough sex then being surprisingly sore the next morning. There is a level of hunger that only the sea bestows, and it always comes on with a delayed but mighty roar. Once the pangs hit, you feel the need to fill that empty stomach with urgency. It is the same stomach you did not realize was empty until the pangs hit. Only the ocean and her ubiquitous salty currents and ceaseless rocking motions can do this. A swimming pool never can. It's just not the same force of nature, and it only comes from her most bountiful resource: seawater and her ceaseless unending motion. The earth's rotation insures this eternal propagation. Ocean-based hunger is therefore time and tide, a guaranteed cause and effect.

    The evening went well. The rising moon laid its silvery path across the darkened waters of Waikiki. She and Jimmy went for a walk after dinner and somewhere near the Royal Hawaiian Hotel, they kissed, the legendary pink masonry behind them creating a picture-perfect backdrop. What started out as a slow, delicate light brushing of lips quickly turned into a deep, passionate longing, and emphatically driven tongue wrestling match. They'd been attracted to each other from the get go. All of the waiting and anticipation seemed to be for this singular moment; the time when his body would introduce itself to hers in an intimate way. As is with most lovers to be, it is with some hand holding, which softened their inhibitions for intimacy. And their first kiss was electrifying.

    He asked where she was staying; it was some generic poor man's Hilton, like a Holiday Inn, six blocks away. Her roommates would all be there. A room on the main strip would cost a touristy ransom, so Jimmy walked her two blocks east and found a motel, not quite a fleabag but good enough for this urgency, this emergency call. This was the backside of Waikiki, the part not meant for vacationing families or upscale leisure travelers. The nitty gritty behind the flashy curtain draping the main boulevard. If Waikiki was the beautiful Persian rug, then this was the veritable dirt swept under it. To get an affordable room, Jimmy had to get away from the bright lights and go "off Broadway."

    Registering seemed to take an eternity but once inside, she and Jimmy attacked each other, they were young, in their prime, tanks full from good touristy Japanese food, so the conditions were right and the episode proved memorable. To this day it was probably still the best sex he'd ever had.

    She had three days left on her vacation. She and her gal pals spent the days on preplanned, prepaid sightseeing ventures, but her nights belonged to Jimmy. They agreed not to fall in love and just enjoy the time together. She even introduced him to her friends so they would not worry about her nocturnal activities. Her two traveling companions were told never to call her by her real name in front of this new, albeit passing, flame. They instantly liked "Daniel" and approved of him once they gauged that he posed no threat. He was a well-heeled polite Hawaiian country boy with a private school education. They gasped when they first met him; they had never seen so beautiful a male specimen. Muscles toned and hardened by an outdoor adventurous life, face chiseled from superior genes, and skin baked to a lustrous bronze by the Hawaiian sun; he was a big league hotty who approached story book mythology. Although he used a pseudonym, she herself never once mentioned her own name. "Daniel" inquired once and, rebuked, never asked for it again.

She and Jimmy spent every night rutting like wild animals. Every morning was then spent enduring that sweet sorrowful parting. He would drop her off at the front of her hotel. They agreed they would never kiss each other goodbye at these morning drop offs. They did not want to foster deeper affections, she and Jimmy knew this party would be over soon and neither wanted any kind of heartache. Besides, the way they went at it on the drop of a hat, a single kiss was all it took for them to make a U turn and have at it again, and they both had things to do during the day. Make their respective hay while the sun shines. He had classes to attend; she had friends to vacation with.

On her last night she and Jimmy had a simple dinner, some Portuguese and Filipino food, in the same establishment no less, then retired to their quarters. The elephant in the room was that she and Jimmy were obviously becoming attached but neither dared speak a word of it. They knew there would be pain should they break this protective shield of silence and nondisclosure. He asked her what time she was leaving. They both knew he would not be seeing her off. Anyway, it would be right in the middle of Jimmy's British Lit class, a subject he struggled with and he could not afford to miss any further lectures. They intentionally did not give each other their names. This was initially a sore spot for him when he first tried to ask her. She said, with very little provocation, that she'd prefer not to give it for fear of attachment among other considerations. He could not understand this logic but acquiesced when she told him she would discontinue this torrid affair should he ever persist. She also told him she knew his name was not really "Daniel."

"Daniel's too dorky a name for a guy like you. Plus you stammered just before you gave it. You gotta learn to lie better, but I'm glad you're a terrible liar Daniel."

So he stopped asking and just enjoyed the remaining phenomenal sex they were having. She and Jimmy just used pet names like Hon or Babe. He sometimes called her whitey or haole girl, and she sometimes called him Kahuna or kanaka. He didn't bother to correct her. That term is misused in the mainland surfing community. The Kahuna was actually a sacred spiritual medicine man, a valued member of the tribe and community in ancient times. And it pisses Hawaiians off royally that it gets abused in those campy surfing B movies.

The day of departure arrived. She left that afternoon. He knew he would never forget her. But he was a man, and it was in Jimmy's nature to sow many wild oats, so women would come and women would go, and he knew that with each passing encounter she would fade into memory. Fade but not forgotten.

The next two years were uneventful. He and Mark surfed, hunted, studied, practiced, and played. Jimmy and Mark even played the vaunted University of Southern California one year which featured the future Heisman Trophy winner at the legendary USC tailback position. Their defense could not stop him and, despite a heartfelt and earnest effort, the University of Hawaii was crushed 52-3.

Jimmy had put on fifteen pounds of solid muscle going into his junior year. He was a full-time starter now. But junior year was going to be unforgettable in other ways as well.

Creaking Door

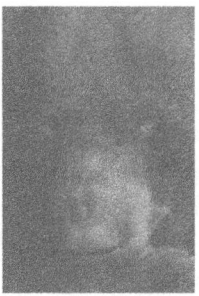

Junior Year

DURING THEIR JUNIOR year at the University of Hawaii, Mark and Jimmy both grew busy for various reasons and only saw each other at practice and at games now. Mark had obtained his own car so they no longer carpooled. Plus they each had a different class load so driving into town together became impractical. Mark had been acting differently as of late, strangely like a man being detoured by another priority, like a person with distractions and focus issues, like a man in love. Sure enough, a few weeks later while surfing at a local break, when Jimmy pressed Mark he revealed he had met a gal and that he was crazy about her. They had two classes together and spent most evenings studying together.

Mark and Jimmy had always fooled around together, sometimes trading spots as wing men during female pick up excursions. Jimmy always thought he and Mark were alike on this matter, birds of a feather, the eternal Playboys, so this new flame must have been special, or Mark was just ready to fall in love, or a combination of the two.

Jimmy asked when he would get to meet this new love. Mark said soon, and that he was in no rush to initiate her into their laid back Makaha Valley life. The University of Hawaii, like all big colleges, has a huge campus and a gazillion buildings, tons of dormitories, and the usual rows of Frat and sorority houses. Try as he might Jimmy could never spy a look at the happy couple. Besides, Jimmy was too busy trying to further his education while starting for the football team.

They'd just returned from surfing at a beach a few miles down the road in Maile. Tumble Land was a beach that had no sand other than the shoreline, with nearly perfect tubes due to a large flat reef located along its entire bottom. For this reason, many avoid it. The locals however know how to navigate it but are not entirely immune to its trappings. Mark took a scrape on his left elbow. Jimmy's father is known for many Hawaiian skills and was considered to be the local modern day Kahuna, or healer.

The cut was fairly deep, about a quarter inch, but only about three inches long. Jimmy's dad clipped some herbs and plants from his backyard, made a poultice, applied it to Mark's cut, then wrapped it in a ti leaf and gave him a shot of scotch and a beer. Jimmy joined them. The shot and the beer turned into a bottle of twelve-year-old, two cases of imported, and a full on barbecue for what Hawaiians like to call pupus, or appetizers that are not the full meal but usually plentiful enough to be so. They became a little tipsy as the evening drew on and both Jimmy's mother and father asked Mark about his new girlfriend. Mark shot Jimmy a look, part disappointment, part surprise.

"Relax," said Jimmy's father, "we also noticed you been acting different brahddah."

"Why no bring 'um ovah fo dinnah dis weekend?" chimed in mom.

He relented and agreed. They were family. They were happy for him and wanted to finally meet her.

She would meet his parents Alex and Esther Tam first, and then drive over for dinner later that evening. That was the plan. It was all scheduled for Sunday, three days from now. Mark, like Jimmy, was an only child. To each other, they were the brother neither one had.

Creaking Door

On Sunday, the big day, the Kanohos spent a good amount of time preparing multiple courses, keeping in mind this young woman was a haole from the heartland. They prepared some traditional Hawaiian foods and of course expected her to politely decline most of them. Having owned the hotel for years now they knew how to be demure about such epicurean matters.

As the orangey-red sun was setting in the distant horizon, submersing itself into the darkening azure waters, Mr. Tam's familiar faded blue, four door Chevy Nova SS pulled into the yard, parked on one of the rutted paths created by other vehicles over the years, and four people exited at about the same time. Jimmy was in the front yard with dad grilling some more of those homemade pork sausages and drinking a beer. His jaw dropped. Jimmy instantly recognized Mark's companion as the farm girl he'd had a tryst with during his freshman year. HIS farm girl. She recognized Jimmy as well and also did a double take. They quickly regained their respective composures. It didn't need to be verbalized; they would act like complete strangers tonight. This just may prove to be the most interesting evening of both of their young lives.

The menu that evening was very Hawaiian. They were served lomi lomi salmon, a kind of Hawaiian ceviche made with ocean going salmon, onion, and tomatoes with of course, a little Hawaiian rock salt which was sprinkled in pretty much everything. The Kanoho's also served lau lau, fatty pork with fatty fish encased in taro leaves and steamed in a ti leaf wrap until the contents melt in your mouth.

They also had steaks to grill and were merely waiting to ask Mark's new girl how she liked hers done. She asked to see the steaks, used her bare hand to pick one up, looked it over, squeezed it between her thumb and index finger, then gave her answer: Rare. This gave the Kanohos a measure of relief about serving poki, a Hawaiian raw fish salad. So Jimmy threw on some extra Keawe and briquettes on the fire, James broke out a huge homemade woven rattan hand fan made just for this purpose, it had a loop for a handle and was shaped like a an overgrown bloated albino spade that had escaped from the middle of an ace card in a Vegas dealer's blackjack deck. It was a Hawaiian style country bellow.

James Sr. then began fanning the flames until the grill and the fire must have unofficially been over five hundred degrees. The glowering angry coals were spread out, embers flew as the delicate, fire softened wood protested with a miniature fireworks display, ejecting fireflies that rose and extinguished as quickly as they had been cast aloft. Jimmy used a big stick to hoist the grill up and out of the way while his dad grabbed a plastic gallon jug that had been cut in half and contained some kind of soft, fleshy, white chunks. It was beef tallow and a little pork fat. James Sr. began tossing the fat and tallow right onto the coals and the fire erupted into a supernova. Jimmy lay the grill back down. They then threw the steaks indelicately onto the sturdy scorching iron grate, a kind of masculine expert mastery of un-finessed meat handling; it was all reminiscent of steer wrestling, a bit symbolic that, in honor of their guest, most of the steaks would be eaten with their insides still a little bloody (Kui and Esther liked theirs medium-well). The steaks were then immediately engulfed in primordial flame, a perfect three-minute char on each side and they were done; the steaks were a perfect rare. The temperature had to be just right to cook it like that, and the Kanohos use of tallow, briquettes, and Keawe were so spot on it should have been filmed for an anthropology documentary, so hypnotic was their process that it was an elevated, ethereal quality of Zen that would have made Siddhartha's journey *and* conversion more delicious *and* sinful.

Jimmy finally learned not only her name but a lot of her personal data as well. On this night a lot of long-forgotten blanks were filled.

Kelly was a Nebraska gal of all things, who was seven eighths German and a one eighth Cherokee. She was a farm girl who attended a junior college for two years near Omaha and traded threshers and vast prairie oceans of crops for lush rain-forested valleys and the deep blue waters of Hawaii.

Kelly ate the poi. She was officially indoctrinated.

Before attending school here on a chemistry scholarship, her parents were tragically killed about ten years ago in a needless car accident on a rural country road.

Alejo Melendez

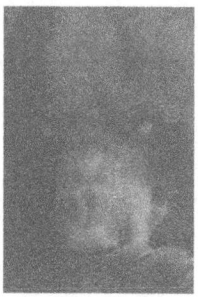

Jugs

ON THAT FATEFUL day, the sun rose hot and the corn and soy fields were already blistering by mid-morning. The stalks shimmered and waved with the prairie sirocco and the imprisoned silk hostages peered out through their husks seeking out the sear in hopes of growth to freedom and the wilting and weakening of their fibrous captors.

    The Stinson Farm was twenty-two miles away from Halsey and the Herzog spread. They housed a rudimentary still in the back of their largest red barn. Zeb and Orin Stinson had just opened the vat containing the current batch of liquefied corn mash. The sugar and yeast they had added yesterday was doing its job perfectly. The fermentation was right where it needed to be. Like all competent and knowledgeable manufacturers of a time-sensitive product, the process is staggered so that the product at various stages is ready as needed. They would add barley and let that batch ferment for about a week. Much of it depended on temperature and the stubbornness of the mash; some corn would be more sugary than, say, last year's crop, some summers hotter than others, etc.

    Large thermometers helped them keep the propane flame constant. They knew many unique tricks of the white-lightning trade as passed on from generations of Stinson moonshiners.

Creaking Door

Gypsum and iodine were sometimes added in small measured quantities depending on the sugar levels. Their copper still's tubing dripped finished product into one-gallon empty plastic milk jugs, which would be sold to the regulars who were ceaselessly on a budget. The shine was transferred into glass for the higher end clientele.

The boys were nostalgic and liked to drink from their grand-daddy's ancient civil war era little brown jug via their pinky finger looped off the shoulder. It was no small feat considering that a full three-gallon jug weighed twelve pounds, five when empty. They'd learned from their pappy to master the leverage. It was a thick ceramic made of red clay from the banks of the Mississippi and fired in an oak-and-ash-fed brick kiln at a scorching three thousand degrees. The brown glaze was made from a dark silt scraped off the bottom of a Louisiana swamp. Legend had it that alligator shit gave it its unique glossy and lustrous quality.

By 2 p.m. the Stinson boys were plowed. They'd grown famished from the hard work in the corn fields and in the moonshine barn. They decided to get a bite at the Janzen Diner a few miles away just off the highway. The food was good but the Janzen's daughter Willa was a real beaut. She alone was worth the trip. She was only nine but they were depraved enough to already have sick fantasies about her.

The boys, with their constant grungy unkempt appearance stood no chance with the young Willa, but seeing her was always a lightening experience. The Janzens were quite used to serving people of that ilk, farmers who'd been in the fields all day, sweaty and grimy from good old-fashioned farm work, bits of straw poking out here and there, and who'd come in looking to refuel and spend time with families their parents and grandparents had known. But there was an uncouth and almost hazardous quality to the Stinsons, something a little scary about the way they would sit and stew while in the diner. Everyone knew they were mashers. Every town, every county had them. Willa was not afraid to serve them but she never offered anything but a blunt smile of professional courtesy. There were other boys who'd come to eat; equally sweaty, sun baked, hardened, muscular, and fresh from the fields. She would offer them different smiles and even flirt. Those boys were never drunk, attended church every Sunday, and had smiles free of tobacco abuse. Good looking people get better service and are always treated differently.

Appetites at the ready, the Stinson Boys climbed into their Chevy pickup and headed south toward Janzen's.

The Herzogs had finished their simple grocery shopping that day—some sugar, salt, a sack of flour, a new roasting pan, and a few canned goods; for Kelly and Ken, some hard candy scooped with a stainless-steel ladle from a tilted glass bin into a paper bag and weighed on a good old-fashioned Toledo hanging scale. They knew the older boys would steal a few pieces so they bought an extra pound or two, like they always did.

The little country general store was ancient, made of wood, and had been owned by the Janzen family for three generations and was located next to their Diner, which was not so ancient and erected where it was so the family could manage both businesses in close proximity. The Herzogs were going to stop into the diner to get some coffee and say hi but Mrs. Herzog reminded her husband she had yet another roast in the oven. So they skipped the banalities and got back on the highway and headed north towards their farm.

A drunk driver and his forlorn passenger had hit Mr. and Mrs. Herzog head on; all occupants were killed. It was later revealed that the responsible party was the Stinson boys, drunk as skunks with blood alcohol levels at a whopping .3, more than triple the legal limit. No one can say why they crashed on this particular day. By all accounts, .3 was normal for the boys. Kelly's brothers were bequeathed the farm and took over all operations immediately thereafter.

All of the things on the Kanoho menu that evening were Hawaiian delicacies; they were simply awaiting her reaction to most of them. They wanted her to be comfortable and this was also a barometer of how she would adjust and fit in to Hawaiian life. There was almost no question Mark was going to marry this girl and would never follow her and settle on the mainland if it came to that. They didn't know it at the time but Kelly had no intention of going back to the farm.

The evening went well. Jimmy and Kelly continued to avoid eye contact without being obvious. It was uncomfortable but not unmanageable. Dinner was served on a beautiful large table made from koa. It was unstained and varnished a golden amber. There seemed to be no knots, no imperfections. It had been handcrafted by James' father Kalani, who was a construction worker by trade but a carpenter by training. He'd helped erect many of the high rises that seemed to sprout overnight back in the early days just before Statehood. When local lumberjacks were clearing out a heavily wooded area north of Honolulu there were many choice cuts to choose from. To the developer it was just a pile of wood that needed to be disposed of. Many Hawaiians grabbed up the bigger pieces and put their ancestral resource to good Hawaiian use. The most ambitious object to come from that scrapheap was a twenty-five foot outrigger canoe that was used as actual transportation up and down the coast. It was also enrolled as a racing vessel in the popular paddling competitions that are still held today. Alas, like its smaller brother the surfboard, other lighter materials such as foam and fiberglass have rendered the mighty koa obsolete as water craft. But as a sturdy wood, it rivals the mighty oak and accouterments made from it are durable and timeless.

Despite the Kanohos' apparent wealth, the chairs, oddly enough, are a mish mash of thrift store and garage sale holdovers. The wooden ones are sturdy and inconspicuously refurbished. Their guests used these. The plastic lawn chairs in different colors were being used by the Kanohos. No one seems to notice or care, it's a country thing, and everyone at the table most certainly is that.

The tough part for Jimmy was the emotion of seeing her again after so long a period of time. To then see her in love with his best friend was confusing, overpowering and almost unbearable.

    She ate and enjoyed everything on the menu, including the poi. She was half fair and half olive skinned now after a year in Hawaii. But for her Midwestern accent which was slowly dissipating, she fit right in.

    Jimmy remembered her healthy appetite, and not just for food. She and Mark were affectionate throughout the evening. Jimmy had mixed emotions about that as well but was genuinely happy for both of them. Jimmy knew he had to be protective of their happiness and that nothing should get in the way of it, including and especially his previous involvement with her.

    After all of the guests had left, the Kanoho men were cleaning up outside, extinguishing the grill and the small bonfire everyone sat around after dinner. James was scrubbing down the still hot grill and Jimmy was putting some folding chairs away. James noticed an odd look on his son's face during dinner. He already suspected what it was about but he asked his son anyway.

    "Dad," Jimmy started, "I had a short fling with Kelly two years ago when I was a freshman. I nevah know her name at da time, and we was jus having fun. I nevah expect fo see her again, fo real kine! I when kinda fall in love wit her. But no worry brah, I can handle."

    "I hope so," said Sr., "look like Mark stay in love and probably goin' marry da wahine too. You know Mark not as smooth wit da ladies like you Jimmy boy. She ate da poi. I tink he wen fine his keepah."

    Jimmy, Kelly, and even James continued this charade for the next few years, never daring to schedule some kind of clandestine meeting to discuss the situation; there was nothing to discuss. It happened, it's in the past, they've moved on, there was nothing for her back in Nebraska and Jimmy himself was busy helping to run the hotel and being an outdoorsman. The longings and other feelings still lay just beneath the surface but they were both sure to quell them and continue on with their masqueraded silence and

Creaking Door

secrets. Again, it was uncomfortable but not unmanageable.

A few months after that dinner, Jimmy found out through Mark that Kelly had admitted to a short-lived romance with a local boy while she had visited Hawaii after her high-school graduation when she was seventeen and on vacation. It had come up in the kind of conversations new couples inevitably have about exes, the kind used to discern and compare his or her tastes in mates. She told the truth when she said she'd never learned his name but lied when she said she hadn't ever seen him again, a deception Jimmy was grateful for. Mark asked her what she would do if she ever saw him again.

"I'll flash him my wedding ring," she said unabashedly.

"What wedding ring?" Mark asked dumfounded.

"Exactly," was her curt and sly reply.

Two blissful months later Mark finally felt sure and secure enough to pop the question.

Technically there was nothing wrong with Jimmy and Kelly's past. She'd not even met Mark at the time, but of course the situation was far more complicated than a simple ex-boyfriend story. So, out of necessity and to keep the peace, they continued the awkward charade. Mark entered his senior year at the University as its starting free safety, and newly married to a beautiful young sophomore chemistry major. It was a charade and a secret that, as they almost always do, would come back to haunt each and every one of them.

Alejo Melendez

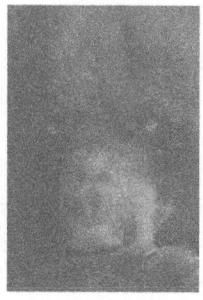

Squeak

FAST FORWARD NINETEEN YEARS

JIMMY'S FATHER, NOW semi-retired, has since bequeathed to Jimmy forty percent ownership of the Hotel and Mark a three percent share. James Sr. is still vibrant and healthy but he wants to enjoy more of his life before his body stages its inevitable mutiny.
Along with his famous surf camp and fishing charter Mark nets a very tidy and comfortable life for his family. Jimmy himself does some freelance contract work for the Department of Defense as a computer scientist. His security clearance is ultra low and his obligation to them is part time only. His computer skill set works best on a consultation basis. He is on a large team of geeks who study internet activity and incoming source codes in the attempt to prevent cyber attacks and viruses. He is on contingency so only does the amount of work he feels like doing. It pays well and Jimmy gets to work from home in a secure office set up by the DOD. There is always work but again, there is also a large team of geeks to tackle it.

Jimmy's involvement in National Defense is minimal but will most likely become significant in the future.

Creaking Door

Mark and Jimmy remain avid outdoorsmen. They have since been on many hunts all over the world. They absolutely love the balance of being watermen and hunters. For them, a seafaring life combined with life on terra firma make for a more even keel.

Their youth was dominated by the ocean and the surf. As time went on and they matured, hunting became the larger passion among their hobbies. It was probably because they had mastered every break on the island and, big or small, they knew just what to expect when it came to wave patterns and breaks. Besides, the lineups increased each year, especially the famed North Shore, or as they called it the North "Sore." Their sacred north side had been infiltrated by outsiders looking for the perfect wave, for their "endless summer." The influx, especially those rude Australians, had been as of late a thorn in their side, a "sore" spot.

But with hunting, the world was their oyster. Surfing provided a kind of instant gratification. With hunting, the patience required was excruciating, the tactics hard earned, and the payoff unlike any other. To hike for hours, then sit in silence and remain motionless for such an extended period of time was like long, drawn out foreplay, the kill like the greatest physical and emotional release ever. You become so worked up when the animal comes into view that you want to explode, very much like a lover being teased by their partner for hours or even days. When the animal is hit then goes down, the physical discharge cannot be described as anything but intensely orgasmic.

Compared to that, sexually and metaphorically, surfing seemed more like masturbation now. They could return to the same hunting grounds annually and never see the same things, never see the same animals or animal behavior. Plus, it fed well when they were successful. Taming a big wave was still special, but bringing down big game, especially a wild animal that was more alive and animated than any wave and that could kill you just as easily, was a rush beyond any they had ever known. And unlike a surfing lineup anywhere in the world now, there was solitude in the wilderness. Hunting was quiet, pristine, primordial, and in the areas they sought you almost never encountered other people while engaged in it.

For Jimmy and Mark, the epiphany came one winter day when they were walking the third floor of the Awaawa. James had told them of a squeaky door in room 309. They brought along their tool belts in case they encountered any other maintenance needs. They had people to perform these everyday tasks but it was lunch break and the boys were bored and decided to do some actual physical work. A large swell was forecast the next day and every big wave rider in the area was looking forward to it. Makaha was that kind of epic once every five years or so. The boys were jazzed.

When they arrived at 309 they tested the door. Movement caused a high-pitched squeak. Jimmy repeated the movement a few more times, then did it more rapidly, then quicker still until he got the right pitch. Jimmy and Mark looked at each other and laughed their asses off. It sounded exactly like a rutting bull elk. They laughed because they remembered the first time they'd heard that particular call of the wild. They were surprised at how such a big powerful animal could make such a high pitched, almost effeminate call. Bucks grunted, bears growled and roared, and even pigs made low pitched scary groans. So they started calling stags "Tysons" because of former great heavyweight champion Iron Mike Tyson, who was a destructive, unstoppable pit bull in the ring. During his interviews, however, he spoke with a laughable, squeaky, high-pitched voice that took everyone who hadn't yet heard it by surprise. Of course no one dared laugh to his face, but that was the reason for the nickname and the reason they were on the ground laughing now. They were both thinking the same thing: "fuck the waves, let's go hunting!"

They Called Ray Espinoza an hour later and tried booking a Big Island hunt for mountain goat the next day if possible. It was not really dumb luck that he was available, most young hunters were also surfers who were also waiting for the big winter waves

Creaking Door

and it was just too cold and wet for most of the older hunters. Plus compared to most other states, Hawaii's per capita hunters were among the lowest.

Jimmy is still single, while Mark's marriage seems strong but there are signs of stagnancy, unrest, and unhappiness. But what eighteen or nineteen-year old marriage is immune to that?

As very healthy and much needed diversions, Mark has his business and safaris while Kelly is dedicated to volunteer work she does down the coast with local youths, mostly teenagers. Their daughter Lei has just left for her freshman year at Columbia. The entire town are all very proud of their little hapa haole wahine. She remained, by choice, an only child, so love and attention were never a problem for this supremely confident *kekoa*. Like her old man and Uncle Jimmy, she hunts, fishes, and surfs with the best of them.

Alejo Melendez

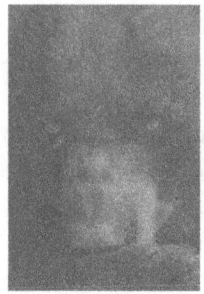

Alberta

THE PAIR HAVE been on many hunts now, and with each trip Kelly and Lei would stay with the elder Kanohos rather than the elder Tams. Even from before Lei was born Kelly would stay the duration with James and Kui. The accommodations were better for one thing, and Mark's father was also suffering from arthritic knees, had trouble walking, and required his wife's help full time. Sometimes the boys were gone for over a week, but usually theirs were mostly two- or three-day excursions. Either way, there was no way an attractive vulnerable young woman like Kelly was to be left on her own for ANY period of time. Both sets of parents were willing but, unlike the elder Tams, the elder Kanohos were able.

They have decided their next hunt will be a return to Alberta, Canada, the black bear capital of the world. Jimmy and Mark have hunted here many times over the years and have made many friends among the many fellow hunters and outfitters they have used and hired. Jimmy and Mark try to distribute their business as evenly as possible so it is natural that a certain faction may have their feelings hurt if, upon their return, Jimmy and Mark opt for a different guide. All of them have competitive boundaries but by and large most are friendly toward each other and understand they reflect upon each other and their industry as a whole.

Creaking Door

    This year Jimmy and Mark are going with an outfitter they've used several times in the past named Jacques St. Pierre. Everyone calls him JSP for short.
    They touch down at Edmonton International just after noon; grab a quick bite, then hop a United Airlines Saab 340 express to the Grande Cache Airport. The flight in the small turboprop is rough but is made manageable by the pristine air, the ground view scenery, and their anticipation of what's to come. They unload their stowed gear from the small craft's storage compartment below deck and acquire their rental vehicle straight away, a mid-sized, copper-colored Chevy Blazer with four-wheel drive as the pair remain ever mindful of their rough and untamed Northern environment.
    They then hop on Highway Forty to begin the fairly short drive to JSP's place. Initially the road west towards the mountains is mainly clear. But when they junction on to some barely paved roads that skirt the Rockies there are a still a few snow drifts around as they ascend. They then take an unmarked main road that serves as the unofficial highway in these untamed parts for the rest of the way before finding the *rock*.
    JSP's camp is situated on an unmarked road just off this obscure country highway outside of the famous and protected Willmore Wilderness Park. Familiarity allows them to recognize the turn-off, but otherwise the spot is marked with a huge fifteen-foot high granite boulder, an untouched vestige from the last ice-age and left alone during original construction done in the nineteen-forties. It could not be moved so the highway and the camp entry road were built around it. The forest and some shrubbery have since grown around it and at its base to make it more inconspicuous. Only an exclusive few in the know are familiar with its symbolism. Otherwise, it is just another big rock from the Canadian Rockies that tumbled down the hill eons ago. There are enough other boulders along the highway that no one pays any mind to it.

Alejo Melendez

An attempted sculpture of JSP's grandfather, the original landowner and lodge builder, was abandoned when Grandpa and the sculptor had artistic differences too diametrically opposed to overcome. The large section of rock protruding from its middle was to be his grandfather's nose and was left to give it a discreet distinction, enough to mark the property entrance but not enough to make it look anything but natural. Time and erosion have helped its cause.

Jimmy and Mark arrive at the massive log-cabin lodge just before sundown and supper is already waiting. At just under thirteen thousand square feet, this massive cabin, which also serves as the main hunting lodge, is about a quarter of the size of the White House. It is designed to accommodate ten hunters and their plus one guests in complete log cabin luxury. There are also several smaller outlying cabins designed for those on a budget or choosing to rough it and forgo the four-star amenities. It never feels crowded, even during peak season, and yet always seems intimate, even when there is only one set of guests on hand, as is the case at present with Jimmy and Mark. More guests will be arriving within three days but for now, as was planned, the boys have the place all to themselves.

Upon arrival, they are hit with a tidal wave of cooking aromas. The smells are a godsend, strong and aromatic, hinting of game and spice and very strong dark-roasted coffee, the latter of which they are offered only to perk them back up from the long flight, but then nothing more due to an early start time.

At just under a thousand feet up, JSP's digs are situated near the base of Mount Becker, one of the larger bumps in the Alberta section of the Canadian Rockies. It is located at the midpoint of Alberta's westernmost borders with British Columbia, a truly beautiful and wild territory. The salmon are running in every nearby stream and Jimmy and Mark enjoy that particular seasonal local harvest along with some delicious aged moose meat that has been brined and cooked medium rare. It practically melts in their

Creaking Door

mouths.

Sometime during dinner JSP gets a phone call. Jimmy and Mark try not to eavesdrop but they cannot help but hear that it is a somewhat distressing call. JSP is clearly arguing with someone but returns to the table composed and looking as if nothing has happened. Jimmy and Mark don't ask. Some after-dinner scotch by the fireplace and in no time the three of them are sleepy. Jimmy and Mark pretty much fall asleep as soon as their heads hit the pillow.

As usual they are all up very early the next morning. Gear has been prepared and loaded beforehand. Jimmy and Mark need only to take the drive with JSP, make the hike, and then climb their already mounted tree stands. A thermos of hot coffee would be most welcome but the smell would surely drive the bears away.

On the forty-five-minute drive to their destination, they pass the kinds of things Jimmy and Mark do not usually have the pleasure of seeing back in Hawaii; heavily pine-forested flatlands and mountains, snowcaps, snow drifts, wandering wildlife, steam billowing out of a crossing moose's nostrils, the once reddened and yellowish autumnal leaves that speckled the landscape now dried by nature to a sugarless brown, organically composted by the ton in great wind-gathered heaps.

Jimmy asks JSP about the phone call last night. He says it was a fellow outfitter named Bart Ronde, a guide Jimmy and Mark know well. Mark and Jimmy have used him before but they did not care for his style. He was cantankerous and not really a people person. If you want to survive stranded in the wilderness than he might be your man, but for tourists on a vacation hunt, he could use a little polishing. On their one and only session with him, about two years ago, Jimmy and Mark got skunked and Bart complained bitterly that they'd made too much noise and that Jimmy and Mark must have smelled too strong, things Jimmy and Mark had never, as experienced hunters, had a problem with over their many years. Of course it pays more for the outfitter when hunters like Jimmy and

Mark reach their allowed quota, or *fill their tags* as it's known, so his attitude was no mystery to them. It was still, however, very much unappreciated.

JSP claims Bart was accusing him of hogging all of the clients this season, but most visiting hunters would agree JSP is about the finest guide/outfitter/tracker/host there is in the territory. Most, like Jimmy and Mark, prefer JSP over not only Bart but most of the other outfitters in this area.

It is about 7 a.m. when Jimmy and Mark, after the long hike through weighty woodland, climb their tree stands and secure themselves into position. Round about 9 a.m. some bears start wandering nearby. JSP has set up empty fifty-five gallon drums secured to tree trunks with thick gauge steel cable and some smelly bait near their bottoms and holes strategically pierced so the bear can stick his head and his arms through these openings and sample the daily specials. Jimmy and Mark are bow hunting today. They love this form of hunting as it requires close contact with your prey. The boys are about twenty feet up their respective trees and often bears will walk right past the base. The barrels are about forty feet away so the shot required is still a difficult one. Jimmy's setup is virtually identical to Mark's but the boys are about a half mile apart. Later Mark would abandon his post and move a quarter of a mile closer to Jimmy to ground hunt. There, another feeding station was positioned, another tree stand as well. Mark would inexplicably opt for the ground shot.

A cold wind blew through the forest; leaves kicked up and swirled in a nearby open meadow. Thankfully Jimmy was properly insulated in his warm winter camouflage; even though technically it was spring, the chill in the air was still a strong one. An old Siberian creed Jimmy lived by was paying dividends: "There is no such thing as poor weather, only poor clothing".

There was still a little frost on the ground, but not enough to keep the now starving bears from emerging from their hibernation.

Actually, bears feed very little for about a week after

emerging from their winter dens. It is only after this period that their appetites become voracious and their search for food becomes truly aggressive.

This was the first season bear hunting was allowed again. It had not been the last six and a half years, with disastrous consequences. A few liberal minds felt hunting of all kind was cruel, so they pushed forth a movement to ban it, their efforts gained momentum and pressure was brought to bear on the local legislators, who then passed probably the worst law in Canadian history. In the three and a half years hence, several businesses went bust: local outfitters, hunting camps, mom and pop stores of all kinds; eateries, lodges, and small motels that relied on the seasonal hunting trade that brought visitors from all over the world to partake in this rich harvest of a natural resource.

What also happened was that the bear population exploded and they began to infiltrate urban and suburban areas, interacting with humans in a most frightening and unnatural fashion, and these bears were killed anyway as nuisance animals, their bodies disposed of in a most wasteful and inhumane manner.

Jimmy and Mark remember watching the news about three or four years ago. It was a piece about the doings in Alberta in a town called Cadomin at the southern end of their Rockies. A bear had wandered into a suburban neighborhood most likely looking for food. It was a nice middle-class neighborhood with nice families and had children who played safely on the streets.

When the bear was spotted the children ran screaming which of course brought out the adults, who then tried to chase the bear off. The poor bear became frightened and confused and found itself suddenly surrounded by two-storied tract housing, seven-foot high wooden fences, and a multitude of parked vehicles. It could find no escape route readily available. So it took refuge in something familiar: a tall Maple tree in someone's front yard. It climbed up to a level of about thirty feet and stayed put, certainly scared out of its wits. Animal control was called. They waited the bear out for only about thirty short and impatient minutes before they decided to tranquilize the animal. Two men stood at the base of the tree with a Browder life net, an apparatus used by fire departments back in the day. It was designed to catch falling objects; it looks like a trampoline but is handheld and without legs.

    The drug takes effect sooner than expected, too big a dose it was later confirmed. The bear fell and the inexperienced duo tasked with catching it were not ready. The bear landed head first on the side of the tree where the Browder life net grippers were not. The bear broke its neck, remained alive and suffered for fifteen minutes, and then died. This was Canada and nearly everyone owned a gun, animal control personnel and most of the residents alike; the great conundrum was that shooting a bear was still illegal and, with news cameras and smart phones rolling, no one dared do the humane thing and put a bullet through its head.

    The unedited news video made it to YouTube and showed the paralyzed motionless animal on the ground wailing and groaning in pain, sounding very much like a human in distress. The sounds were haunting, excruciating, and heartbreaking. A better option would have probably been to have the residents shelter in place, have an armed police sentry posted down the block (police were legally allowed to shoot anything that threatened public safety), and then sometime in the middle of the night let the bear quietly find its way back to the wilderness. That would have been Jimmy's choice. He remembers seething with anger at the foolish and inhumane choices that were made that day. The chain reaction from the moronic law showed not only the catastrophic cause and effect, but revealed that the law had obviously not been thought through. After a few years of totally unnecessary debate, the knee jerk moratorium on bear hunting was lifted.

    In a beach house in Milford Connecticut Dr. Susan Zao had been watching the same news program. It reminded her of the National Geographic shows she watched as a child in which veterinary scientists would sometimes tranquilize a wild animal, take data and samples while it slept, then inject it with an antidote that revived the animal rather quickly so as to traumatize the animal as little as possible. She had been working on a similar project at work and that specific news report and the memory of those National Geographic shows gave her new inspiration to a possible solution to something that had been deeply troubling her for years. She could research those same drugs comparatively against her own results and obtain a better idea on using the body's own natural responses and defenses in allowing a safer biological reaction, thus turning the corner on a project which had provided only failure so far. She and the FDA needed it to be far safer than the animal antidotes they were inspired by. This new approach to her old theory was definitely a pitch she could take to her bosses.

Alejo Melendez

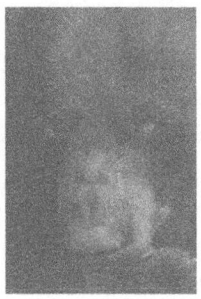

Junior Prom

HERA HAD GROWN fat from a well-stocked barn on her owner's farm. She lazed her way all day on or near the front porch, then lived her second mysterious life once the sun went down. She never listened to anybody and would only come if she heard the familiar sounds of food or drink being put out for her.

Hera was the teen girl's black and white cat. The girl begged her father for her when she was ten and Hera but a kitten. As soon as she was brought home she began chasing mice and rats all over the property. Upon seeing this, Willard, the patriarch, her strong but quiet father, liked the animal right away.

Hera grew up, grew fat, and, like most farm cats, became utterly bored with her humans and lived virtually independent of their care. She had all she needed in the barn. An endless supply of vermin in the nooks and water in the troughs; she wanted for nothing. Hera was also not above stowing away on visiting truck beds to prowl neighboring farms. She came to know each individual truck or vehicle and also knew just which would take her to the most fertile hunting grounds. She became a common pet in the territory, each farm an extended family. Everyone appreciated her house cleaning services and treated her like she was their own, providing bedding and clean water et al. on the occasions she chose

Creaking Door

to spend the night, or even the week, with her calabash family du jour.

Frank Dumbrowski was the high-school Prince Charming. Shock-top blonde hair, a farm tan, and Hollywood straight and white teeth. He'd been eyeing the three musketeers, as Zora, Kelly, and Willadean became known, for weeks now. They all giggled when he would walk by. He would always say the same thing: "Hi Ladies", he'd tip his head in acknowledgment and sometimes even wink.

No one was sure who he was going to ask to junior prom. The other three cheered each other on. None of them would have a problem finding dates, but the prize was Frank, a true babe. He was the second-string quarterback, got some playing time, and was the crown prince waiting to inherit the throne once the starting senior quarterback graduated.

But a week before prom Frank mustered up the courage to ask one of them out. It was Kelly. Zora and Willa were devastated but showed only happiness for their friend.

Kelly, ever sensitive of her two best friends, spoke nothing of it the rest of the day, and the three of them even went out for their normal root beer float at the drug store after school.

***

When she got home she locked herself in her room and cried. She lay in her bed with salty tears trickling until, surprised, she heard her ma calling the clan to supper. She looked out her window to see it was indeed twilight.

She was pretty, had always been told so by other boys. She got good grades, a 3.6 GPA and was unquestionably the smartest of the three. But he asked Kelly and it hurt bitterly.

Her claim that she was not hungry did not fly with her parents who promptly ordered her down to the dinner table or be dragged down by her older brothers. She cleaned herself up, washed her face and brushed her heartbroken, tangled, bed head hair and sat at her place. She barely tasted the pot roast and roasted herb potatoes. Her obvious moping was thought to be nothing more than her monthly visit from "aunt flo".

Her father suggested she go out to the barn and make sure the horses had water for the night knowing she could probably use the fresh air. She stepped into the darkness. Everything looked surreal, like a charcoal drawing with carefully placed intentional smudges to enhance and soften the hard edges of structures, like the barn and the pen. Soft breezes caused rippled puddles that cast dull reflections of moving starlight that shimmered like billowed campfire embers.

Pungent fresh manure and the semi-sweet smell of wet hay filled the clear Nebraska night, the stars above twinkled their somber sympathy at her, and Hera purred and rubbed at her ankle. She bent over and petted the cat, stroking the stiff fur caused from farm life spent mostly outdoors. Hera looked content and had probably just eaten a fat rat or something. The girl paid it no mind and dwelled only on the frustration and heartache of Frank's perceived rejection. She was angry and didn't even know it. Having yet to check on the horses, she picked up Hera and carried her into the barn, continually petting her and putting both of them at ease. The trough was full, fresh hay had been laid for the horses to bed upon, and she just stood there taking it all in. There were cracks and knotholes in the ancient grayed wooden planks and faint light crept in from the house. The tools were hanging quietly on the western wall so as to be illuminated with the sunrise for easier picking. She walked over to that wall and stared at the old rusty iron and steel tools. Her father would probably put them to the grinder in a few days to make them polished and corrosion free again. The axe hung solemnly, its head nestled between two nails. The hammer end was red while the blade end shone its unrusted edge proudly due its continual use for firewood and the like. Even as she plucked it off the wall Hera lay calmly and trustingly in her arms. As if unconscious, she lay the cat on an old stump just off the side of the barn next to a pile of yet to be chopped logs. The whump and thud of the blow broke the silence, Hera's head separated and lay on the wood platform while its body, with its last vestiges of nerves and life, jumped off the stump and scampered about a yard before being permanently stilled.

Whatever happened was visceral. She would not remember it the next morning. She didn't snap; she wasn't even angry. She was compelled.

It only took five minutes for her to grab the shovel and dig a shallow hole at the edge of the nearest plot of corn about twenty yards away. The earth was still soft from the plow and the regular irrigation of the family's lifeblood crop. She tamped down the mound she had created and the family pet, which she once loved and begged for, was no more. The sweet innocent girl was buried along with it. The dour moods would continue, and they would always trigger the dark, horrible secrets that lay within her.

Alejo Melendez

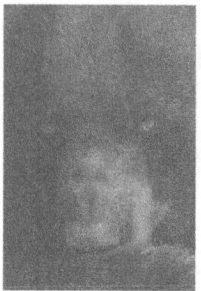

Breakfast

COUNTRY HAM AND hot lard fill the air. Fresh eggs are sizzling away as the Janzen kids come down to breakfast. As usual, Willa checks the porch where her cat Hera sleeps in an old wooden box layered with old blankets. Hera often leaves dead rodents near their front door as homage to her beloved benefactors, but the stoop is clear of both hunter and hunted. It is strange because Hera loves ham and comes running before it ever hits the griddle.

Willa then remembers a strange dream she had last night. She saw Hera's headless body running about, clawing at mice in the barn but no way to capture them, not without sight or smell, her main arsenals. She wonders now if it was a dream. Hera sleeps indoors during the winter, but it has been an especially hot summer and Willa, working hard at her chores, has suffered from dehydration a few times, the fiendish ailment sneaking up on her and her willowy frame. She has blacked out three times in the past week and a half. She has told no one and wonders now if it happened last night as she cannot recall events past dinner. She thinks she went to her room and slept it off, but it was another particularly hot day and her weakened state, once again surreptitiously sneaking up on her, caused her to eat little and discard her memory. Her father always told her to drink plenty of

Creaking Door

water in this Midwest sauna; if you drink when you are thirsty then it's already too late.

Sixteen-year-old Willa has been distracted by her impending junior prom, and happily so. But for now, Hera is missing and she can't recall the night before.

Alejo Melendez

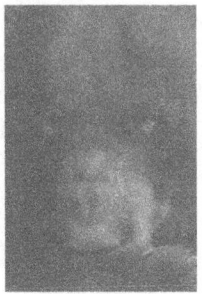

Death

JIMMY KANOHO SITS quietly in a tree stand twenty feet above the forest floor. It is mid spring in Edmonton, Alberta and the weather is very cold. His layered clothing has just the right amount of insulation. There is no such thing as poor weather, only poor clothing.

He has come here looking for the black bear that are now emerging from their winter dens and looking to feed after months of deprivation. He's been sitting on the tree stand's collapsible mini stool for so long he can identify each grated hole through the soles of his thick and impervious hunting boots.

A cool, dewy mist hangs in the pine-scented forest air. This part of western Alberta has come alive with the arrival of spring and two very good friends have come here to hunt.

Jimmy Kanoho and Mark Tam occupy tree stands a half mile apart. The bears here are so plentiful that they know they each have an outstanding chance of bagging one.

There are green and white buds and shoots popping out of the branch tips on nearly every deciduous tree. Along with residual snow dotting the forest floor, it makes for a nice, sharp contrasted landscape. The light colors against the darkened earthen scenery has always been conducive to good feelings, and that is exactly how the boys feel doing one of their most favorite things in the world.

Along with the flora and fauna, the vegetative smells have also made this spring morning come alive as well; pine resin, flowers, loam, musk, and even the faint smell of things the animals do to let hunters know they have been in the area.

The sun rises higher in the sky. The forest warms, and Mark takes a healthy pull from his brand-new water canister.

Usually a patient and experienced hunter, Mark changes tactics and foolishly decides to ground hunt for the black bears. Normally Jimmy and Mark erect and use tree stands for the obvious reasons including vantage point, safety, to keep their scent above the wind, etc. But Mark was certain his hunting prowess would take the day. The area in this Alberta forest is teeming with bears, and while he focused on a mammoth twenty yards away, an even bigger one stealthily crept up behind him and mauled him to death. Jimmy was about a quarter of a mile away in a tree stand at the time. Jimmy heard Mark scream, climbed down, then ran toward the ruckus and arrived in time to see this huge black mass with meaty bits and blood in his mouth and a carcass beneath him. Jimmy drew his sidearm, a Taurus Raging Bull .454 Casull, sporting an 8.4-inch barrel but without its scope for an easier fit in his holster. It is for emergencies only, and this qualified. Although it is a mini cannon, when Jimmy shot at the bear in urgency he managed to hit only his hind quarter where the bullet lodged and did little to mortally wound him. A second shot, aimed higher, went right past the bear's front right paw. But that highly explosive noise it makes shattered the forest quiet and drove the bear off at a full but gimpy sprint. Jimmy's Taurus is a revolver so it will not jam, and thankfully that was very useful in this case, but nonetheless it and Jimmy were too late.

A chunk of Mark's neck, where the jugular would have been, had been ripped out, probably causing death within fifteen seconds. When he stopped struggling the bear most certainly went after the soft "underbelly" as most predators do. Mark's entrails were spilled out over the forest floor. Trembling and with his head on a swivel, Jimmy waited a full five minutes before placing the 911 call for help. He fully expected to see that enraged and humongous bear or others like it come tearing back to reclaim the kill. Jimmy waited with both trembling hands on his fully drawn weapon.

Most hunters today mount multiple mini cameras to record their hunts for posterity. These digital cameras are sometimes smaller than the size of a pack of cigarettes. Hunters will even submit these videos to websites or television shows dedicated to such pursuits, often on that very same day, at home through the internet. Mark had three, and one was mounted on the tree four feet behind him. This was the video that confirmed his focus on a bear in front of him when the aft bear charged. All three cameras revealed in great detail the sequence in which he was killed. Jimmy was told about it but could not watch the actual footage until a week later when Jimmy was forced to finally give statements in the investigation by Canadian authorities.

Jimmy's only regret is a very miniscule one. He shot in haste and did not take the chance that a better aimed, more time-consuming shot could be taken. If Mark were perchance still somehow alive beneath the grisly chaos, seconds would have counted.

Even a missed shot might not have driven the bear off and could have easily set the bear to attack Jimmy. If he knew how far gone the damage had been, he would have paused a beat and gone for a kill shot, in the upper torso, at the bear's heart, perhaps even a head shot. Now this bear is wounded but not mortally and hopefully Jimmy or a fellow hunter will take him down so he needn't suffer any longer nor pose a danger to the other humans it will surely encounter in the remainder of its life. Finding it and killing it would also prevent an already horrible situation from becoming worse. The police, but especially the game wardens, were informed of this and have put that bear squarely on their radar. They will keep a prioritized eye out.

Creaking Door

The tremendous guilt Jimmy experiences at the time of Mark's death is from his inability to somehow save Mark's life, either by not allowing him to hunt alone or by being quicker and truer with his pistol.

The Edmonton authorities, especially the game wardens, have seen this kind of thing before, and the victim's grotesque condition, with its torn flesh and horrific dismemberment, could only have been done by a large wild animal. This immediately but not unconditionally puts Jimmy in the clear, and Mark Tam's death, for the time being, is completely unsuspicious.

Not only is this bear disadvantaged with its injury, but it is now a confirmed man eater, and an injured and desperate one at that. It poses a significant danger to all human hunters that now cross its path. It will surely be handicapped and limping and therefore take a beating from other bears during the rut or over a kill, so to NOT seek it out and humanely destroy it would be cruel. The injury will most likely mean denial of food from an inability to hunt normally or protect its kills from other healthier bears. This would lead to greater hunger and therefore greater desperation. Meaning humans will now become a viable food source instead of objects to fear. And, for Jimmy, there is that small measure of revenge that seems to come naturally to competitive people like himself.

He recalls how, at the time immediately following the attack, there was the nightmarish logistical matter of dealing with his very best friend's gruesome death. How, with great anguish and difficulty, Jimmy had to tell Mark's parents, his wife and daughter, and Jimmy's own family who loved Mark like their own son, that unbearably devastating news. More bad news is on the way; Jimmy just didn't know it yet.

Alejo Melendez

Alanitrol

JENIFER AGUILAR, THE attractive young receptionist at Bannon Industries, a leading global pharmaceutical company based in Asbury Park on New Jersey's far Northern end, watched in wonder as the company's top three managers, Jack Dillon, executive VP, Lance Redman, VP in charge of Sales, and Megan Dunkirk, CFO, all entered the main conference room at about three p.m. Men's leather soles and Megan's slender clog heels could be heard slapping and clicking the polished linoleum floor—white with decorative black splatter patterns and, thanks to their internal maintenance team, nary a scuff mark in the whole building.

Jenifer sits behind a large twelve-foot crescent shaped cherry wood reception desk. It is two tiered. The top level has inlaid grey marble Formica with two chained pens and a sign-in sheet which, at the close of each day, Jenifer places in a properly marked folder in a locked oak file cabinet built in to her station. There is also a vase of fresh cut flowers which are replaced daily. These are the only things at her station that are visible to visitors and guests of the building. This top layer provides a kind of roof for the cubby holed work station beneath, where it houses three phones connected to seven separate lines of communication, a computer hardwired only to the

Creaking Door

in-house server, and six closed-circuit security monitors for her secondary scrutinizing; she is to notify security at once should she see anything out of the ordinary. Their private security detail views those exact same images and twenty more for the four buildings that comprise the campus. Jenifer's are merely an extra set of eyes.

There was a giddy but restrained look about their three normally drab and worried managerial faces, as if today was somehow cause for difference among people notorious for favoring routine, people who did not like surprises, people for whom the word "different" was a sin. They favored and lived by uniformity and routines one could predict and set atomic clocks to. Megan was wearing a floral patterned full-length skirt when she normally, almost exclusively, wore dark, serious solids and pants.

Five minutes later, Julio and Rigoberto, the food services supervisors from the company cafeteria, come strolling by Jenifer's reception desk with two covered carts that they promptly wheel into the same conference room. The covers are black and linen and they are dome shaped at their tops, revealing, by design, nothing of what they might contain.

"What's in there?" asks Jenifer using her best irresistible smile.

"It's a secret, sugar pie," replies Rigoberto, using his pet name for her. All the company males, even and perhaps especially the married ones, flirt with Jen.

Ten minutes later the company CEO and owner, Wellington Bannon, who is rarely seen in this building, also enters the room. Jenifer is quite naturally situated next to the building's main entrance so Mr. Bannon's surprise and sudden appearance means he has used a rear service entrance of some kind. The conference room door is closed behind him. There is no fanfare but obviously something large is brewing. Jen knew this the instant handsome Rigoberto declined to share any information with her. Rigoberto was one of Jenifer's reliable gossip partners, had a big crush on her, and would normally spill the beans at the flash of her smile, or her cleavage.

Alejo Melendez

Three minutes later Jenifer's intercom buzzed. It is Jack Dillon asking her to page Doctor Susan Zao. Dr. Zao, the company's leading research scientist, answered the page and is put through to the main conference room.

With the push of a button, Jenifer is dropped from the conversation. Via speakerphone, Susan is asked to attend an impromptu meeting in the lobby. She is filing reports for her department, nothing urgent, so she drops what she is doing and makes her way down the western staircase to attend to matters. The adjacent western wall is comprised of segmented floor to ceiling windows, each piece ten feet high and braced with polished steel framing. It was designed to view sunsets and a subconscious message that long hours were appreciated and necessary in their cutthroat business. Their late afternoon view is of the sun setting over the Freehold Township, a pretty town of affluent homes. The Trenton skyline is a bit too far to see, but bits of the building tips can be made out, particularly when silhouetted by the golden glow of dusk.

Upon entering the room, she is handed a flute of Dom Perignon and knew instantly that she is about to hear the news she had been waiting for. Her only question to the bigwigs is if they had hit the trifecta. With great big beaming smiles, they all nodded yes. The drug Dr. Zao had been working on for a little over three years had passed its FDA trials and was deemed safe for use by humans, was granted its patent, and was approved for marketing and distribution immediately.

Rigoberto cuts the German chocolate cake baked especially for this occasion. Everyone is handed a slice on small black paper plates festooned with printed orange and yellow balloons. It is Dr. Zao's favorite and she relishes the finely shredded coconut baked in between velvety soft chocolate cake layers. To complete its decadence, a mocha butter-cream frosting sprinkled with crushed almonds graces its rich, dark exterior. It is a glorious ending to an endeavor born of tragedy.

Creaking Door

Over several years a growing number of very specific sex crimes had infected society in general, but particularly hard hit were college campuses. The crime is known as date rape, and a drug that a rival pharma had developed as a prescription sleep aid is being used to perpetrate this hideous deed. Dr Zao's daughter, Alanis, was a junior at Stanford when Dr. Zao received a phone call late one night from California all those years ago. It was a Palo Alto police officer telling Dr. Zao that her daughter had attended a frat party and was unconscious and being treated in the Stanford Hospital ER.

They assumed she had imbibed on whatever they were serving and when she could not be revived, 911 was called and an ambulance dispatched. Because of the circumstances, it being a frat party, a pelvic exam was performed and when signs of vaginal trauma were evident, a rape kit was taken.

Knowing her daughter, a health nut, triathlete, and straight A student, would never have taken any kind of drink or drug, she asked that her blood be tested and for some very specific compounds. Knowing the results would not be available for at least 12 hours, she hung up and booked the next available flight to Northern California. It was one in the morning in her Milford Connecticut home. It overlooked a rocky beach and the Atlantic Ocean lulled gentle waves upon its earthen and stony shores. The sounds were soothing but Susan could not at that moment hear them. Nearby, a New England White Onshore Skeletal Lighthouse beamed its light seaward in a comforting oscillating sweep. Her daughter and her friends used to climb the squat structure and throw paper airplanes off its observation deck. She watched and imagined it guiding potentially lost and wayward craft safely into Milford's embrace, and she was going to fly west, grab her daughter and do the same. She could not wait to touch down at San Jose International.

Alanis's test results revealed the presence of Rohypnol. A recovered pubic hair was enough to eventually convict the perp, an undergraduate senior loser named David Mackin whose wealthy parents fought hard to buy his way out of a conviction, but the evidence was clear and the crime considered too heinous. Rohypnol was found in his room as well, sealing the conviction with a bow tied neatly on top. He was given five years in State Prison when he should have gotten ten. The cumulative effect planted the seed in Susan's mind that was germinated years later by seeing the news item about the inept handling of the loose bear in Cadomin. That provided the impetus for the work Dr. Zao had been doing, and now her hard work was coming into fruition.

    She had developed an antidote to the date rape drug, a drug that attacked primarily the Rohypnol molecules but also the depressant GHB and successfully rendered them ineffective and removed them from the victim's bloodstream. The remnants of the Rohypnol were still there of course, just transformed by her new drug into a harmless protein, soon to be processed by the usual culprits: the kidneys, the pancreas, and the liver, then expelled by either the number one or number two bodily function soon after. Taken in the correct dosages, it would effectively negate the Rohypnol's effects but also remove all traces of it, the latter being an unintended consequence. Dr. Zao's objective was strictly to revive people who'd been drugged against their will.

    It is a miracle of modern molecular biology, but no researcher was ever more motivated than Susan. She named the new drug Alanitrol after her precious daughter, who had dropped out of school after the attack. After several years in the wilderness Alanis had eventually returned to her education, not in California but back in the northeast, closer to home in New England.

    Unlike Rohypnol, Alanitrol did not come in pill form. It was developed as a resuscitation and rescue drug with the obvious limitation of oral delivery being the crucial element of time, so it was developed as a serum sold readymade to inject directly into the victim's blood, like an EpiPen. If a girl/woman suspected she had been drugged she would have enough time to counteract the

Creaking Door

Rohypnol by using the Alanitrol as soon as she felt woozy. A very important component in Alanitrol's development was to ensure its harmlessness in the case of a false alarm, if there was NO Rohypnol in the subject's system and the ill effects were from something of an entirely different nature. So a stern warning was issued and written in bold print on every label to never take on an empty stomach, like Ibuprofen, which would lead to tummy aches and possible ulcers. Alanitrol on an empty stomach would not be fatal, just give its user, like Ibuprofen, discomfort. In this case headaches from its attacking of red and white blood cells and platelets.

Not only would Alanitrol solve a huge social dilemma that was becoming rampantly out of control, it would also make everyone in the conference room rich and the shareholders very happy. It is a win-win situation, and they all knew that a truer definition of that phrase could not be had.

As they were toasting their massive success, thousands of units of Alanitrol were already being shipped to not only all fifty states, but the four corners of the world. It was designed to empower women with a means to combat a horrible violation committed by any person who would do them bodily harm. Of course men, particularly gay men, who were also targeted sexually, were not excluded as candidates for use of Alanitrol. A bigger demographic was even better news for their sales department. Win-win.

Somewhere deep in a lush green valley on the island of Oahu's west coast, a young punk named Kimo Kealani and a middle-aged man whom he'd known since childhood would soon discover Alanitrol on an internet news page. The middle-aged man would then attempt to use it in tandem with Rohypnol to try and remedy an unbearable situation he had found himself hopelessly overwhelmed by.

Alejo Melendez

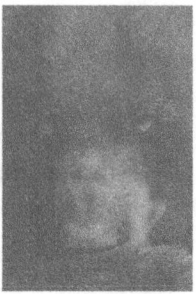

Suspect

NOW, ABOUT A full month later, after all the pain, grieving, and no amount of closure, Jimmy receives a call from the Royal Canadian Mounted Police asking Jimmy to come back to Canada for some questions. Mark's videos gave excellent close up footage of the bear and its unique markings, which were then catalogued and distributed to all hunters, lodges, and game wardens. There was no way to tell if the bear was now dead, or just wily enough to remain hidden. But that face, those markings, and especially those eyes are indelibly etched into Jimmy's brain. Yet he has a bad feeling about his impending visit to the Canadian authorities, that he may be their prime suspect and that he may never get the chance to hunt this killer animal down.

When the plane touches down and it is deemed safe to do so, Jimmy places a phone call to his lawyer, Preston Akahana, a former Hawaii State Senator and a distinguished long-serving member of the Hawaii State Bar Association. The temperature is much lower here, but the deeper, more profound chill comes not from the region but from the memories of what this area represents, especially as he looks west towards the vast spread of Mountains that alter life and meteorology alike. The spacing, the cold, the very pristine Canadian nature of everything surrounding him

Creaking Door

presently, once held pure majesty, a sense of wonder, and even innocent fascination. Now it holds only sadness and fear, visions of blood and guts and intestines, the savagery within its wilderness, and indifference from its smiling citizens and their tart beers. It is all a matter of perspective of course, and Jimmy's vision of Alberta has since been tainted a dark, very opaque shade of crimson. Jimmy and Pres have had discussions prior to Jimmy's departure and Jimmy has been briefed on what, and more importantly, what NOT to say.

A man Jimmy's never met before, Henri Laplatt, is the lead inspector in the investigation and he is the one who meets Jimmy at the arrival gate.

Henri is six two and about two hundred twenty pounds. He carries his frame with a kind of cop like swagger that makes him appear a few inches taller and a few pounds huskier. He has dark brown hair, deep probing eyes with black irises, and a lantern jaw to further invoke his tundra masculinity. His smile appears warm but could very well be another police tool; the disarming warm veneer and façade.

Jimmy and Henri exit the semi empty terminal and his car is parked right at the curb, a police privilege for which they are both grateful. The last thing Jimmy wants to do is walk a half mile to some cold concrete parking structure in The Great White North. It is just the two of them and Jimmy is sure this is designed to put him at ease, but he still can't shake his anxiety that something bad is about to go down. It is the way Henri greets him, the very way he looks at Jimmy, through what appears to be a cloud of suspicion and a thirst to close the case, his case, the stain it has become on his home, his province, his world of Molson's six packs and the singing of "Oh Canada" before every puck is dropped onto the ice with the cast iron weight and gravity Jimmy feels now. This is beyond the weight of the world; it is cosmically enormous and interplanetary. It is the immense investigative and prosecutorial weight and specter of an entire solar system.

Henri has done preliminary research on Jimmy, knows he comes from money with a hotel magnate for a father and a beauty queen for a mother. He knows Jimmy has gone to private schools his whole life and is seen frequently with a different woman every week. He travels regularly to seek out adventures in the great outdoors. And he is devastatingly handsome with the supreme physique of a well-conditioned athlete. Henri cannot wait to put this pretentious prick behind bars.

The Police headquarters are nicer than Jimmy expected. Jimmy is told it is fairly new, built only three years ago. It is three stories of concrete, glass, and steel and takes up the entire block. The Jail is two blocks over. Like every structure in Edmonton that Jimmy has encountered since Mark's death and his current arrival, it is cold and impersonal, but this building and this man taking him inside of it especially so, like lifelessness and cruelty, devoid of warmth or heartbeat or pulsation of any kind. It is Transylvanian, sinister and colorless. The blood leaves Jimmy's face and he feels himself paling.

Jimmy and Henri go to Inspector Laplatt's office on the third floor. It is smallish at ten by ten feet with six metal file cabinets squeezed in on two sides. All six cabinets are a weird mismatched color and show signs of abuse; drawers slammed in anger and chipped paint by careless rushed movements within the small enclosure, some dings, some dents. Three cabinets are grays and the rest are various shades of black. All of them are scuffed and look like reclamations from an office supply surplus sale. A laptop sits on one side of his desk, files and papers strewn about the rest of the blotter. The entire building is warm, but Henri's office is furnace-like by comparison. It must have been over eighty degrees. It felt cozy at first but soon, doffed in his thick wool-lined leather jacket, Jimmy begins feeling trickles of sweat down his back and armpits and suddenly realizes why Henri was wearing short sleeves under his bulbous trench coat. Jimmy goes to hang his jacket and looks for a nearby stand. There is a small rack of deer antlers for this purpose, a ten pointer with nice polished tines. They are mounted on one side of Henri's office, just abreast of his smoked-glass door window with his name and title stenciled in black paint. The antlers stand out like a huge white Lima bean atop a tray full of lentils moving along a conveyor belt in a legume factory waiting for some quality control person to pick it out. It also should have been the first thing Jimmy the hunter noticed but he obviously had other more pressing matters on his mind.

Henri invites Jimmy to sit down, he is still cordial. With that impish Canadian smile still plastered across his lips he begins asking questions. His chair is some kind of expensive, ergonomic padded, swiveling gizmo with large easily reached levers for adjustable height and backing. The armrests are padded for good measure. It is the one concession in an otherwise drab and utterly standard Government Issue office. Jimmy's chair, by comparison, is varnished wood, no armrests, and a straight backing with a slightly curved shoulder board amounted atop two pieces of three-inch diameter dowels, about as cheap as an office chair gets and entirely like something out of the depression era.

"Do you know anyone who would've wanted to harm Mark?"

Jimmy says no at first even though he knows of a couple of Mark's adversarial relationships back home, but none who would fly to Canada to commit that sophisticated level of crime. Jimmy is nervous enough to forget the sinister deed could have been done beforehand.

"Anyone at all, even someone who you do not think is capable but has a grudge."

This gives Jimmy pause as he ponders a townie back home who had hit on his wife Kelly, also a hotel customer who once threatened him with bodily harm though Mark would have dispensed with him easily, some boyhood football rivals, and a few others any normal person would have confrontations with as a part of normal everyday modern life, but no one with the wherewithal to actually plot something as clever as timing his death on a bear hunt. Or was Jimmy not giving this mystery person enough credit?

Now the rival outfitter Bart Ronde comes to mind and the nasty phone call the night before the bear hunt. Jimmy's mind starts quickly rolling through the possibilities. He tells the inspector all about it. JSP has already been routinely questioned, as was Jimmy, at the time of Mark's death, about a month ago. It appears JSP will soon be brought in again. As will Ronde. Jimmy tells Inspector Laplatt that Ronde's grudge was against JSP but it involved the clientele, and this raises Henri's eyebrows, but only for a split second. He regains his cool, impartial demeanor and continues his questioning.

The interrogation continues for another half hour, then Inspector Laplatt asks that Jimmy not leave town for a few days, that they have further questions they need to ask him. He suggests Jimmy go on a hunt to pass the time, not realizing how insanely morbid and crude that sounded. Although it feels wrong, like a setup, Jimmy agrees to stay in downtown Edmonton, at least for a few days. After all, he is innocent. He feels like a hibernating lemming and Laplatt is the stomping Polar Bear anxious to unearth the protective layer of snow and feed. Three minutes after exiting police headquarters he calls his attorney Pres. They agree Pres must fly to where Jimmy is so he can provide counsel. He will stay a few days at a nearby Hilton courtesy of the Edmonton Police Department.

That Ronde angle is new but quickly quashed as the man had an airtight alibi. An hour after Ronde's nasty phone call, phone records and witnesses verify that JSP contacted two incoming clients and rerouted them to Bart claiming his lodge had needed unanticipated maintenance and would be closed. They were brought in earlier than expected the next day. Bart was two hundred miles away with a husband and wife hunting team bagging elk in Kakwa, further up north and closer to British Columbia. They filled their tags. The clients, JSP, and the Park Rangers verified it. Unless he had conspirators, Ronde was cleared and off

Creaking Door

the table. Besides, why would Bart Ronde kill Mark Tam? Hunters, predominantly visiting hunters, were the outfitter's lifeblood; it made no sense to bite the hand that feeds you.

For now the focus remains squarely but quietly on Mark Tam's best friend Jimmy Kanoho. To Henri, he is the kind of privileged pretty boy he would love to see in prison, denied his freedoms, eating powdered eggs and grey processed meats, and taking it up the ass on a regular basis.

Alejo Melendez

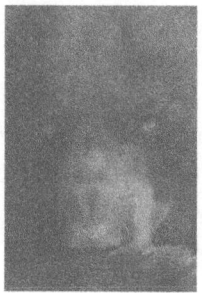

Henri and Pauly Boy

"WHAT THE FUCK were you thinking?" yells Captain Ronald Kipana. "We have a potential fucking terrorist attack and you sulk off to meditate!"

He is red in the face and beads of sweat roll down his forehead. Kipana is royally pissed off, eyes bulging, collar loosened. Before him stands the object of his ire; Pauly Boy Magat, who is standing at attention and not daring to move a hair before his commanding officer.

"You're command Pauly Boy, practically brass, and you go and pull this shit!"

The door to the captain's office has been closed but the blinds remain open and everyone is gawking. Kipana has done this intentionally to send the very strong message to his troops: no one is above policy or his wrath.

The captain finally sits, not at his oaken desk with the high leatherback swivel chair but on the vinyl couch beneath his wall of fame, chock full of awards and commendations from his eighteen years of service to the HPD. The hiss of his cushion breaks the silence. He pauses for a beat, takes a deep calming breath, then invites Magat to sit in the love seat opposite him. The Captain hoists his size twelve wingtips onto the large golden finished koa coffee table. It is only then that Pauly notices the manila folder he has been holding, which he now slides across the table.

"You know about the Mark Tam death?" he asks

"Yeah," says Pauly, "an open-and-shut, up in Canada right?"

"Yes and no. It's been reopened and you are to liaise with one of theirs, an Edmonton homicide detective named Henri Laplatt."

"Homicide?"

"Yeah Braddah, look like our local legend was da victim of foul play."

Alejo Melendez

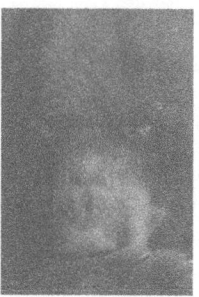

Rousseau

JANET ROUSSEAU THOUGHT graduating from Toronto's Ryerson University was the happiest day of her life. A lifelong Ontario resident, she remembers the happy looks on her parents at her commencement ceremony. Her uncles and aunts, brothers and sisters, and even most of her cousins were at the after-party in her backyard in rural Owen Sound, Ontario. She was born and raised in the same house on a plot of land located at the mouths of the Pottawatomi and Sydenham Rivers on an inlet of Georgian Bay, a connected body east of massive Lake Huron.

The land had been in her family for five generations. As recently as the 1950's, her ancestors still made their living as fur trappers. Her father did it as a boy and occasionally still traps a beaver or a hare, but nowadays it is strictly for its meat, although the pelts are not wasted and are sold to local furriers.

She particularly likes when her mother makes fresh Lapin a La Cocotte—French Rabbit Stew. Although her parents have roasted, baked, barbecued, fried, and even stewed it, Janet somehow never acquired a taste for beaver. It was a little too gamey, too musky for her palette.

Although Owen Sound is considered to be Southern Ontario, it is 282 kilometers north of Niagara Falls in New York, which is

Creaking Door

the closest US point yet still about three and a half hours away. Considering Niagara Falls once froze over in the late 1800's, the winters here at Owen Sound, in *Southern* Ontario, are very cold indeed.

Attending Ryerson was a cultural shock to the young maiden from Georgian Bay. At 191 kilometers away, it was the furthest she had ever been from home. Toronto is also the most populous city in Canada, the provincial capital of Ontario, and a foreign country as far as young Janet was concerned. She had never seen so many people, so many buildings, so many of everything crammed into such crowded spaces; the street traffic, the pedestrian traffic, the houses and buildings, and the lines for everything from shopping centers to movie theaters to class registration.

She endured, acclimated, made lifelong friends, and graduated on time with a degree in criminology. Janet excelled in forensic science, and when one of her many applications for employment was accepted, she had a brand new happiest day of her life. She was the newest criminologist and forensic scientist for the Edmonton Police Department. Her parents were overjoyed that it took less than a year for her to find such a good job. She'd already dormed four years in the blight of urban Toronto; Edmonton would be a piece of cake. Her English was better than decent and she'd shot and killed a polar bear at the tender age of twelve. She was ready for police work in the western part of her beloved country.

On her first day at her new job, she was picked up at the airport by her new boss Ian Fournier. When she read his name in her acceptance letter she was overjoyed she would be working with a French name. She found him at the arrival gate holding a placard with her name on it. She promptly bid him an enthusiastic "bon jour" but the oaf spoke no French. Imagine that! He actually did but very little, not enough to carry a conversation. His mother was from Seattle. That explained a lot. Still he was kind, patient, and moderately good looking although very married.

When they arrived at Police headquarters she found a slate-grayish-white three-year-old (she'd been told) three story building of inlaid pebble concrete, glass and steel that took up the entire block. For this country girl it was intimidating. Their designated work area is on the second floor. Fournier took the stairs and Janet, who always votes green, appreciated that.

When they get there she finds it clean and organized. There are only five other people in this department and all five are in the exterior lounge waiting to meet and greet her. She shakes everyone's hands, tries not to have too much of a French accent, and is welcomed with big smiles and big hopes. They'd been waiting months to fill the vacancy left by Sam Richard who retired at age sixty after twenty-seven years with the department. Janet was a rookie but treated like a godsend. For now. She would have loved Sam Richard, a true French Canadian who did indeed parlez-vous français and insisted on the proper French pronunciation of his last name: Ree-shard.

In life, timing is everything and Janet had just missed a potential master mentor. He was the most knowledgeable, the most experienced, and because of his grandfatherly age, was also the most patient worker in the often hectic, fast paced lab. And he could have taught her in her primary tongue. That Sam would not be present for Janet's development would prove crucial in the coming days.

The lab space is particularly well lit and actually a bit too bright. Janet will learn later it is a necessity for the very small particulate matter they often are tasked with examining. She is shown the equipment and will spend several weeks being trained and tutored, reading manuals and performing the mundane tasks of police forensic science. And she couldn't be happier.

Janet is 5'4, 105 pounds, thin, wears black horn-rimmed glasses, has black hair and hazel brown eyes, is a direct descendant of the first Europeans to settle Ontario, and is pretty but mousy, confident yet quiet, clean looking and nice smelling. She is a

Creaking Door

feminist and has never had a boyfriend and is, in fact, "untouched." She's kissed boys on occasion and come close during her Ryerson years but she knew it was not the time for these boys who were just trying to accumulate conquests and sow some oats. She was saving herself for the right man, not some beer swilling juvenile.

She once had a crush on her handsome math professor, but so did a lot of other girls; taller shapelier girls with bigger breasts and bigger tolerances for accommodating his gregariousness. It actually helped with her scholastics; no social life meant more attention on academics, and a very good student she was. Top of her class in fact, and that was one big reason she had ended up here in the big leagues rather quickly. She was more than happy to be out west and away from crime-ridden Toronto. She did in fact receive offers from constabularies in that area but she turned them all down. Spending four years away from home meant she could never be happy living with her parents again. She had fled the nest for good. Of course she still loved and missed her parents and quaint little Owen Sound, and she would be sure to visit at the appropriate times, but for now she was an overjoyed fledgling glad to be able to spread her wings and take flight out in the open spaces of glorious Edmonton, Alberta.

Alejo Melendez

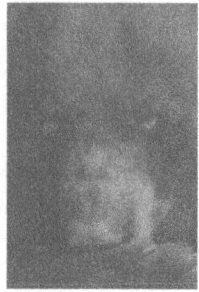

Randall

RANDALL WHITAKER IS very excited as he unpacks his new rifle from the back of his father's Jeep Grand Cherokee. He turned fourteen yesterday and his father is taking him on his first real hunt, a hunt where he will actually get to finally shoot his gun at live game.

His father Chet has bought him a brand-new Remington 700 ADL Bolt-Action Rifle and Scope Combo. They had spent all day yesterday at the range practicing with it. Randall checked his gear and his clothing. When he confirmed to his father that his clothes were buttoned up and his boot laces tight, they set off down a trail Chet was very familiar with; he had hunted for whitetail in this exact spot since before he was Randall's age.

They'd walked about three miles through brush and rugged terrain. This spot was chosen for its short and easy hike. Just about the time Randall was going to ask, Chet told his son they'd reached the spot. The pair promptly cut through the brambles, crossed a small creek, and then came upon a bluff overlooking a wide meadow with wild spring alfalfa and clover growing in sporadic patches. He did not have to instruct his son to now sit quietly and await any deer roaming the area. Young Randall was very excited.

After two hours Randall had to pee. A single doe had

Creaking Door

wandered by thirty minutes ago but no bucks followed yet. His father told him to do it into the small creek about fifty yards back so the scent would wash away. He would respray him with scent killing extract upon his return.

Randall unzipped and began urinating when something shiny caught his eye. He was in a thicket covered by some tree canopy. It was an unnatural glint that the speckled sunlight had dabbled upon in the slow trickling waters of this creek. He reached down to grab it. It was a medicine bottle of some kind, the kind that was meant for use with hypodermic needles, the kind with rubber tops held fast with a metal rim. The name on the bottle's label was faded, but it bore the name Alan followed by a few spaces and another "L". It had obviously been in the creek for some time. Curious, he placed the bottle into one of his pockets to inspect it later.

Randall took a shot at a decent buck about an hour later but missed high. They waited another ninety minutes before Chet, seeing his son disappointed and growing antsy, decided to pull the plug and call it a hunt. He promised Randall they would try again next weekend. Buoyed by the buck he'd almost bagged, he readily agreed to the return trip and some pizza on the way home.

Three days later Randall's mom Etta was doing laundry. Chet and Randall's weekend camo gear were among the garments in their hamper. Like she'd always done, she began checking pockets for things that could damage the washing machine like money, or paper that would disintegrate in the wash and embed itself as pulp on all of the other clothes. Once she even found bullets in her husband's pockets and on another occasion, an eight-inch folding buck knife. While checking pockets, she found a bottle in Randall's pocket. It was a drug of some kind, an injectable drug. They'd caught Randall with a small amount of marijuana two months ago and had smelled beer on his breath at least three other times. They knew he was at that vulnerable age when young boys experiment, but this was something altogether new, something very alarming.

She showed it to Chet that evening when he'd come home

from work as an insurance adjuster. They did extensive online research and found the only drug that fit was called Alanitrol, a new drug used to mask Rohypnol, the date rape drug. Rohypnol had been on the news the past couple of years so Chet and Etta were familiar with it. They began piecing a conjectured theory together. Was their son some kind of serial rapist using these drugs to attack and molest unconscious females, then cover his trail? They were horrified.

They phoned Chet's hunting buddy on the police force, Henri Laplatt, an inspector of seven years and a twenty-year veteran of the Edmonton police force. Chet asked him about any rapes in the area and the public details. Thankfully, there was only one. It occurred forty miles away about three months ago and the date rape drug was not used. The young woman was assaulted by her forty-five-year-old alcoholic step-father. That was the only instance.

When Laplatt inquired as to why they were asking such strange questions about a very specific crime like rape, they happily unburdened everything. Chet and Etta wanted to turn over the drug to Henri because quite frankly they did not know what to do with it. They also asked Henri to question Randall about it.

So Uncle Henri came over that night, gathered parents and son in the living room and got right to the point. Randall swore he'd found it in a stream last weekend during his and Chet's last hunting trip. When asked where exactly, Randall told him, "near Miller's crossing in the creek about a hundred yards back of the alfalfa meadow". Laplatt knew it well, he and Chet had hunted it many times together in their youth and also about a year ago when the whitetail were running hot following a rainy Spring that caused their food supply to explode. It was in the Mount Becker area.

Etta asked the obvious question if any rapes had occurred in that remote area. Laplatt said no and that the only thing he could think of was some hunter being killed, mauled, and partially eaten by a black bear about a year ago.

Creaking Door

The Whitakers nodded in recognition, they all remembered the incident. It was big news in their little township of Wildwood where nothing, especially drug induced date rapes, ever happened. That was big city stuff.

Uncle Henri asked Randall for a paper napkin of some kind. He wrapped the medicine bottle in it, placed it in his coat pocket, and then stood to leave. They offered him coffee and dinner, he politely declined. Father and son made him promise to go on a hunt with them soon, and he agreed. It was something for Henri to look forward to in the miserable and thankless world of law enforcement. Whatever was cooking in the kitchen smelled damned good but Henri was anxious to get back to his office so he could look up a few things about that mauled hunter, some American named Mark something. It was his case and had gone cold. At least he considered it cold. Officially, it was closed. A slam dunk, straight up, no doubt about it bear mauling hunting accident. But something about that death always struck Laplatt as odd and it stuck in his craw. That Mark guy was an experienced hunter, over twenty years, had been to JSP's lodge and others in the area many times, so the territory was not unfamiliar to him, and yet he was taken by surprise by the very animal he was on the lookout for.

Alejo Melendez

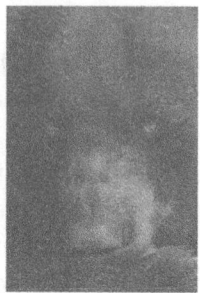

Investigation

LAPLATT DUG DEEPER, found the medical examiner's report and discovered to his surprise that Mark Tam's blood was only tested for alcohol, a common find in the local hunting related accidents. It was many a Canuck who had tipped one too many and accidentally shot a nearby companion or himself in the foot. Despite forensics being shorthanded, he placed an order to run a full screening on Mr. Tam's blood. The boys in evidence and the labs would be miffed, but fuck'em thought Henri, he was going on not just a hunch but a *bona fide* new lead. Young Randall's incidental find may finally crack the case after all this time.

Two mornings later, the sun rose on a lovely Canadian spring day, crisp air, trees budding with their annual regrowth. Moose mothers could be seen escorting their new babies across busy thoroughfares. Canadians knew to slow for this phenomenon not only to respect the newborn life as a natural sustainable resource and national symbol, but because hitting moose could often prove fatal. They were as big as Amish plow horses and as heavy as a 1950's Buick. Many an automobile insurance policy premium had skyrocketed from the damage caused by moose during non-fatal encounters.

Laplatt actually slowed down twice for moose crossings while on the way to work. The second crossing took long enough to afford him a look at the surrounding hillsides. He could make out white and green budding offshoots springing out of the branches and draping the slopes with speckled dots of lightness to contrast with the stark dark brown of the winter-weathered mountains. Seeing this reaffirmation of life made him temporarily forget about something he'd been eagerly waiting almost two days for.

Approximately thirty hours after Henri's request for a more thorough screening on Mr. Tam's blood, the results had come back. He was right. Rohypnol, the date rape drug, had been found in Tam's blood. It was in a dosage consistent with an amount designed for a quick nap, not a deadly dose of Rohypnol but enough to incapacitate him long enough for some mischief to be pulled off without his knowledge. It was intriguing to say the least. There was not enough left of Tam's body remaining to adequately test for sexual assault at the time of his death, and no one had even considered that remote possibility then. Tam had already been cremated, his ashes scattered into the Hawaiian waters he'd loved so much his entire life. And now it was up to Laplatt to forge ahead and answer the mystery of why this man had that particular drug in his body, and since Alanitrol was used specifically to counteract the same Rohypnol found in Tam's blood, the fact that it was found about a mile away from the mauling could not possibly have been a coincidence.

Because of Henri's diligence, a provincial prosecutor has reopened the investigation and the tissue and blood samples previously untested that have now revealed the presence of Rohypnol has forced the government's hand. It was clearly evident at first that a bear had mauled Mark to death but now everything has changed. With these latest test results, it appears Mark was murdered, and not at the hands, or paws, of a giant black bear, which has still not been caught.

Any forensic evidence left on the bottle of Alanitrol had long ago been degraded. That it was found in a running stream also made any kind of evidentiary forensic testing seem a waste of time, but not out of the question, not to Laplatt who now insisted on thoroughness from his subordinates. No more half-measures to embarrass the department and leave the victims' families wanting and disrespected. He was determined to solve this killing that he now knew in his gut to be a crime.

As expected, his latest test request to examine the Alanitrol bottle proved negative. So Laplatt would now pound the pavement and go old school with a modern twist, he would use his laptop to follow any possible trail its owner may have left.

The Edmonton Police Department covered a wide swath of jurisdiction that extended out to some of the more remote surrounding areas, including some that were four or five hours away. There was local law enforcement in many of these outlying areas but when a major crime was committed the Edmonton Police, the big boys with the heavy equipment, were called. Most townships, like Wildwood, the one the Whitakers lived in, had a single sheriff with volunteer deputies to handle the virtually nonexistent crime amongst the good peoples of the territories.

Knowing this, Henri plotted a strategy to move forward with the limited resources he would have once he took the investigation back to the mountains where it had originated. His first objective was a return scouting trip, to re-examine the facts and the geography to help determine the team he'd like assembled, one he knew he would battle with department heads over. He wanted to bring at least seven people on board; he knew he would be lucky to get one. He would have to make use of the locals. He would never say it to their faces but Henri thought of them as backwoods hicks when it came to serious crime solving. He would have them handle the mundane chores and be used as muscle only.

Alanitrol was still in its probationary phase with the FDA so obtaining it could not have been easy. It was only distributed to doctors and outlets that were mandated by law to keep tight inventory controls under penalty of criminal prosecution by the

FDA and the governing medical state boards. Abuse and theft of Alanitrol was a federal offense. His online search had shown seven possibilities. One bottle had gone missing at a gynecologist's office two months ago in Baltimore, Maryland. Too soon for Laplatt's purposes but not discounted just yet in his eyes. The remaining six instances were all over a year old, one being in Hawaii roughly fourteen months ago. Henri smiled and felt he had hit the jackpot.

Alejo Melendez

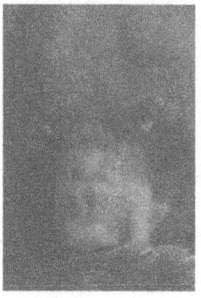

Hawaii

HE TURNED HIS attention to a Doctor Russell Mallari, a general practitioner with an office in Waipahu, on the leeward side of Oahu and, interestingly enough, only about a twenty-minute drive from Makaha, Mark Tam's hometown but more importantly Jimmy Kanoho's as well. Laplatt had already begun formulating a list of suspects and topping it was still Mark Tam's hunting companion. But all reports and indications were that the two were thick as thieves, virtual brothers their entire lives. All witnesses said they loved each other unconditionally and would never have harmed each other. They may have been like brothers, but so were Cain and Abel Laplatt thought.

Doctor Mallari submitted a list of employees past and present and was made to recall first from memory, and then with the help of his receptionist, who else had come into the office in that time frame. The length of time made it difficult for any of the office people to recall any helpful detail, big or small. Dr. Mallari's inventory records were combed and a list of all deliveries was followed up. Laplatt started with this because a patient list was of course off limits and would require a subpoena.

Fourteen months ago a company simply named Aloha Medical Supplies had delivered three boxes of standard disposable supplies;

one box had latex gloves in small, medium, and large sizes, one box had surgical masks for patients and employees alike during flu season mostly, and a third box containing several bottles of betadine, a standard disinfectant for the many lacerations the doctor treated in the course of a year. Tucked in with the betadine were five complimentary sample bottles of a new drug called Alanitrol. According to the records, a day after that delivery it was discovered that a bottle of Alanitrol was missing. This was promptly reported to the local board. The report steadily made its way up the chain to the federal authorities. The incident was placed on a federal and national watch list as standard protocol. When taken alone, Alanitrol was harmless. No real effort or priority was made to investigate its whereabouts. The interesting thing, when looked into further, was the parcels delivery man, a guy named Kimo Kealani.

    Mr. Kealani lived in Nanakuli, a town only ten minutes away from Makaha. Kimo also worked summers at the Awaawa a few years ago when he was a teenager, the famed hotel owned by the Kanoho family. Some loose ends were finally being tied and this investigation had just gotten a lot more interesting.

Alejo Melendez

Nei

IT TOOK SOME strong persuading but the Edmonton brass finally agreed that a travel voucher for Laplatt to Hawaii was germane to the case. The Honolulu Police Department was duly notified and another local detective, Pauly Magat, who had consulted on the Hawaii side of the case with Laplatt a few months ago, was assigned to be Henri's liaison.

Magat, who was dark skinned, 5'10 and 185 pounds of stocky well packed muscle, greeted Laplatt at the arrival gate with a cup of fresh-brewed Kona Coffee. Laplatt, who had never tried the Hawaiian brew, exclaimed his delight by saying, "Wow! That's some good shit!"

Magat laughed as they strolled to the curb where his unmarked crown Vic was parked. Laplatt, who had left a forty-seven degree Canadian spring morning, was now traipsing in eighty-five degree Hawaiian sunshine. He'd worn a fur-lined leather jacket for both his departure and return to Edmonton. Even without his jacket, he was working up a healthy sweat, an embarrassing one. He'd not yet acclimated. His office might have been toasty but it lacked this local cloying humidity that was sure to bring him to his knees, a Hawaiian punch.

The Crown Vic's light gray leather seats were scorching hot.

Creaking Door

The car had been sitting curbside in the sun for only twenty minutes. Despite the cracked windows, the interior temperature had risen past the mid-nineties. Magat grabbed a nearby towel and used it to insulate the steering wheel, which was sizzling to the touch. He blasted the air conditioning as Laplatt swore his life in gratitude to the clairvoyant Hawaiian. After some customary exchanges of pleasantries, Magat told Laplatt that their boy Kimo had already been picked up and was back at HPD HQ in an interrogation room being sweated by detective Robert Fernandez for details. He was denying having anything to do with the missing Alanitrol.

Kimo Kealani was a year older than Jimmy and Mark. He was one of several drug dealers on Oahu's west side, but he was perhaps the most well-known. Growing up impoverished, he'd gone to public schools all his life including the notorious Waianae High School, an institution known for their winning football teams and the massive Polynesian players that came out of its program. Many Samoan, Tongan, and Hawaiian-blooded players out of Waianae now play in the NFL, many more are scattered throughout the landscape of big-time college programs.

Kimo has a mildly long rap sheet. He was first arrested for shoplifting when he was just twelve. A few burglary convictions followed during his high-school underclassman years, then a leap to the big time when he assaulted a teacher, Mr. Apisa, during a junior year math class in which he could not grasp the concept of fractions. He was expelled, did time in juvi, and never completed his high-school education. He'd had ample opportunities to acquire his GED but felt it unnecessary when copious amounts of money flowed in from his criminal enterprises. He dealt weed, coke, acid, Quaaludes and other pills, and occasionally robbed a house or two on the more affluent sides of the island. He'd learned well as a minor; he'd never been caught as an adult despite the fact that everyone, cops included, knew he was perpetrating crimes. Kimo had been picked up for questioning and like the experienced criminal that he was, he never broke a sweat over it.

His persona of ultra cool played well with his thug friends and the females that gangster life attracted. Bad boys were in vogue again at the Nanakuli end of the coast.

They lied and told him his prints were on the recovered bottle. He saw right through the trap they were laying. They then told him their secret witness confessed and named him as an accomplice; again they were caught in another lie. Kimo was not smarter than they were, just not as desperate. He maintained his stone-cold silence and waited for the right time to invoke his lawyer if needed.

After two hours without a break, Kimo stood up. He'd had enough of this balderdash. His legs were stiff and his gluteus had partially fallen asleep but, like a hit batsman, he would never let on to any kind of discomfort or pain. He merely wanted to appease five oh knowing they would roust him if he at least didn't stick around to answer most of their inane questions. He was playing the game, the cop/perp game.

Continuing his tough guy routine, he asks, "so, am I under arrest or what?"

Fernandez shook his head no. Kealani headed for the door.

"Thanks for coming in Kimo, we'll be in touch."

"Sure thing Bobby," says Kimo with a bit too much sarcasm. He's had previous dealings with detective Fernandez and knows he hates being called Bobby.

Laplatt later asks that they subpoena the security footage from the Awaawa. There are twelve cameras set up throughout the five-acre hotel grounds. With their three golf courses averaging one hundred forty acres each, their entire property totals much more than that. Thankfully, there is no need to inspect the very few golf course cameras.

Pauly and Henri obtain footage from the day the vial went missing to the day of the murder, roughly a two-month span. They review everything but pay particular attention to the entrances and the parking lot. It is tedious, exhausting work that shows no sign of Kimo paying a visit. It was a long shot. If the exchange happened, it was probably at one of their homes and definitely off hotel property. It would be hard to pin because Kimo was one of the boys, a known surfing companion to both Jimmy and Mark so his presence at any time on hotel property was justifiable.

Tailing Kimo would be useless without audio. His phone was already tapped but he seemed to know it. All of Kimo's calls were now made on a burner cell. A female police associate, a rookie ten months out of the academy, asks Pauly about the video, and he tells them to go over it again just in case.

The next day Pauly and Henri review facts and gathered evidence. They wrack their brains trying to piece together a very complicated puzzle. They know they are very close to finding their Rosetta Stone but so far it has proved elusive. They decide to take a break and hit up a trendy restaurant in Waikiki. The scenery was great, the food's reputation only a little better than mediocre. Henri knew it was more the venue than the fare, but he was being treated and he'd skipped breakfast to get a head start on the case.

At the restaurant they were seated favorably in an open lanai. Pauly was a regular. The famous Waikiki Beach with its sandy white shores lay just across the street. There were a lot of pedestrians roaming the sidewalks, a great spot to people watch. Magat orders chicken curry with rice while Laplatt orders a Ruben with an ice-cold apple cider. The trade winds are blowing and it creates a nice balmy atmosphere out on the open lunching area. Coconut trees sway and pedicabs bustle to beat the momentum-killing red lights. Tourists are everywhere and are easy to distinguish simply by their skin tone but also their apparel, which seems completely out of place to everyone but themselves. Ignorance is bliss. He laughed. A few uniforms patrol the area. It is extraordinarily congested for the middle of the week.

"Ever work this beat?" asks the Canadian.

"Sure," replies Pauly. "My first two years. I made seven busts and was almost stabbed by a druggie who'd lifted a purse off a tourist. He made a run for it."

"And?" inquires Laplatt.

"And I was young, dumb, in shape, and faster than the punk."

They both chuckle. A few war stories are exchanged until the food arrives. Laplatt's sandwich is large and surprisingly delicious. It arrives on an oval plate that is warm to the touch. A nice pile of French fries is mounded alongside the sandwich with a stainless-steel soufflé cup of ketchup. When his red linen napkin is unraveled, he tucks it into his front collar and under his chin, old school and perhaps a little uncouth. He is the only one in the crowded restaurant to do so. Magat says nothing and begins eating. Henri is surprised when Magat opts for the chopsticks. He was not expecting to taste a Ruben this delicious so far from New York.

As they dine Henri notices there is no trash on the street, at least not on the touristy section of the beach before them. There are also no ubiquitous street sweepers or sanitation workers, like in other big tourism based cities. He'd been to the Philippines once and one could not mistake the sanitation workers who were all decked in loud red and yellow outfits with "Metro Manila" stamped in bold, contrasting black on their T-shirts. He notices because the trade winds are blowing, and one would expect to see at least some scattered urban litter bandying about.

Henri politely offers to pick up the tab, an empty gesture, and Magat tells him to get the next one. Oahu is notorious for its traffic jams but Magat knows the back roads and gets them back to headquarters in less than twenty minutes.

They touch bases with their video team and they still have not seen hide nor hair of one Kimo Kealani anywhere near the Awaawa. Laplatt has an idea; he goes through Dr. Mallari's employee jackets, scanning faces in his mind, assembling copies of the photos in an array and tells his scouting team to look for ANY of these mugs. Thirty minutes later they hit pay dirt. Francine Cajugal, a dark skinned beauty and one of three registered nurses employed by the

Creaking Door

good doctor, is caught on video not once but three times making contact with Jimmy. The body language indicates an obvious romantic connection. In the videos they are seen giving each other brief, welcoming kisses, holding hands, and leaving the grounds with their arms around each other as they pile into one or the other's car to go on their outings.

There are no overt signs of material exchanges so the transfer of Alanitrol is not caught on surveillance. But now they have another solid lead to go on.

Alejo Melendez

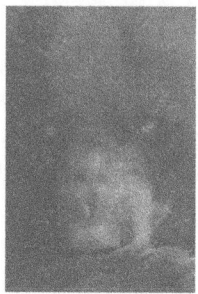

Francine

FRANCINE IS ASKED to come into the local precinct, the Waipahu Police Department. The Waipahu PD HQ looks like what it is, or rather what it used to be: a plantation style manor with eight long, two story Classic Antebellum columns fronting its once grand entrance. The white exterior is painted over every couple of years so it still looks presentable, perhaps even majestic if one uses imagination to hearken the days of yore. It is an old two story wooden structure built in the twenties when Waipahu was still a booming agricultural town. A French sugar baron, Jean Luc Verdant, erected the grand structure to run his massive sugar operation using Asian immigrants and local native Hawaiians as labor. The wages were criminally low and they revolted in 1932. The baron and his band of enforcers were killed by a mob of workers, mostly Hawaiians, who joined the growing and persistent movement against outsiders exploiting the people and the land of their beloved home. A rumor that old Frenchy was roasted on a spit and eaten like Captain Cook two centuries ago cannot be verified, or dismissed according to local legend.

The sugar mill is still standing, though long dormant, as an artifact and a government-declared historical landmark. The cane fields have all been paved over for modern subdivision housing and

Creaking Door

supporting businesses: shopping centers, grocery stores, various shops, goods and services, municipalities, etc.

There are twelve jail cells in the basement, hardly ever at full capacity but also never completely vacant. The chief and a few higher-ups have second floor offices along with a spacious reception area. There is a tall, judicial bench-like desk for the watch commander, usually a sergeant, who mans the post from which he or she directs traffic, and screens all visitors.

Sergeant Tommy Borges is behind the front desk today, he and Magat know each other well enough that they exchange friendly barbs on the way to one of three interrogation rooms in the lobby.

"Pauly Boy how's your wife and my kids?" says Tommy.

"Better than your current ugly wife now that those brats take half your salary," is Magat's playful reply.

The cops nearby laugh and Tommy tells them, "she's in three."

They make their way to interrogation room number three and find Miss Cajugal seated and seething. She has beautiful smooth mocha skin and runway model good looks.

"Sorry for the delay Miss Cajugal, you know how downtown traffic is."

She says nothing and continues her icy glare. It softens a little when Henri brings her a cup of coffee and a bottle of water. She takes this as an offering but the cops know it was given because this was probably going to take a while.

They start off by asking her the nature of her relationship with Jimmy Kanoho. She tells them they date every now and then, nothing serious, nothing steady, just good times. They went to grade school together so have known each other for over twenty years. They keep her talking and she tells them that Jimmy, because of his rugged good looks and killer surfing body, is considered a trophy catch by all the local girls. The family's multimillion dollar business is also quite the carrot.

Jimmy is smooth with the ladies and is careful about his standing, knowing one accusation or paternity suit could bring down their humble empire. He has not had a steady girlfriend since high school. It was not Francine. They started their off-and-on dating only about three years ago. She wanted something more serious at first but Jimmy said he was not ready for that level of commitment.

Now that the detectives understood the nature of their relationship and that Jimmy held most of the cards, they began probing a little deeper. They started by asking her how long she had worked for Mallari and how she had gotten the job. They were actually wondering if the Kanohos influence had come into play in placing her there. It hadn't. She earned her nursing degree at The University of San Francisco, which she attended for two years after her first two at Kapiolani Community College here on Oahu. She'd worked hard, maybe slid a little off of those good looks of hers, like all attractive people do. They delved deeper. She innocently revealed the massive student loans she was struggling to pay off.

They took that as their cue to begin a harder level of interrogation. They asked her if she knew anything about the missing bottle of Alanitrol. Imperceptibly, she squirmed and paused before saying no.

They knew they had her then. They pressed harder but in a slow and gentle manner, expertly negotiating her psychology. The fish was nibbling but not enough to set the hook, if they moved too fast and were too aggressive they would lose her. They knew how much money she made as a clinic nurse. Her bank records had already been subpoenaed and revealed a biweekly deposit of three hundred extra dollars above her automatic direct deposit salary. They asked where that money came from. Pausing for just a beat, she told them a lie she had conjured twenty-four hours ago, once she knew the cops were going to be asking.

"It's embarrassing but I perform outcall massages."

They were prepared for that kind of rebuttal and said that her phone records had already been checked and it showed no such extraneous activity. They asked if she had a website for it. She said no. They were closing in and continued to press. Where was this extra money coming from? She continued on with her massage story and said she accepted only cash and business was done word of mouth. They asked for a list of her clients. She refused. They told her they would get a court order, a search warrant to turn her apartment inside out, and hold her for obstruction until she gave it up. That is when Francine inwardly panicked and asked for a lawyer.

The day Francine received the phone call asking her to come in for questioning she immediately went to a payphone and called The Awaawa. The man who answered the phone chimed in with the standard hotel greeting pleasantry. When Francine told him who it was the nature of the man's voice changed. He gave her a number, the family lawyer Preston Akahana, and told her to call it once the magic words were uttered or implied: *jail time.*

So Francine was given a phone call and asked for her legal assistance. Glenn Kaneshiro showed up in a two-thousand-dollar suit and a pink silk Armani tie. He'd just come from court and was a third- year associate in the Akahana firm.

He burst into interrogation room three and exclaimed: "Not another word Francine."

He asked if his client was under arrest. Kaneshiro was told that she was not, at least not yet.

He patted her hand and said, "let's go Francine. All other questions can be directed to me." He placed his embossed business card on the table. The detectives didn't need it. The Akahana Law Firm was famous, practically on the police equivalent of their speed dial.

Francine exhaled a huge sigh of relief. The Kanohos had come through again. It looked like everything was going to be all right. The direct link between the stolen Alanitrol and Jimmy Kanoho had not yet been established and left the two cops frustrated but more determined than ever. They could smell that they were getting close. A bigger, clearer picture was emerging. And the beautiful Francine Cajugal was an intricate part of it.

Dr. Mallari was also questioned further, but informally and over the phone. The only people in his clinic who would have had access to any drug would have been the two doctors or the three nurses. The other physician, the squeaky-clean Dr. Ben Batchu had been hired after the bottle went missing so his involvement was dismissed. Again, the three nurses, especially Francine Cajugal, were placed under a microscope. Pressure was brought to bear on Mallari, who then pressed the only possible people, his three nurses. The police had shared Francine's information with him, that she'd acquired extra money, that she also claimed she ran outcall massages, and that they knew she was lying but could not prove it. So Dr. Mallari's help was again solicited. He did not want that kind of reputation or odious activity associated with his practice or among any of his employees, let alone his caregivers. He cut Francine's hours and let her know in very specific terms that he was not happy that she was the target of such intense scrutiny, and more importantly, that she was the prime suspect in the burglary of such an expensive drug.

Mallari did not need to be schooled on how to take meticulous notes, to document them in Francine's personnel file, and to then use them to terminate her employment without repercussion. She would be blacklisted in the entire state thus rendering her hard-earned nursing degree all but useless. Her world was spinning, exactly as the detectives had planned. Francine knew the other shoe was falling, and her desperation caused her to eventually confide to her boss that she had taken the bottle. She knew her job was a lost cause now. Theft was definitely grounds for dismissal. She was now more importantly trying to avoid jail time.

She was brought in again, but this time to the big house in Honolulu, where statements were taken, and it was revealed that she had been paid two thousand dollars for the five-thousand-dollar bottle of Alanitrol. It was Kimo Kealani who had paid her.

Kimo was playing billiards near Pearl Harbor in a bar that off-duty sailors frequented. Kimo liked to hustle the Navy boys on payday. He was picked up in that pool hall during a nine ball money match. He was about to combo the five ball into the nine when his name was called out. He looked up to see two huge Samoan cops, one waving a familiar light blue arrest warrant and the other a pair of hand cuffs.

"Oh, shit," was all he could say.

Alejo Melendez

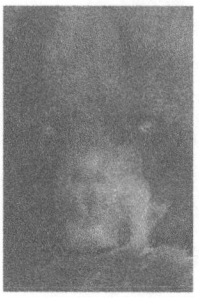

Kimo

AT THE STATION, Kimo was filled in. Francine had cracked. The noose was tightening and Kimo squirmed. "Stupid bitch," he muttered to himself.

After letting him stew for about an hour, Pauly and Henri leisurely entered the syrupy warm room armed with several manila folders and the knowledge that they now had a huge piece of the puzzle. They grilled him with the standard techniques, local brahddah Pauly Boy was the good cop, haole boy Henri the bad cop; they plied him with food and drink, deals via prosecutorial discretion, attrition, all the while peppering him with the fact that he was going down for paying off Francine and conspiring to steal a controlled substance. It was all in an effort to expose some kind of link to Jimmy Kanoho, a link they knew existed beneath some very complex and annoying layers. Layers like this punk Kimo.

They knew that not only was he *not* smart enough to mastermind a long-distance murder like that but he really had no motive; he and Mark were on best of terms as far as the investigation turned up. They had no history of bad blood, no feuds past or present, and in fact had not seen each other socially for over two years.

Kimo had gravitated to a rougher crowd early on while Mark

Creaking Door

attended private schools and was a model student and grew up to be a model citizen. Mark went on frequent hunting trips and ran his charter business dutifully. The birth and upbringing of Leinaala had also drastically altered Mark's social behavior. He and Jimmy *did* hang out with Kimo on occasion for the occasional excursions like surfing, attending local Waianae high-school sporting events, but rarely for any social reasons other than local get-togethers or parties. They ran in different circles but were all on very amicable terms.

More importantly, Kimo had never left the state and neither had anyone else within the circle of reasonable suspicion. Passports were checked and no one had left Hawaii for Canada within their time frame except Jimmy and Mark. They checked activity from two years ago, all connecting flights, all shipping vessels like cruise lines or passenger boats. They even checked transports from two years ago in case some patient psychopath was willing to lay in wait, but to no avail. No one fit the profile. Their only chance was to press Kimo. There was another person involved in this conspiracy, they were sure of it. Kimo was just another rung on the ladder, another cog in the wheel.

The questioning was getting them nowhere closer to Jimmy Kanoho. They fashioned the interrogation to skirt any direct connection to Jimmy. They were trying to trip Kimo up, but he either wasn't biting or he actually had no criminal connection to Jimmy. As time wore on, the detectives were beginning to believe the latter. After they had worn out their circuitous options, they decided to drop the hammer on Kimo. They told him if he didn't cough up his connection to Jimmy and the Alanitrol he would take the fall for the murder of Mark Tam.

Kimo seemed genuinely surprised by that accusation. They had great instincts on human behavior as homicide detectives, and it looked authentic to Pauly and Henri.

"Murder?" stammered Kimo, "I don't know anything about any murder! All I did was bang a few haole tourist chicks, I swear!"

They played it cool and acted completely unsurprised by this.

"We already know about that Kimo. We wanna know about Jimmy. Tell us more," answered Magat.

Kimo went on to detail how he had obtained some Rohypnol from a mainland source about a year ago. When one episode went badly and a female tourist almost OD'd from Kimo's careless exploit, he decided to carry the antidote as well to avoid any unnecessary and accidental deaths. He knew Francine had access and also knew she needed money so he recruited her in obtaining some Alanitrol after asking her if Dr. Mallari's office carried it. He also instructed her to deposit his large cash payment in small amounts over time to avoid suspicion.

Henri pulled out a small evidence bag labeled "Edmonton PD" with the beat-up vial of Alanitrol and shoved it in Kimo's face. Continuing to pretend that they knew all about his exploits, they pumped him for more.

"Tell us how you got to Canada without us knowing?"

"Canada? What the fuck you talking about Homey? The farthest I been away is Northern California brah. I ain't ever been to Canada and that ain't my bottle!"

The detectives were skeptical but allowed Kimo to take them to where he said his Alanitrol was. The search warrant for his house in Nanakuli turned up some recreational drugs in small amounts, a mere misdemeanor. His real cache was somewhere else. He wasn't stupid.

They drove him and his lawyers, Mr. Kaneshiro and Ellen Ilima, to the Waipahu branch of First Hawaiian Bank. The police escorted him into the bank but were stopped by Kaneshiro once the door to the safe deposit vault was reached. Their warrant did not cover his safe deposit box so Kimo went in alone. Two minutes later he emerged with a big "fuck you" grin on his face.

They left the bank while Miss Ilima stayed. The cops were sure she remained to collect whatever contraband was in that safety deposit box before the cops could get a warrant to search it.

Creaking Door

Kaneshiro and Ilima initially arrived at the police station with their briefcases, not uncommon for people in their profession. But Ellen Ilima, who looked young enough to have been in high school, most likely sported an empty attaché for the purpose of being Kimo's "mule."

Francine corroborated his story but more damaging was when Kimo actually produced, through his lawyer, the partially used bottle of Alanitrol. Its serial number and lot number confirmed it was from doctor Mallari's sample inventory.

This was a huge blow but not an entirely fatal one. They assigned the remainder of this new investigation, the one that would bring down the mainland Rohypnol ring, to another local criminal division as well as the Feds. Kimo was willing to tell all now knowing they had slyly gotten him to spill the beans on a crime he wasn't even brought in for. His lucky streak was over. But they couldn't do what they set out to do; pin a connection to Tam's murder on him with the ultimate end result of implicating Jimmy Kanoho.

Francine and Kimo would get their day in court, but so far the man they were targeting, Jimmy Kanoho, had been elusive.

Alejo Melendez

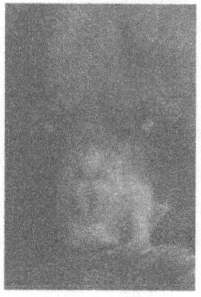

Kin

A WARM MIDWESTERN breeze blew across the bright and bountiful corn and soy fields, stirring their crops' feathery tops as they rolled on for miles in every direction. It looked like giant pond waves rippling throughout the golden ocean of grain, the sheer moving vastness like cosmic energy bouncing and radiating amid its own topaz universe. The sun was low, just over the horizon and it cast a very flattering and romantic bronzing light across the prairie and his farmland.

It reminded Ken Herzog of a college football game he had once gone to. The crowd was huge, and everyone wore red. When a yell leader instructed them to do the wave, the stadium suddenly came alive as throngs rose and fell rhythmically section by section, row by row. It felt like a massive human energy fluctuation, and he felt its electricity coursing throughout his body when the surge approached, arrived, and even as it departed his section. The vigor of that human oscillation was real power, its force palpable. It was a flowing sea of crimson rising and falling like big red living dominoes.

He was with his late father then and it was just the two of them. None of his other five brothers had been asked, just little Kenny on his special day. He had turned nine that day, and he never

Creaking Door

forgot the smells and sounds and sights of big time college football that day; the popcorn, hot dogs, caramel, beer, and the roars seemingly louder than a dozen jet engines at full throttle whenever Big Red scored.

His fondest memory was when he actually laid his eyes on the field for the first time. They'd walked a good distance, almost a mile, having parked in a general section well away from the stadium and the reserved VIP parking for the thousands of dedicated season ticket holders. During that long walk, he saw the color red adorned everywhere together with miles of drab black asphalt, grayish white walkways and grayish white smoke rising from the hundreds of grills sizzling in the Autumnal chill. They scaled the mountainous pale, cold, and dull concrete stairway that sawbacked up to their seats in the nosebleeds, walked a cavernous concourse through many concession stands and past countless people scurrying to get to their seats. They finally arrived at a tunnel entrance, walked through its short distance, and promptly entered what for Ken constituted another world, a Shangri La. The verdant world before him looked surreal, and its massive Ireland green opulence swallowed him like a black hole sucking in light. The football field with its white grid, the perfectly straight parallel and perpendicular lines, shone like a dazzling one-acre emerald to him. Its particular shade of brilliant green was unlike any he'd ever seen and, when contrasted against the massive red sea of humanity before him, felt like he was on a real-life movie set. What he didn't know at the time was that it took dozens of men, professional groundskeepers, to make the football field that way and that no pasture of grass could ever look like that naturally. That was neither here nor there, for the young Kenny Herzog all that mattered was that he had entered a fantasy world with his beloved Father. He was certain he would remember it and this day for the rest of his life.

Big Red won that day, Father and son went home happy, both of them smiling and giddy the whole two hundred and thirty-two miles home. It made Ken smile. Tragically his mother and father would be dead ten years later, killed on the very same main road they had driven that day.

They'd first taken a detour; his dad had wanted to check on a plot of land they had just turned over. The summer corn had been good and he wanted to see if the fallow soil now had the right color. The right color for his soil was something only his wisdom and experience as a lifelong farmer could determine. That field was as dark as roasted coffee with infinite staggered rows of tiny mounds and valleys that stretched forever. Leafy corn detritus and fading green husk filaments poked their crisp sun-bleached whiteness up and out of the dirt, the field crying for another pass of the tiller to masticate the fibers and splintered stalks into oblivion and pray grant uniformity to its sacred earthen scape.

After a good long look, Kenny's dad said nothing, smiled, got into the car and turned the ignition. The old Chevrolet coughed and belched black leaded supreme gasoline exhaust before its engine caught and started. They got back on the old country highway and continued the short drive to their stead. When they got home, Ken ran to his mom to tell her what a great time they'd had. In his childish excitement, he could barely manage cohesive statements when he tried to parlay the whole day into one long sentence and in just under a minute. Mother made him go upstairs to bathe in their old porcelain claw-footed bathtub and to be dressed in clean clothes and down for supper in fifteen minutes or his brothers, all older than him, would leave him nothing to eat. She reminded little Kenny to "warsh" behind the ears.

Dinner was a large pork shoulder coated in maple syrup and roasted with heaps of carrots, potatoes, parsnips, and turnips underneath it. The pork juices rendered and softened the roasted vegetables, which were separated and removed from the oven a full hour before the pork, then reheated and re-crisped in a separate baking tray just after the pork roast was pulled. All of it was delicious, the way only a mother could make.

A large oak dinner table passed on from four generations of

Creaking Door

Herzogs was set with a clean white linen sheet that would later be washed and used on someone's bed, the usual modest cycle of rotation for all Herzog bed spreads. The children were warned not to stain the table cloth. If it didn't wash out in the laundry, whoever did it would be using that as their permanent bed sheet. Everyone always sat in the same place so stain culprits could always be traced. Family seating assignment routines were common in farms across the Midwest, the Herzogs proving no exception.

All throughout dinner Ken expounded on the doings of the day. He was annoying his brothers but since it was his birthday they were all told to leave him be under punishment of Daddy's weather worn leather strap. The only one who listened raptly was his baby sister. His parents' attention was merely obligatory and gratuitous. They smiled and ate while his brothers cast evil or indifferent looks.

The sounds of supper made their farmhouse dining room come alive; knives and forks clinked, porcelain plates were scraped and sopped, milk and water were gulped down voraciously, and finally the pervasive requests to be excused five separate times concluded the meal. The two youngest always remained to help clear the table until they were old enough to work in the fields like their big brothers.

The memory was hypnotic. A distant train whistle caused Ken to snap out of his reverie. He was now looking over some of the fields for no apparent reason other than his need for fresh air despite the freshly lain manure which he'd grown up with and was more than used to. He was set to mail his sister a gift. It was a medicine bottle of some kind. A tiny one. She'd given him a thousand dollars for it and he was out here clearing his head before sending it off in the mail. All of his sensibilities were telling him it was most likely a dangerous drug probably meant to either be abused or do harm. The potential trouble it implied and the hellacious deal with the Devil he was making told him to give this directive a very wide berth. A thousand dollar check he'd already cashed and a final big brain-clearing whiff of the pungent country air told him to go ahead and send it.

    This section of land belonged to him now, this and about fifty more acres of it. With his worn Stetson pushed a little forward, and faded jeans dirtied at the thighs from wiping, he would occasionally become a cliché and get down on one knee and grab a fistful of freshly plowed soil, then let it trickle through his widened fingers like a Pearl S. Buck promotional photo, and muse.

    Like his father, he knew the dirt was sacred and he liked to gauge its texture regularly to remind himself of who he was and what he did. His brothers had gotten about the same amounts of land when the farm was divided among them. There was no bickering following father's death. The brothers accepted their inheritance and moved onward with the business of agriculture. His sister was given money in trust in accordance with her wishes to leave the farm and move to a big city elsewhere. An uncle they all loved and respected was placed as executor. Ken had not seen his baby sister in years.

Creaking Door

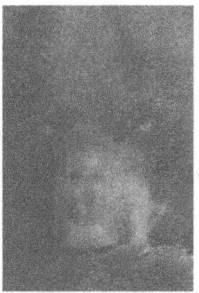

Vile Vial

LATER THAT MORNING, Ken placed a shoe box on his kitchen table. It was first lined with foam peanuts and some straw for shock absorption and insulation. A small box about the size of a deck of cards and containing the vial was then placed within. The shoebox was sealed with packing tape then wrapped in plain brown wrapping paper and heavily wound again in clear packing tape. He addressed it to his sister, whom they'd always called by her pet name; Baby. It was her birthday. She'd been asking for a certain hard-to-come-by gift, and today he would grant her wish.

She'd also told him she knew a man who would pay one thousand dollars for it. Unbeknownst to Ken, the tiny bottle was worth upwards of five thousand and could even fetch up to eight thousand in some places. In any case, he wanted to help his sister and a thousand bucks would buy a lot of beer and chaw.

It took some doing to obtain this rare artifact, but he used a connection through his brother Kerry, who was married to a woman who'd kept her maiden name.

Eunice Paxton, the woman who was the direct link to the object Baby needed, worked as an office manager at a medical supply company in North Platte, Nebraska. It is just south of Dunning where she lives with her husband of ten years, Kerry

Herzog, whose fifty-two-acre farm spills over to the next town of Halsey where Kerry grew up as a boy and still has family, his five brothers.

Eunice was pretty but a big gal, wide birthing hips and large breasted, she was what the pioneer homesteaders would have dubbed a trophy wife, a breeder, able to spit out kids on a regular basis to help run the homestead or farm. She and Kerry had only three children; ages seven, nine and ten years old.

Eunice's employer, Husker Medical, received shipments from all over the world and sent them to individual facilities throughout the Midwest but mostly within the state. They were middlemen who stored vast quantities of mostly non-perishable and disposable medical supplies. Some of their inventory involved, on a very limited basis, pharmaceuticals, but mostly it was non-descript things like latex gloves, O.R. scrubs, hospital gowns, hypodermic needles et al. They had three warehouses full of stock that every hospital and clinic within the state needed, and it was through her that Ken was now able to obtain and package the gift item for his baby sister and ship it off discreetly.

Ken had offered Kerry and Eunice three hundred dollars for the small item. Eunice wanted the extra money for a new top-of-the-line food processor. She had taken a fancy to fruit smoothies during those endless steaming prairie nights. Her nearly twenty-year-old Osterizer blender was not only a dinosaur and limited in its functions, but despite being American made in an era of quality manufacturing, it was finally on the fritz.

When she looked up the item Ken needed on her company desktop she'd seen that they carried thirty cases of it, each case containing one hundred twenty-four individual boxes of this item. When she looked up the actual product she saw it was no bigger than her thumb. She figured she could pocket one of these tiny bottles, leave its little container box empty, and no one would be the wiser once it was shipped off. What Eunice failed to do was research its true value and discover that it was a federal crime to steal any drug, especially *that* drug being it was still in its probationary phase, not to mention its very existence was based upon a very specific crime. She would not realize until it was much too late that her stolen item was under very heavy scrutiny.

One day during the company lunch break, she slipped quietly into warehouse number three. It was a warm Nebraska day and the sunshine beamed down on all of the Corn Husker state and made its colors shimmer and seemingly more vibrant. The fields seemed more golden, the orchards and woods more green. Waves of heat rolled off the asphalt she walked on to get to warehouse number three, the smallest of their storage units by far. They seldom carried perishable items but when they did, they went straight to warehouse number three, their only refrigerated storage facility. She used her cardkey to enter the secured space and was hit with a cool icy blast of goodness and relief.

It was a nice escape from the Midwestern bake, and she wished she could languish in there all day but she had a specific task to perform. She found the lot stacked on a wooden palette near the rear. She'd brought her box cutter and a roll of packing tape with her. She sliced the taped seal cleanly off of the top box, then opened it to find several rows of small container boxes that were no bigger than the box a roll of film came in. She took one, opened it, removed its content, and then placed that empty box back into the void she had just created. A quick re-taping and it looked as new as the day it left the factory. Pleased with herself, she calmly walked back to the office knowing she would soon have a brand-new fancy appliance in her kitchen.

Ken had finally first heard from his baby sister about three years before and they'd steadily kept in touch. She plied him slowly and had been informing him of the decline of her once whirlwind marriage. Baby also said she needed help, but not in the form of his physical presence, and make no mistake Ken and all of his brothers were large, hulking, Teutonic farm boys. But little sister needed another kind of material aid; she could always take care of herself.

Alejo Melendez

After all, she had the same country strong Herzog bloodline they did, but she was a lot smarter, which is why everyone knew she did not belong on a farm. She also mentioned that once she'd gotten Ken's gift, she would probably not contact him again for a very long time. Despite that red flag, Ken was determined to help his baby sister no matter what the cause of this unusual request.

The parcel, which was shipped via the US Postal Service, would be delivered by ground service and arrive in five to seven business days according to Vernon Bosworth, his longtime boyhood buddy behind the post office counter. Vernon weighed it on a modern digital scale then printed and stuck the paid postage on Baby's gift.

She told Ken not to leave a note anywhere on it, not even a return address, which Vernon, by law, had asked for. Ken lied and told Vern it was a surprise birthday gift for Baby, whom Vern remembered well because he'd had a severe crush on her. Vernon had also given her birthday presents while they were all growing up on adjacent farms so he remembered her birth date as well, which at the time of the mailing would have been the following week, and it all seemed kosher, plus Vernon recognized Baby's real name on the box, so he dropped the package into the delivery bin where it would be sorted and separated into geographic destinations.

In high school Vernon and many other boys had developed crushes on Ken's younger sister. She was the prototypical Daisy Mae beauty, often wearing cut-off jeans and an old blouse tied in a knot to perform her chores. Many of the boys would use their daddies' high-powered hunting binoculars to hide in the crops and sneak peeks at her. Many an adolescent male proclaimed his love for her, and Vernon was no different. His fairly close relationship with Ken often brought him into close quarters with the Herzog family, so he got to know Baby fairly well. He was shy and awkward, as most boys that age are, and kept his passions inward lest he stammer an awkward proclamation of some kind, become publicly embarrassed, and find himself branded MC Stammer or something similarly ridiculous and demeaning. Or worse, be out and out rejected by the girl of his fantasies and quite possibly her entire family. Vernon would lead, as most teen boys with crushes do, an adolescent life of secret despondency and longing.

Ken left the post office very happy knowing Baby too would be overjoyed in a few days. He hoped his gift would help resolve whatever it is that she is going through. He'd gotten her the gift but had no idea what it was or what it could be used for. In many ways he did not want to know.

Later that afternoon, a Postal supervisor, Josh Coleman, returned Ken's package to the front and asked Vernon why that explicit package had no return address. The supervisor reminded Vernon that nothing could go through the post 9-11 mail service without a return address due to terroristic threats. He was severely reprimanded and told he might have to interview with Federal Marshalls on just who dropped it off. Panicking now, Vernon claimed the package was his and said it must have slipped his mind and that he would take care of it. Thinking he might get lucky and rekindle any kind of past friendship as well as possible ongoing communication, he innocently jotted down his name and address on the parcel. The supervisor was mollified. Vernon knew Baby would realize it would have come from Ken, and if she asked why his address was on it he would explain it with the very simple truth; that Ken wanted it to be a surprise. Wanting it to arrive safely and ignorant of little sister's instructions, Vernon also went the extra mile and took out a small amount of insurance on it and registered the package as well.

When the package was finally received, she saw Vernon's name on it, swore, cringed, and then burned the boxes, thankful that Ken had not been nor would be implicated. The memory of Vernon's adolescent pining made her nauseated.

Alejo Melendez

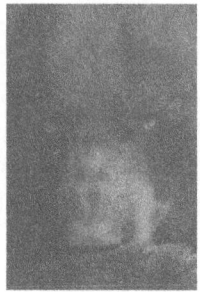

Plan

AS LEINAALA AGED she began bearing a striking resemblance to the male Kanohos. Mark joked about it at first, and then became increasingly suspicious as more time passed and the Kanoho genes began to manifest themselves in her mannerisms as well.
He pressed Kelly and Jimmy until finally, in separate corroborating confessions, they both admitted to an intimacy once upon a time during Mark and Jimmy's freshman year. It was fully two years before she had ever laid eyes upon and fallen madly in love with Mark. It was a huge weight she and Jimmy were actually finally happy to shed.

As his dating relationship with Kelly bloomed, Mark kept her existence hidden from not only his own family but the Kanohos as well. Dating a haole girl in isolated Makaha was akin to a white southern preacher's daughter marrying a northern black urban jazz musician in the 1950's.

It was an overreaction on Mark's part, but so were his other perplexing actions, like asking her not to attend his football games, claiming an athlete's superstition. He loved Jimmy but so too did the ladies. On more than one occasion has a woman Mark was interested in fallen for or gravitated toward Jimmy. And through no fault of his, Jimmy was always apologetic and could not seem to stem that particular tide. They were both handsome and affable but there was just something about Jimmy.

Kelly snuck into the big USC game but, devoid of a program which would have had photos of the players, she would never know that her one-time lover "Daniel", helmeted and fully padded, was playing on that very same field as her boyfriend Mark.

Jimmy and Kelly begged and pleaded for Mark to believe them and they swore on every oath it was the truth, and it was. Jimmy and Mark were almost always together since kindergarten, so there could seldom have been a chance for any kind of infidelity. Jimmy profusely detailed the timeline of that fateful, long-ago time of freshman year, the time Mark nailed that chick at the zoo in his dad's car. It rang a bell for Mark, and he trusted his friend implicitly. Jimmy, like his father, was as honest as the day was long. It was one of many admirable Kanoho traits. Mark also did the math; at the time of Lei's conception he and Jimmy were away on a week-long deer hunt in Montana. Upon their return Jimmy had departed on a two-week business trip with his father for a symposium on hotel management.

Still, the timeline was not bullet proof. Mark knew quickies could be accomplished inside of five minutes under whatever conditions were available. He loved and trusted Jimmy but this was something worth lying about. Back then, Jimmy was a young magnificent magnetic beast and, given Jimmy and Kelly's past, he continued to believe Jimmy to be the father of his daughter. The trick was going to be his ability to mask his growing anger and resentment.

As for Lei's mannerisms, Kelly said Lei was always around the Kanoho household so it was no small wonder that she would act like they do, use the same phrases they do, and have the same traits. Kelly claimed the resemblances, which she maintained she could not see, were purely coincidental.

Mark acquiesced, or at least seemed to. Life went on. He and Jimmy remained best friends and continued their adventurous life together. Mark was caught in a conundrum of loving Jimmy as his lifelong best friend but believing he was being lied to. All the while Mark's feelings of anger and deceit festered. Finally when Lei turned eighteen and was preparing to depart for her freshman year of college on the mainland, the resemblance could no longer be denied. Mark snapped. He told no one and showed no outward sign of the evil that lay in his heart.

The only one that noticed the very subtle change in Mark's demeanor was James. From Jimmy and Kelly he'd learned that Mark fully suspected Jimmy of fathering his beloved daughter. Mark still adored Lei but was now openly contemptuous of Kelly and secretly with Jimmy. But he kept it to himself. He would use the kind of deceit perpetrated upon him to allow him a means of revenge and justice.

All the while James knew something was brewing. He'd known Mark since he was a baby and had a father's instincts when it came to familiarity with Mark. He saw a certain glint in Mark's eye, and it wasn't a good one. Of course, he'd known about the word that Mark was putting out regarding Lei's looks. That he suspected Jimmy of fathering Lei was no secret now among the families. As time passed, some of the other townsfolk also began to notice not only Lei's resemblance to Jimmy, but the somewhat quiet tension brewing in that part of the valley.

It wasn't instinct or intuition by which James knew that the pair's latest hunt in Alberta was going to be the reckoning. He'd been receiving intel from a very concerned Kelly and a vigilant hotel employee as well. Kelly's information was sparse and involuntary. His female employee's was not. James had begun soliciting her help when he noticed a growing rift between the younger Tams. Kelly kept telling James that Mark was definitely planning something; he was seething and spoke often to her about Jimmy's sins and how he would be made to pay. His faithful employee confirmed it. James was going to do something about it but never discussed his ultimate plan with Kelly, choosing instead to keep her ignorant for her own protection, legal or otherwise. And for fear his malice aforethought would be revealed to whomever and ultimately used to implicate him.

One glorious warm sunshiny day before their impending trip to Alberta, Mark's new field canteen was laced with enough Rohypnol to render him unconscious but not kill him. James' plan was to tail them into the forest, unharness Mark from his tree stand, drop him to the ground head first in hopes of displaying signs of breaking his neck, then inject him, still alive, with the masking agent Alanitrol, and manually snap his neck. That would hopefully end the life of the kid he loved like a son and the evil that lurked in both of their hearts. James could not extinguish one without the other. He would then leave him for the many hungry bears that were coming out of hibernation just then. Alanitrol must be administered to the living if its intended purge was to be fulfilled. Whatever physical and bodily traces of Mark remained would be devoid of the drug that incapacitated him, the end result being a completely unassailable appearance of a hunting accident.

Among the many things James Kanoho Sr. was or had been—loving husband and father, successful entrepreneur, outspoken Hawaiian activist—he was also a Vietnam veteran and former Marine. Not only did he know how to snap a man's neck, he knew how to do it without making it look like another man had done it. This involved a technique requiring a precise angle of twist so only certain vertebrae were affected.

James booked his trip to Canada under the pseudonym Brett Lopez. He initially called in favors from the many people he'd met over the years who'd come and stayed at his hotel, powerful and connected people he'd bonded with and went out of his way for. James would use that influence and the wealth he'd amassed in the resort hotel business. He'd smartly arranged each favor separately so as to not reveal nor connect the entire diabolical plan to any one entity. On its surface, each step was made to seem like an innocent favor. But these efforts were all for naught.

In the end and with painstaking care and caution, he instead obtained everything he would need, including a phony passport, from a better, more covert source. He studied the drugs intensely before he planned on using them. Brett Lopez was booked on a five-hour flight to Los Angeles, caught a twelve-hour bus ride to Sacramento, and then boarded a plane to Edmonton for his final leg. The bus ride would be the undetectable gap in his long distance international commute if and when the investigation progressed to the commercial travel stage. That was also contingent on if they ever discovered Brett Lopez. It was well thought out. If the crime was ever solved, it would be done without connecting this segment of the plan to it.

Brett Lopez was also furnished with the outfitter the boys would be using. He'd accidentally already asked Mark claiming he would want to take Uncle Kaimana on a bear hunt of their own next year. Now he knew exactly where the boys were staying without having to tail them from the airport. He calmly waited until the morning of the hunt, renting a Subaru Outback four-wheel drive, the smallest all-terrain vehicle he could find, then, at a safe distance with his lights off and using night vision goggles, he followed them in the pre-dawn darkness. The goggles also came in handy when it was time to follow them on foot to their respective locations.

He lay in wait about five football fields away, glassing Mark with some high-powered binoculars, the kind the boys used on their hunts. He knew it could be hours before the right moment presented itself so he calmly sat and waited. Unlike a hunter, he COULD bring a thermos of strong coffee. When he had to, he peed right where he was situated. The coffee not only kept him awake and warm, but the foreign smells would likely keep predators away. He had not masked his scent for this express purpose. James was armed in any case. He had no intention of using his sidearm on Mark; it was merely a precautionary measure against natural predators.

Creaking Door

At about ten a.m., for some strange reason Mark abandons his current tree stand and takes a fifteen-minute walk northward. This is totally unexpected and puts James on high alert. Along the way Mark drinks from his canteen twice. Having focused entirely on Mark, James is unaware this is also the direction of Jimmy's location. He sees Mark finally stop and mount three very small portable video cameras on nearby tree trunks, a sure sign this will be his new hunting locale. James also notices there are feeding barrels about forty feet away from where Mark is standing. Mark attempts to climb a second nearby tree stand but mysteriously stops. He holds the first rung and hesitates, James suspects the drug is taking effect, although from this distance that cannot be readily determined.

The sun is getting higher but it is still cold, the increasing sunlight casts a spectacular woodsy tapestry before him, and James suddenly realizes the boys' infernal fascination with this cold, seemingly inhospitable place. He has never hunted in Canada or anywhere this far north for that matter. There was plenty of game on the outer Hawaiian Islands, particularly the Big Island, but the animals were supposedly bigger and more diverse here. He'd yet to see any big game here, but the proof was indisputable. He could sense that big elk, deer, and especially bear roamed these woods despite their eerie silence. The odors of the wild wafted about; pine, loam, fir, the earthy muskiness of the damp, and the snow-thawed moisture-laden soil. Chattering chipmunks and squirrels bandied about; sweet, ornate songs from waking birds filled the air and lingered as if ensnared by the forest mist. There existed a very pure and pristine quality to this place. The remoteness had given it an untouched, virgin like eminence, as if he'd been the only man ever to lay eyes on this place. It was a pleasant but also distracting feeling he quickly relinquished.

Suddenly Mark ditches all efforts to scale the current stand and sits with his back braced against a tree. It appears he is opting for a ground shot, and James eyes him intently as he awaits the moment to make his move. During Mark's mysterious hike, James has followed suit and has paralleled Mark. In the interim, when Mark was slowly mounting cameras, James has also moved closer in anticipation of Mark becoming unconscious. James now stands about two hundred yards away in an area thickly populated with spruces, maples, and firs. He also knows he must dispose of the mounted video cameras once he is finished. He knows for a fact that Jimmy's portable hunting cameras store all captured data on an internal SD card and do not transmit wirelessly, he can only hope Mark's are the same.

He sits in the cold, crisp Canadian wilderness no longer ambivalent about what he is about to do. He has already shed his tears and answered the difficult questions. He has begged God for forgiveness and is sure he will receive none. No more wrestling over the subject; it HAS to be done. He knows he will burn in Hell for this but the very life of his own real son, his own flesh and blood, is at stake.

After the short but strenuous hike Mark takes several more hardy swallows from his canteen. It is what James has been waiting for. The entire canteen is the required amount to place Mark under, but from what he has been told half that amount will inebriate him. James can see by the tipping of it that it is now only about half full. Mark has not yet consumed the requisite amount. He eyes Mark with the intensity of an eagle flying over a jackrabbit. It would seem James had underestimated Mark's supreme physical condition and his ability to hold his Rohypnol.

James knows the drug will fully affect its user within approximately ten minutes. After about twenty, he still cannot tell if Mark is under its spell, Mark merely sits calmly with his back still up against a tree. He may already be unconscious.

The tree tops rustle and a few squirrels sprint across their trunks. Mark is stock still, it may be because he is in hunt mode or because he is unconscious, James cannot be sure. He also cannot give up his position at the moment, so he waits patiently. James is

Creaking Door

looking for the telltale lull and sideways drooping of Mark's head. He is prepared for the spring chill and lays in wait in supreme comfort, padded thermal underclothing snugly beneath his camo, a necessity to a man used to tropical weather.

A fairly large bear enters the feeding area in front of Mark and begins exploring the steel drums. Mark quietly raises his bow but has not yet drawn it. He is awake and displays no ill effects, although it is impossible to determine that from his vantage. James watches attentively. More squirrels chase each other, kicking up leaves as they run indiscriminately on the ground, looking to mate without a care in the world. In his camos and scent killer, Mark is invisible to the woodland fauna. The bear pays the playful and amorous rodents no mind. Mark, too, is entirely focused despite the chatter and chaos of a half dozen rampant chipmunks and squirrels sprinting vociferously less than fifteen feet away.

For the first time Mark displays signs of being affected. When he raises to his knees he stumbles a bit and lumbers in what is normally a springing movement and quick as a whip. And he seems to be having difficulty drawing his bowstring once the device is upright.

James has been warned about this contingency: that Mark maybe unwilling or unable to consume the full amount. He was told to go ahead with the planned physical assault, and that Mark will be in no condition to fight back or leave evidence of a struggle. James is not so sure at this point.

Suddenly James notices an even larger bear behind Mark. To Mark's rear is a low canopy that obscured the view and now this behemoth has come out of nowhere. It is sauntering slowly towards him, pausing every few seconds to eye his target and sniff at the wind. James cannot believe what he is seeing. His first instinct is to yell and tell Mark he is in immediate danger, but of course, he does nothing of the kind. Unsure of who else is in the vicinity, James knows that no one must ever know he was here.

When the larger bear is about ten feet away, probably having made some kind of a sound, perhaps heavy footsteps upon crinkly dead foliage or the snapping of a crisp, brittle twig, perhaps even his breathing, but whatever it is, it causes Mark to suddenly try and swivel his head toward what lies behind him. He is not in time to see this huge creature and cannot even hope to draw his bow; it is far too late for that. In an instant the bear pounces and covers the short distance in the blink of an eye. Sometime after that Mark lets out an involuntary blood-curdling scream. James watches in dismay as the bear smothers Mark, who has disappeared under its black furry mass. The movements of the bear are lightning fast and murderously violent, its arms flailing and head shaking as it rips through human flesh. James is horrified. He can do nothing and is stricken with revulsion. He knows there is nothing to do but endure the wave of nausea and watch the gruesome scene play out. His mind is racing and twisting with contradiction; to lend aid as a loving surrogate father and friend or to watch apathetically and help prevent his own actual son from being murdered. In an instant he understands there is no dilemma. He has not yet realized it but the gods of fate have smiled upon him; nature has performed his evil task for him. He continues to stare in stunned silence, stifling an instinctive scream he knows can never be let out.

    About eight minutes later Jimmy comes upon the scene. Knowing where this particular bait station was located, he quickly ran toward it once he heard that awful screech.

    Upon seeing that, James quickly packs up his limited amount of gear, looks around to police his area to make sure he has left no trace of himself, and then bids a hasty retreat, but not before witnessing Jimmy firing upon the beast with his trusty emergency pistol. The shot is loud, and once he sees the attacking bear scamper James flees the scene secure in the knowledge that Jimmy is safe. A bottle of medicine is tucked snugly on his vest in the external appendage designed for twelve-gauge shells; James confirms its presence before bolting. He fails, however, to remove it and place it within the total confinement of any one of his ten utility pockets.

Creaking Door

He has just witnessed eight long minutes of savagery, of a huge wild animal tearing apart not just another human being but a man he has loved since that boy's birth. He was beyond numb but somehow forced himself to function.

James' rented Subaru is located only about three quarters of a mile away across a ravine and at the bottom of the hill he had originally perched himself upon. His adrenaline causes him to reach it in record time. It is close for this very reason; to effect a quick escape if needed.

After sprinting to the car and obtaining scratches to his face and hands from the ubiquitous thickets and brambles, the trusty Subaru thankfully fires right up and he quietly drives away hoping the impending harsh Canadian Rocky Mountain weather and his diligence will eradicate any traces of his ever being there. He has to remember to drive calmly in case other hunters have sighted him or if quota-minded, citation-issuing police are nearby.

He is still trembling when he reaches his hotel room. James quickly undresses and throws everything into his rollaway soft luggage, not even bothering to fold or check them. Following a quick shower, he dons a simple gray T-shirt, some heavy black jeans, laces up some thick leather high top sneakers, and slips on a quilted-down Columbia jacket. He grabs his gear and leaves the room still quaking. His plane leaves in three hours, but he will spend a good chunk of that time at a nearby diner, in front of witnesses just in case. He also cannot be alone at the moment for fear of a nervous breakdown. James is an absolute total wreck. He'll order a meal he knows he is not hungry for and coffee he will never be able to drink due to his frazzled nerves and the cyclonic whirlwind presently occupying his fast spinning gray matter.

An attractive young blonde waitress brings his platter of sausage, baked potato, bowl of minestrone soup and a cup of coffee. She tells him there are scratches on his face, so he gets up and goes to the bathroom. The mirror partially reveals not only his own treachery, but the one he has just witnessed and will never get out of his mind. He uses soap and water and several of the dispensable paper towels to clean himself up as best he can. The blood is gone but red lines remain. They are not so bad he tells himself. They look much better than they did five minutes ago when they looked like bloody lacerations; now they just look like common everyday scratches. He snugs an extra paper towel into his pocket so he can continue to dab at them until it all dries.

Two hours before departure James arrives at the airport, returns his rented car, then proceeds with the slow, meticulous process of airport security. It goes without fail. Brett Lopez is not on anyone's watch list. He welcomes the direct flight home.

When James arrived back in Makaha and began unpacking, he discovered a small bottle was missing. A wave of panic rippled through him. In a frenzy, he double-checked every garment and every pocket, felt between luggage linings and every compartment. It was not there. He hoped and prayed that it was forever lost in the wilderness or someplace very far from the spot in the woods where Mark died, like at the airport or in his rental car where a minimum-wage-earning teenager will probably vacuum it up during the returned vehicle's routine cursory cleaning. Like him, the next customer will turn the keys on a sanitized and deodorized unit awaiting the kind of abuse that comes from non-ownership.

The Makaha Valley and its gingerly rhythms have a way of keeping you in the present. The rich green embroidery of vegetation, the perpetual motion of the ocean, its relaxing sounds, and its ever-freshening salty air all serve to eviscerate whatever objects impede your inner tranquility. It is scenery and environs to get lost and absorbed in like thick double-layered motel drapery obscuring a dull, listless, uninteresting view, whether you want it to or not. It has an all-encompassing quality that is total and compulsory, and James has melted back into its warmth, its embrace, and its entirety as if he'd never left. Despite this and Kui's best efforts, James remained sullen and subdued for a time. A year has passed without incident and the troublesome thought of the lost medicine bottle, which nagged at him daily, begins, like the morning lunar tide, to ebb with a gentle grace.

While James was crossing the thick Canadian underbrush, a small, seemingly insignificant, little bottle full of an innocuous clear liquid falls out of one of the six circular elastic holsters manufactured onto his hunting jacket. They are designed to hold shotgun shells, but he is using just one of them, and he is using it to hold a bottle of an injectable drug so he wouldn't have to fumble for it when he needed it. Because when he actually would need it, it would surely be a matter of haste and no small affair. Now it slips out and bounces off a softball-sized stone that is rounded, slightly mossy, and worn smooth by the relentless winters and snow melts that have sent oceans of water cascading down the mountains every spring, a snowflake, a drop, and a dribble at a time, just as it has patiently done so ad infinitum. The bottle rolls away from the stone and down this hill toward a small creek, which is now just a trickle compared to three weeks ago. The bottle is made of thick glass, does not break, and makes a pinging sound off the rock that, in his rush, is completely inaudible to James. It is stopped by some semi-frozen, partially dehydrated scattered foliage and will lay there until the wind and her sister natural forces clear the undergrowth and allow gravity to help this shotgun-shell-sized bottle continue onward toward the creek ahead where it will drift according to whatever time and tide this humble trickling Canadian mountain stream imposes upon it. And it will bring to bear whatever bidding fate may have in store for it.

Alejo Melendez

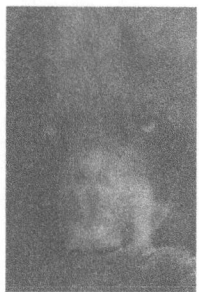

Nebraska

HENRI LAPLATT KNEW once more that half measures could no longer be tolerated and he demanded that all avenues be researched. If the Alanitrol did not come from Hawaii, which only registered the singular incident from Dr. Mallari's office, then they would search the national databases, globally too if needed.

There were no missing bottles of Alanitrol in Canada. Given their model health care system, this came as no surprise. Their first alternative, the Federal databases of the FDA and the FBI, thankfully showed just seven incidents of missing Alanitrol, a testament to both well-thought-out security measures and the drug's fresh entry on the marketplace. Street-wise, it was still a somewhat unknown commodity.

All seven cases were reviewed and nothing stood out. So each was researched a bit further to look for even the tiniest connection to anyone or anything that bore any kind of common thread in their investigation.

A stolen bottle from a small warehouse in North Platte, Nebraska was looked at further. The absentee vial of Alanitrol was actually discovered then reported missing by a pharmacy in Lincoln. The Pharmacy's inspection of all deliveries was performed for this very reason and their thoroughness was garnishing

Creaking Door

dividends for Laplatt. If any Alanitrol had made its way to Hawaii, maybe the criminals were stupid enough to use a traceable method of delivery. "But who or what in holy hell could possibly be in fuckin' Nebraska?" thought Henri. But, as every good detective knows, you follow the facts to wherever they lead you.

So now delivery databases were searched, since every parcel moved in the United States was catalogued in post 9-11 America. And a lone voice in the vast Postal wilderness of stamps, envelopes, cardboard, and packing tape called out to Laplatt; a delivery of insured and registered mail was made from the Dunning post office in Nebraska to Hawaii about fourteen months ago. Laplatt's hunch, a two-story leap of faith and instinct, had just been cushioned by a shipping container full of Styrofoam packing peanuts.

The delivery was made to Kelly Tam at her PO Box in Honolulu. This new tidbit was not only very interesting but also highly surprising despite the fact that the spouse is usually the first suspect in a homicide. Kelly Tam had long ago been initially dismissed as a viable person of interest.

This prompted a closer look at Kelly Tam. Her maiden name was Kelly Herzog, and she grew up in Halsey, a town not far from Dunning or North Platte.

This also prompted a closer look at Husker Medical, the company that owned the warehouse in North Platte. Employees were cross referenced and there were no Herzogs found, so Laplatt demanded a second and deeper search which then found the name Herzog buried deep in a personnel file. That file belonged to Eunice Paxton, and she was married to one Kerry Herzog. His name turned up buried in some seemingly inconsequential company insurance requisition forms for dental work. It didn't take much after that to connect him to Kelly, they were siblings. Husker Medical was not too far from Dunning or Halsey, about an hour. Thank goodness for root canals.

So they started at the beginning and checked the man who'd sent it, Vernon Bosworth. This man lived in Halsey, the same area where Kelly Herzog came from. Nebraska State Police were solicited and data on the Herzog's and Mr. Bosworth was asked for and received. The Herzog farms were spread out over six parcels of huge properties, about fifty acres each, and all in the Halsey area. So this gave Magat and Laplatt six persons of interest so far. Magat had an inspiration and asked that they start with Vernon, and that maybe he could reveal the link to one of the Herzogs. They immediately suspected Kerry simply and obviously because he was married to Eunice. The next attractive suspect was Ken Herzog, simply because he was the same age as Bosworth, but his brothers and Kevin and Kaleb also fell rather inconveniently into that age range.

It was too important a discovery so Laplatt and Magat both booked a flight to Nebraska. They were gathering manila folders, some as thick as an outer island phone book. Magat and Laplatt stacked every file pertaining to this case they could grab and were just about to check out a few items from the evidence room when Detective Robert Fernandez tossed a small black item on Pauly's desk. Pauly first thought it was lipstick or lip balm for protection from the Nebraska weather. But it was too flat.

"What is that?" asked Pauly. Henri was thinking the exact same thing.

"It's a thumb drive," replied Fernandez. "Put all those jackets back you idiot troglodytes, welcome to the twenty-first century."

Fernandez then used his thumb to slide out a small rectangular metallic insert from within this little drive and stuck the object into the side of Magat's laptop. A folder popped up on the screen following some kind of chiming noise to alert the user a new device had been detected.

"Click on da foldah brah," said Fernandez.

Pauly did so and twenty other folders appeared. They were labeled identically to all the evidence jackets they were packing. Magat randomly clicked on a folder in the middle and was amazed to see the entire file on Kimo Kealani.

Creaking Door

Pointing to the briefcase holding all of the manila folders, he asked, "You mean all of that is on this little gizmo?"

"Yeah you knuckleheads. You guys bettah get yo shet togedah. Fuckin' stupid assholes."

It was locker room talk among fellow cops. The kind of universal shop language and levity that was totally understood by all police officers. The pair was grateful to have such amazing and powerful technology at their disposal. It eliminated an extra ten pounds of check-in baggage they had to lug.

They couldn't believe their luck when it was discovered by the agency HPD used that Broken Bow, which was a LOT closer to Halsey than Lincoln, actually had a Municipal airport. However they were ordered to land at Lincoln and drive the rest of the way, even though hops from Lincoln to Broken Bow were cheap, about fifty bucks a man. The pair was even willing to shell out of their own pockets for this convenience.

Alejo Melendez

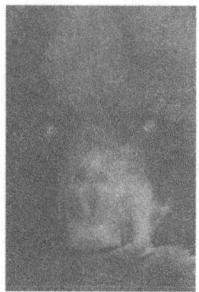

Trooper Cooper

THE MIDWEST RATE for rental vehicles with unlimited mileage was less than twenty bucks a day. Even cheaper, Nebraska State Police would furnish an unmarked as a courtesy to their brothers in blue. Laplatt and Magat were barging into town to possibly accuse and arrest some of their citizens. Checking in and coordinating with the NSP was, in fact, the real reason they were going to land in Nebraska's state capital.

It was warm in glorious Lincoln, a dry heat, almost crusty one would say. A smartly dressed man in a midnight blue State Police uniform stood next to a woman holding a sign that had Laplatt's name printed on it in five-inch high bold lettering. She was a redhead with a trim athletic build. Her smooth calves were showing from under her blue mid-length skirt. Nice firm C cups jutted out from a red safari blouse. She was a clerk from the Lincoln PD on loan because The Staties thought it looked unbecoming for a trooper to be performing a chore most common chauffeurs would do. The trooper had asked for her personally. This also allowed the trooper to perform security detail while they waited for their out-of-town guests, always needed at a busy International airport.

He stuck out his big Midwestern meat hook and asked, "Laplatt, Magat? I'm Matt Cooper."

Creaking Door

He pronounced Magat like maggot and did so in an unsure, questioning manner. Pauly corrected him and knew it was an innocent mispronunciation. Pure Filipino names were surely uncommon here. Henri stifled a laugh until the same trooper called him Henry. Now it was Laplatt's turn to correct and Pauly's turn to chuckle. The four of them loaded into the complimentary Ford Taurus station wagon, a stakeout vehicle from the State Police's Lincoln pool. Magat and Laplatt sat in the rear and found it roomy and nicely suited for the long drive after their tedious flight.

Cooper headed west on 80 for several hours. The backseat duo fell asleep sometime during the long haul. Nothing to see but farm equipment and cornfields. The flight had tuckered them out. Cooper then took 83 north to Thedford and awakened the pair at that point telling them they were very close to their destination, then he turned eastward on highway two toward Halsey. Once in town, they stopped at a local diner. Henri and Pauly were starving and grateful, but it was also done to have a place to review the case files and go over strategy.

Cooper had his laptop in hand when they entered the eatery. Matt removed his Smokey the Bear hat and handed it to Loretta, the clerk whose name they'd just discovered. Something about the way she took it foretold of some ongoing intimacy between them. It was self-seating so they opted for a booth all the way in the back, the place was thankfully uncrowded.

Large clear windows facing south let in lots of that Nebraska sunshine which seemed brighter and more golden to the two. Thankfully, that brighter and more golden Nebraska sunshine was indirect. Maybe it stole its richness from the Fort Knox of prairie gold that was reflecting off of all that corn. Or maybe their retinas had been stained yellow from staring at those endless rows of drying maze. Cooper told them this thirsty phase was a sign that harvest time was at hand. Their table was tucked in the cooling shadows of the eastern corner of the restaurant.

They sat in a semicircular red Naugahyde booth. It may have

been unoccupied for some time because it was thankfully cool to the touch. There were two napkin dispensers and a chrome cage holder of salt and pepper shakers, a rectangular porcelain receptacle of sweetener packets and jams; a few grains of salt lay scattered on the dark imitation wood pattern Formica table top. This station had not been policed in some time.

They waited for the waitress, who first took the extra napkin dispenser away and then wiped the table. The quartet placed their orders, then Cooper opened the laptop and plugged in the thumb drive. Matt copied everything on it and said it was being entered into Nebraska's official crime database as surely as they sat there. He would review it personally but that, as was to be expected, the local Halsey law enforcement would be their main liaison for the duration of their stay in this town.

"Don't worry," he joked, "they have computers, internet, and heck even running water."

A chuckle was raised and the food arrived in no time. They had a pleasant lunch. Henri and Pauly had four cups of black coffee each. First because they needed to wake up and second because it was actually a very good tasting, rich blend, far better than they'd expected from here in the middle of Bumfuck, Iowa and far better than the station-house mud they'd been swilling lately.

Matt told them the local sheriff was just off highway two and that they would take that highway south about fifty more miles where they would drop off Matt and Loretta at the opportune Broken Bow airport so they could fly back to Lincoln and leave the car for their disposal. Cooper doffed his Campaign hat as a sign it was time to go. This time Loretta carried the laptop.

They again piled into the car following the meal and continued south on highway two. After about three short miles the Halsey Sherriff's building was pointed out. It was smallish but at least made of masonry, cinderblock upon closer inspection, and thankfully right on the main road so no searching in this unfamiliar hayseed town would be required. It was painted gray and an electronic digital keypad could be seen mounted on the wall next to the Dakota Inactive Dummy Door Lever, which looked thicker than normal and was probably custom made for law enforcement. Matt said the local LEO's had already been notified of Henri and Pauly's arrival and that their mail clerk, Vernon Bosworth, had been picked up and was being detained on a Federal postal statute violation for seventy-two hours, which is why Cooper was in no rush to get them to the Sherriff. He did, however, have a municipal flight leaving in an hour and the drive to Broken Bow would take about forty minutes, so Matt's clock was ticking.

They dropped them off at the airport, thanked them profusely, Henri shook his big hand again, then pulled him close so only the men could hear what Laplatt, in the passenger seat, would tell him.

"Loretta's really cute and has a killer body you lucky son of a gun."

Matt said nothing and instead looked over at Pauly in the driver's seat. Pauly grinned and winked. So they knew. They were detectives after all. Matt smiled back and offered a polite country boy thanks, almost like the "aw shucks ma'am, tweren't nuthin'" dialogue you hear in old westerns. It was a nice parting for a nice day considering they were here to do a dirty job.

Alejo Melendez

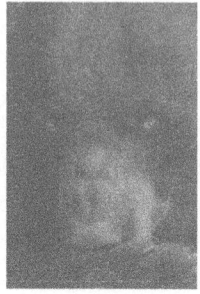

Chaw?

THEY ARRIVED BACK at the Halsey Sherriff's building in about sixty minutes, taking in the rural sights, the magnificent amber waves of corn and soy, the occasional gigantic red barn, the towering silos, the unpolluted sky, and the crisp warm country air. They even enjoyed the pungent, acrid stench when passing stockyards. The pair was not around such rural venues often and decided to soak it in. They were also cognizant of the Federal Statute allowing the luxury of the seventy-two-hour hold Trooper Matt had enlightened them with. That grace period allowed them this very rare leisure time so they acted like tourists for about half an hour on the drive back.

They were given a phone number which they dialed, once parked outside the sheriff's building. Before the first ring another tall, rangy Midwestern farm boy type, decked in the standard beige khaki regulation Sherriff's uniform, came out. He'd been waiting and watching. This probably constituted excitement in these parts. The pair could respect that.

"Howdy all," he said, "Name's Arlen Jessup. You must be Laplatt," he said aiming his handshake toward Henri, "so that makes you Pauly," now aiming the same warm handshake toward Magat. He seemed smart enough to not attempt pronouncing Pauly's

Creaking Door

unusual last name. The pair took an instant liking to him.

He asked them if they needed anything, food, drink, chaw.

"Chaw?" thought Pauly. What backwoods bizarro world did they just enter? Little Dorothy was evidently not in Kansas anymore.

"No thanks," said Henri, "we've just eaten, but thank you. We are just about ready to interview Bosworth."

Good enough thought Jessup, so he briefed them in case these big city cops found any of his tidbits useful. They genuinely did.

When Henri and Pauly entered the Sherriff's building they immediately noticed a strong odor of tobacco, not cigarettes or cigarette smoke, something stronger and more odorous and raw. When Jessup turned his head and spit long distance into an overflowing spittoon about six feet away and the splashback plastered against the wall, Pauly almost dry heaved. The splatter was thick and viscous and slow to creep down the permanently stained wall. Pauly had to look away. Henri had a stronger stomach and withstood it far better than Magat. Seeing their revulsion, Jessup apologized and said that corner was cleaned regularly but he and his two other deputies had gotten busy lately. It was one deputy's normal day off, the other called in with the flu. A single Sherriff on duty could manage this small town so Jessup paid it no mind.

Arlen reiterated what Cooper had told them; that Bosworth was being held on a trumped up Federal charge for their investigative purposes. What they really found useful was that good old Vern was expecting to be interviewed by Federal Marshalls, and on some pretty serious mail fraud charges, which could send him to a Federal Prison, like Leavenworth. This had Vernon frightened, pliable, and fully amenable to volunteer anything that would keep him from being ass fucked daily for the next ten years.

So Magat and Laplatt entered the room where Vernon was being held. He looked scared. He was of slight build and had medium length stringy brown hair in a rural page boy cut. The heat caused him to perspire a little, enough to make him look like a frightened, wet mouse.

They started off easy, using their first names to facilitate an air of trust.

"Hello Vernon, my name is Paul and this here is Henri. May we call you Vernon?"

He nodded, throat too dry from nervousness to verbalize an answer.

The local cops were instructed to not question him and to tell him nothing beyond the postal charge he'd been picked up for.

"Do you know why you're here Vernon?" asked Magat.

There was a visible shift in Bosworth's demeanor and body. Magat, being fairly dark skinned and a non-Caucasian, seemed to have a very visible effect on him. The pair of detectives discreetly exchanged looks. They knew this was something useful and useable. How they would profit by it could be discussed later.

"I'm here because of some kind of package I mailed last year."

Magat looked over at Laplatt and nodded, signaling for him to continue this line of questioning to help put their mouse at ease.

Henri casually stepped forward. Bosworth looked visibly relieved.

"That's right Vernon. Do you know what was in that package?"

Vernon thought about it, furrowed his eyebrows, opened his mouth but retracted what he was about to say. He cleared his throat and tried again. His brain was willing but his tongue would not commence. If the Feds were here, he must have unknowingly mailed something very dangerous. What if it were an explosive device that killed innocent people? Or contained ingredients of chemical warfare? What if Ken had actually been trying to kill his once and forever beloved Kelly? These previously unthought-of images were now overwhelming him. That was when the dam broke.

Vernon began stammering out his sob story, complete with

tears as he crooned like young Sinatra in the forties. He told them his buddy Ken Herzog, a name they were waiting to come forth, brought him a package one day to mail to his sister Baby in Hawaii.

Laplatt interrupted him. "Baby?"

"Her real name is Kelly, but folks 'round here have always called her Baby."

Laplatt nods his head in understanding and with his palm upward and his fingers motioning toward himself like a "come hither" gesture, he signals for Vernon to continue.

He drones on that Ken dropped off the box but without a return address, which Bosworth claims he pointed out and asked for.

"Ken claimed it was a surprise birthday gift for Baby, uh Kelly, and I knew her birthday was the next week so I accepted that as truth, honest to God."

This all seemed plausible so they asked him to continue. The feeble-minded Bosworth, following the sequence of events, states that his supervisor Josh Coleman brought the box back to the front desk and basically made Vern correct the mistake. Unable to remember Ken's exact address, wanting to stay out of trouble, and also hoping to establish contact with his old crush, he innocently placed his own name and address on an adhesive label and stuck it in the upper left-hand corner of the box. Knowing it must have been important as a birthday gift, he then generously insured and registered it as a favor to his buddy Ken.

Henri looks at the two-way mirror and nods his head sideways, a signal for Arlen to go. Jessup knows this means to check out Vernon's story so he takes the quick drive to the Post Office and asks Josh Coleman to tell the story in his own words. It takes Coleman a second to recall the incident. It is almost an exact match to Vernon's version and, so far, goes a long way toward clearing Bosworth of any direct conspiracy charges.

The unrecovered physical packaging has most certainly long since disappeared, so any hope of finger prints was out of the question. The Halsey Post Office did not have security cameras mounted at the time, so video surveillance records were also not available. All that remained was what brought Vernon Bosworth to their attention in the first place; the national catalogue of parcel deliveries into, out of, and within the US borders.

Twenty minutes later a gentle knock on the interrogation room door has Jessup whispering the confirmation to the pair, all out of earshot for the still nervous Postal Clerk.

They know now the investigation is progressing, and moving forward means Ken Herzog is the next man up.

All three cops re-enter the room and Henri tells Vernon he is free to go now, and that they will need to question him again at a later date.

Vernon blows out a sigh of relief then asks the two, "Are you guys FBI?"

Not wanting to lose the legal deception or that ace in the hole, the darker Magat, whom Bosworth fears most, says, "We *are* law enforcement with the government but our agency has to remain a secret for national security purposes."

Vernon looks even more intimidated but is also impressed that a major federal agency has come seeking him out.

It is all Henri and Arlen can do to suppress their laughter. A Canuck and a Kanaka posing as boys from DC. It was a brilliant improvisation by good old Pauly Boy, the flyin' Hawaiian. They'd not blown their cover. Arlen liked these two good ol' boys. He was gonna have to buy 'em a beer one day soon, before they left of course.

They escort Bosworth out to Jessup's official vehicle and drive the exhausted but relieved clerk home. Pauly and Henri follow in their borrowed Taurus. On the drive back Arlen radios the two a few mundane questions about city life, big crime, etc. The transmission is surprisingly crystal clear. The one common thread is they all hunt, so the conversation blooms from there.

Jessup asks if they have a few moments and they say they do.

Creaking Door

Jessup pulls up to a singular building like his own office but painted bright red with white trim. The joint stands out because there are two strip malls nearby; one directly across the street and the other located two parking lots over on the same side. A sign above it reads "Big Joe's Saloon". There are swinging double doors at the entrance but they are only for show. They lead to some black ornately engraved doors with push bar handles, which in turn leads to a foyer in which patrons are obliged to hang their coats and clean their boots on a floor-mounted stationary fourteen by fourteen-inch scrub brush pad with sturdy black steel bristles. It was meant more for the harsh Midwest winters so the trio bypasses the whole shebang. They keep their jackets to conceal their weapons. Their shoes are clean enough to pass a surprise departmental inspection.

It is just past 5 pm, the end of the workday. The place is cozy, dim, and uncrowded. Paul inconspicuously counts five others in a bar meant to comfortably hold at least fifty, none of them look threatening. Also, none of them look surprised to see the cops in here. Only Arlen is in uniform, but one needn't be a genius to see that both the broad-shouldered Paul and Henri are also law enforcement.

Arlen moseys on up to the back end of the bar and orders beers. He looks the two over first and they both nod their OK's. They were on the road, a long way from home, they'd just made headway into the case, and the Midwestern sun was cooking today.

Three beers were placed in front of them. Paul took a sip and marveled at how refreshing it was. It was a Budweiser short neck barrel style bottle, the kind he hadn't seen in years, and it was icy cold. He held no compunctions about downing three fourths of it on his second swig. Thirty seconds later he ordered a second, which raised an eyebrow of Henri's but not Arlen's.

Pauly was just having a little fun, relieving the massive hidden stress this case was thrusting upon them. He was enjoying the Cornhusker hospitality to the fullest that an out of town cop on duty could. Henri was relieved when that second beer of his lasted for half an hour.

Jessup had chosen that spot in the room because, unbeknownst to the pair and especially Pauly, there was a spittoon located in the corner just behind Arlen, who turned his head every sixty seconds or so to expectorate from the fresh wad he'd just packed into his maw. Pauly was grateful the place was dim once he realized what Arlen was doing. They weren't drunk but were loose and laughing as if they were.

Out of the blue Arlen spins a yarn: "One day this here fella walks into this here bar. The spittoon is overflowing and a few cowboys are using it. The stranger pipes up 'I'll bet any man a here a hunnerd bucks I can take a swig off that spittoon.' The thing is overflowing, rancid, and stinks to high heavens with thick, gooey, blackened, mucousy spit. Nearly every man jumps at the chance and soon the stranger has a running bet with just about every man in the place. So he picks up the spittoon, gunk spilling over the sides onto the floor and onto his hands, places it to his lips and begins to sip at it. Everyone is disgusted. The stranger had won the bet. But surprisingly the guy kept on drinking; he wouldn't put the vessel down. He drinks until the damned thing is empty. Everyone is heaving and retching when the bartender asks 'Mister, all you had to do was take a swig. Why'd ya drink the whole thing?' The stranger replies 'the damned shit wouldn't break!'"

A look of disgust crosses Henri and Paul's faces. Soon they are laughing. It was thoroughly nauseating but the kind of morbid humor cops tell and understand. Paul especially knows he might be skipping dinner tonight.

Henri says to Jessup, "Arlen, you are one sick fuck *and* a fuckin' asshole." More laughter abounds, even from the bartender.

The three decide to let Ken Herzog stew overnight, partly because they'd been drinking and having a good time blowing off steam but also because they knew Bosworth would alert him to the presence of Federal Agents in town to investigate the mail incident, the one Kenny-boy was involved neck deep in. They would also spend the time coordinating a concerted effort and making a list of specific questions designed to point them to the ring leader of sorts, specifically to one Jimmy Kanoho.

They ordered another round and some whiskey shots to continue the nice buzz they were starting to get.

Before the next round, Arlen stepped outside and pulled out his phone. The first and only thing he did was notify state police to red flag Ken Herzog and his vitals, which included vehicles and plates, in case he tried to book a flight or catch a bus out of town overnight. He also asked that an eye be kept for movement back at his residence. Then Jessup went back in to continue the good time they were all having. A little over an hour later they drove back to their motel rooms just off the highway and a stone's throw from Arlen's office ready to hit the hay and move forward the next morning. It was only 7 p.m. but jetlag and Joe's saloon were the culprits.

Alejo Melendez

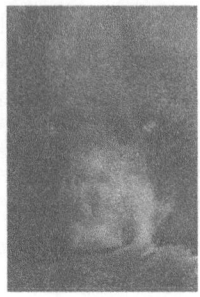

Pone

STILL ON HAWAIIAN time, Laplatt and Magat struggled but awoke at 10 a.m. and headed straight for that restaurant with that great coffee. They filled up, discussed strategy, then drove, as the *corn* flies, back to meet up with Arlen.

Ken Herzog was thirty-seven and lived alone. He managed his spread with the help of just four hired hands. It was all that was needed due to modern farming equipment. One man ran the combine which was closely followed by another man in a separate vehicle that turned over the soil and fertilized it, another to man the grain elevator or silo conveyor belt, and during the harvest one man who was retained as a full-time farm equipment manager and mechanic who performed as-needed repairs and the requisite daily maintenance. The farm equipment took a major full-time beating when in season.

The combine had two modes; one stripped off the kernels and the empty cobs were sold to local piggeries as feed. The other mode harvested whole ears, husks and all. It was an efficient operation, one his Daddy would have been proud of.

Ken lived sparsely despite good money from farming, was not a bad looking guy according to his most recent DMV photo, but for some reason had remained unmarried. When he answered the door

Creaking Door

at eleven in the morning he was in his underwear and sporting an open Budweiser. In a can no less. Ken Herzog might have been thirty-seven, but he looked forty-seven, and his being single was starting to become clearer.

Magat: "Ken Herzog?"

"Who wants to know?"

"Agents Magat and Laplatt. We'd like to ask you some questions about a package you sent to your sister Kelly last year."

He took a swig of his beer and said, "This sounds kinda serious, mind if I call a lawyer first?"

Laplatt: "You can do that down at the station sir. Come with us please."

"Do I have to?"

Magat again: "Postal crimes are a Federal offense sir, so yes, you have to."

"Let me grab some clothes first."

Laplatt: "FREEZE, Mr. Herzog!"

Ken was startled, he froze, eyes wider now. They had his full attention despite his breakfast of champions. Laplatt's thunderous voice splinters the serene tranquility of the farm's silent timbre; distant plovers and meadowlarks shriek and take flight from the predatory hostility contained in Henri's command. Even unflappable prairie chickens nearby stop their pecking and seek burrows stolen by breeding gophers two summers ago.

"My associate, Agent Magat will grab your clothes. Tell him where they are. You will remain here with me sir, is that understood?"

Herzog nodded and complied. The house was messy and stunk with bachelor slob smells; stale pizza, stale beer, unwashed laundry, mold, and even a faint trace of marijuana. Magat could not wait to get the hell out of there. He put on purple latex evidence gloves before handling Herzog's garments, a pair of jeans and a long-sleeved University of Nebraska sweatshirt. These were the first articles of clothing he spotted in the laundry room he was directed to. He couldn't tell if they were clean but they *were* folded. He sniffed at them from no closer than eight inches and they did not stink, it was his main consideration since they would be riding in close quarters with the man back to the sheriff's office.

"Arlen know about this?" asked Herzog.

"He's brewing up a fresh pot of coffee just for you big boy," said Henri.

Henri drove while Pauly sat in the rear guarding Ken Herzog. The ride was short. They'd memorized the way which was good since neither knew how to activate the GPS gizmo on the dash. The Taurus was a smooth ride. The NSP obviously kept their motor pool in tiptop shape. They passed a soy field yet to be harvested and Henri was surprised by three does that came bounding out of it. Henri pressed the brakes in time and slowed the vehicle without skidding or coming to a complete stop, the antilock brakes worked just fine like the rest of the vehicle. He proceeded slowly in case more deer came out. Ken, anxious to get this over with, told them to "go ahead and floor it because those three cunts always travel alone."

The man was charming. Even these two hardened cops flinched at not only the use of that word but the ease in which it was uttered among total strangers. It told them a bit more about the man they were about to interrogate.

They assumed he'd gotten a heads-up from Vern and they were right. Ken, too, believed they were federal agents. He was led to the same room Vernon had been in the day before. The room was sprayed with air freshener ten minutes beforehand but still held its ominous air and aura of fear and intimidation.

"This about the mail to Kells?" Ken asked.

Laplatt: "That's right son. Now instead of us asking a whole buncha questions, why don't you just tell us everything you can about it, like what was in it and why you didn't put a return address on it?"

Herzog sits stone faced and considers his options. He knows it

Creaking Door

was a drug of some kind but he had no idea what it did. As planned, he'd not heard from Kelly since she'd asked for it. Could it have been used to kill or harm someone? He knew he was about to step on a land mine so his curt answer was "lawyer."

Magat strode forward in a most aggressive manner and slammed his open hand on the table making everyone, Henri included, jump in surprise. No one was expecting it.

Magat, voice raised: "Now listen, you dumb corn-fed fuck, you're involved in some serious shit and the only way we're gonna help you is if you come clean right here, right now, motherfucker! Once your lawyer gets here any deals we woulda' cut are off the fuckin' table."

Arlen was ready to jump into the room but restrained himself when Henri seemed to read his mind, looked through the glass and shook his head; negative on the entry.

"All this for a fricking return address mistake? Get me a Goddamned lawyer NOW before this psycho asshole frickin' kills me! And once I ask for a lawyer, you're not supposed to talk to me, right?"

Magat: "Wrong again moron. We're not allowed to *question* you. We can talk all we want Zeb, you ain't even gotta listen."

They now had Herzog in fear for his life and freedom and decided it was a good time to exit the room and let him sweat. They also wanted to confer on the matter away from Herzog's earshot.

Once the door was closed Henri asked Pauly, "What the hell was that about!? I hope you knew what you were doing in there."

Pauly smiled and said, "just give him another ten minutes."

Jessup: "Should we let him call his lawyer?"

Henri: "Arlen, you go in there and ask him for his lawyer's name and number and tell him we'll call him. If he doesn't know the number, tell him we'll look it up. But DON'T make that call until we say so."

Arlen did as he was told and, as expected, Kenny perked up when he saw a familiar face. They'd grown up together and had been boyhood friends. Arlen avoided small talk and left the room once he'd gotten the lawyer's name. He offered an encouraging word or two before he left but was careful not to sound too helpful or amiable. He knew they wanted to keep Ken intimidated and scared. These were the kind of decisions that were tough for any cop but certainly a small-town Sherriff; to criminalize one of its citizens, a friend in particular, versus having to side with the law and in this case total strangers who happened to be toeing the same blue line as him. It wasn't easy, but it always had to be about the law.

A shade under fifteen minutes later the dynamic duo re-enter the room. Herzog was slouched from his beer breakfast but suddenly jerked awake and alert when he saw Magat.

"You guys call my lawyer?"

Henri said, "Yup. He's on his way." A total lie.

Magat moves in on Ken. "We know everything Ken. We know you sent your sister a very expensive drug; a bottle of Alanitrol, and we know it came from a warehouse in North Platte from your sister-in-law Eunice. You're all going to be charged in a federal crime for the theft of that drug and the subsequent crimes that resulted from it. Your brother Kerry and his wife Big Bertha are going to the big house, Child Services will have your nieces and nephews placed in foster care where they will surely be abused and neglected, maybe even molested by one of your moonshining neighbors. Now tell us all of the details; how you got it, who got it for you, and what Kelly used it for or you'll take the biggest fall all by yourself. You, your brother Kerry's whole fuckin' family, and that pretty little sister of yours, you're all gonna be someone's bitches within two months."

Like all smart detectives and prosecutors, they were asking questions they already knew the answers to.

Ken could hardly breathe at that point. The suffocating gray interrogation room had just gotten a lot smaller and a lot warmer. He was almost dizzy trying to process all of this new and overwhelming data, just the way the detectives planned it. Magat and his dark Hawaiian sun-soaked looks had played him masterfully. Ken wanted to wait for his lawyer but the mention of the children and Kelly's name and her involvement sent waves of panic through him.

Spittle flew as Pauly spewed his venom. His eyes were bulging and his breathing rapid. The rage was genuine, he was tired of chasing ghosts, of being close yet finding plot twists at every turn. Of being outsmarted. His deeply embedded frustration was now openly exhibiting itself as a blindingly fast-moving eviscerating sandstorm of rage on poor helpless Kenny Herzog, threatening to grind down and obliterate the staunch barrier of ignorance and deniability he once thought he could hide behind. Herzog recoiled in fear and surprise at the lunatic cop who looked like he was going to punch him in the face. Ken figured he could take old Darky in a street fight, but not sitting here in the blazing red-hot seat of this Federal criminal investigation; they were top cops and they held all the cards. Plus there were two of them, three if you counted Arlen. He saw his options worn down like day old Bondo being sanded in a body shop that catered to Asian housewife drivers. The sands of Magat's desert storm quickly became this suffocating, pressing emery cloth of unbridled exposure; wiping and grinding away at the layers of deception, a rasp of vehemence and wrath efficiently discarding the curled shavings from the once mighty fallen oak tree of the Herzog family lies. Magat's personal brand of anger was a force of nature on this tepid Nebraska day, and all that was left of Ken Herzog's arrogance, disdain, and cockiness was a splintered, weathered stump sitting low and alone on his vanishing, freshly tilled field of un-imprisoned, free range, and free-roaming farm life. So thorough was Pauly's scouring that not an acorn of hope remained from this felled wooden leviathan.

"All right dammit, I'll tell you everything but you gotta leave Kelly out of it."

Henri looked at Pauly, who shook his head. Kelly was a

lynchpin to their man Jimmy. Henri concurred. "No deal," was all Henri had to say.

"Then I tell you nothing assholes. THAT's the deal."

"Assholes?" Says Magat taking a very aggressive step toward Ken. "Listen up Huckleberry, someone was murdered using that drug. The *deal* is you give us the details or you take the whole rap. The deal is you tell us who else is involved or you and baby Kells do the maximum time. The deal is if we like and can verify your info we tell the prosecutors to cut a deal that grants leniency and you may not have to die in Federal Prison. The deal is it's gonna be YOUR BUNGHOLE being passed around like a frat party bong for the next five decades if you last that long. Oh yeah, did I mention you might even get the needle? That's the fucking deal ASSHOLE."

It was a finishing blow, a Sugar Ray Robinson blinding combination, a thing of pure Polynesian warrior beauty. Detective school one oh one on display from a master. It was said with such fervor and conviction it practically made Ken cry AND shit in his pants. Henri stood in admiration for his stocky Hawaiian brother.

There was a painful silence for what seemed an eternity. Ken stared straight ahead. He seemed calm but there was a very slight tremor in both hands and he tried to steady them by grabbing the table's edge harder than normal. This caused some very visible white knuckling. He did not look well but the out of towners didn't care one lick.

Two long minutes pass. Henri and Pauly get up and head for the door without a word.

"Wait."

It was said in a soft, mournful, and defeated tone, like its speaker didn't want to wake the baby *and* had just gone fifteen asthmatic rounds with Joe Louis without his inhaler. And it was the one word they'd been waiting two whole minutes, possibly fourteen months, for.

Laplatt and Magat's thorough investigation had brought to light virtually all of the players, at least in Nebraska.

Creaking Door

Seeing no other alternatives and knowing the gig was up, Ken spilled it all. Kerry Herzog and his wife Eunice Paxton were later brought in and prepared for questioning. They were looking to possibly extradite Ken to the beautiful 50th state depending on what Kelly gave up. He may soon be reunited with his baby sister if all went well. So far, so good. The right connections were being made, but did they have them all? That was the sixty-four-thousand-dollar question.

They disclosed their findings and filed their reports with the Nebraska State Police, thanked Cooper on the phone personally, then made the long drive to Lincoln to return the Taurus and catch a flight back to Hawaii.

Alejo Melendez

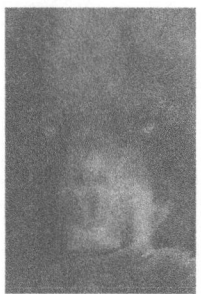

Bulb

KEN, KERRY, AND Eunice were all placed under arrest and being held at the Lincoln State Prison. Further discussions would be needed as to their final judicial destination. There were logistics involved in extraditing them to Canada for conspiracy to commit murder. The US Attorney's office and the Postmaster General wanted them for mail fraud and to be tried here in the United States first. And then there was the question of the reopened case of Mark Tam; he was a US citizen but killed in a foreign country. All of this and still no direct connection to Jimmy Kanoho.

But at least they were back on Hawaiian soil and getting closer to their man, geographically if not forensically. With the involvement of Kelly, they were now at the doorstep of Makaha family entry level when it came to the Kanohos.

Laplatt, who had been away from home now for a good long week, was actually glad to be back in Hawaii. Like the Polar Bears that roamed some areas of Northern Edmonton, he had a winter layer that made him far more comfortable in sub-freezing temperatures. Leaving the sirocco of Nebraska's natural sauna behind suited him just fine.

When the plane touched down at Honolulu International he actually felt like he'd come home. It was still far too warm for him,

Creaking Door

but at least the trade winds provided some relief, and the economics of it all dictated that most buildings, which thankfully included all of the police departments, were air conditioned. Nebraska folks were used to their oven and cared nothing for the comfort of its visitors while Hawaii's economy absolutely *depended* on keeping those very same tourists cool and comfortable.

Wanting to be more thorough, Laplatt takes out files on all family members of the Tams and Kanohos. Everyone thinks it's a waste of time and that the focus should be on Kelly but Henri is patient and knows the investigation will stall when their three corn pone musketeers stonewall authorities. Every criminal, in Henri's experience, holds back a trump card.

Focusing on their next known connection, they both study Kelly's profile a bit more. She is a very attractive woman. They both wonder if somehow her looks tie into this. From what they know Mark was pretty much gone most of the time. Every family member's photo is blown up and stuck onto the eight by five-foot white board they affectionately call the "murder" board.

Henri and Pauly stare at the photos, mostly at Kelly because she is hot and they are both men. But also quite a looker is her eighteen-year-old daughter Leinaala. Henri stares at Lei's photo for a long while. There is something about her that he just can't put his finger on, something familiar. He asks Pauly to take a closer look, he sees nothing but a typical beautiful young Island girl ready to break some hearts, including theirs.

They read a few of the files a little more thoroughly. Henri continues to sneak glances at Lei's eight by ten glossy. She truly is beautiful. They know she is presently home for a short break from her studies at Columbia. She has that strong magnetic island beauty that comes from Hawaii's melting pot. The one that the influx of immigrant labor has provided. Superb harmonious genetic mutations have all but been perfected and bound cohesively with the aid of decades of the agricultural boom super-glue; first from sugar cane and then pineapples. Now it is tourism that dominates with the help of, ironically, the beautiful progeny of that ongoing superb harmonious genetic fusion. Fruit is cheaper imported from Central and South America. The industry now is a very different kind of fruit; that produced of Hawaii's unique multi-racial, multi-cultural, and continuously evolving ethnically blended hodgepodge of people, and all beautifully woven into the tapestry of that very unique aloha spirit found only in Hawaii. That, as much as the scenery and the climate, is what people from all over the globe come here to experience.

Henri stares with anger and contempt at Jimmy's face. He knows in his gut that he is their killer but they somehow cannot find a viable connection or a rock-solid motive, and this is driving them mad.

A light bulb goes off in Henri's head. He doesn't know where the inspiration comes from and he dares not question it at this point. He gets up and removes Jimmy and Lei's photos from their current positions and sticks them to a vacant area of the board so they are right next to one another.

"Pauly Boy, you see what I see?"

Magat stares. It takes a few seconds but now his light bulb turns on as well.

They take their theory to Honolulu's District Attorney George Watanabe. Watanabe is sold and assigns the case to his top ADA Byron Abercrombie, who then procures the warrant compelling DNA samples from Kelly, Lei, and Jimmy.

Creaking Door

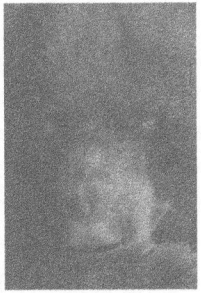

Probie

JANET ROUSSEAU IS enjoying her training in Edmonton's police forensics lab. She has been introduced to so many things; its major mass spectrometer, its chemical composition testing kits, its ultra-high-resolution digital microscopes, the kind that record evidence straight to the D.A.'s computers for file storage to be used in court, fingerprint analysis, fluorescence spectroscopy / fluorometry, forensic DNA analysis, forensic toxicology, gas chromatography equipment, histology and pathology laboratory equipment, and even the plain old centrifuge which for some reason fascinates her. Separating plasma from blood is proving an amazing lesson and process for the young Ontarian.

So much crammed in so little time yet her coworkers are highly impressed because the mousy, cute little newbie does not seem in the least bit overwhelmed. Quite the opposite, her enthusiasm is almost annoyingly overly-abundant. She has trained hard for this kind of work and now she is like a kid in a candy store.

Everyone is enjoying their new probie, probably because she is the only female in the department. Naturally she gets a lot of attention. Her confidence as a forensic scientist grows daily and her training goes well.

At the start of her second week there is a flu bug going around and three of her five coworkers have been afflicted, leaving her and two others to run the busy lab. Their boss Ian Fournier is away at a technology symposium in Olympia Washington. A test kit arrives and is labeled *PRIORITY*. It has come all the way from Hawaii and is from their chief homicide inspector Henri Laplatt. He wants the results emailed to him on the secured police server yesterday. They get right on it.

    Larry Tang is in the middle of six rape kits from five different provinces. Jack Remedios is busy with backlogged skin tissue analysis, so the package is delegated to the probie. She's been trained on the test procedure. She is told to ask any of them if she needs help. She remembers performing this very exercise at University. But now it is the real deal, and from what she's heard, Laplatt does not like slow or wrong.

    The test instructions are specific, she is told exactly what to look for. She finds it. Sample A is a paternal match to Sample B. Sample C is also a mitochondrial match to sample B. The process itself is slow and intricate but she sends her results off as soon as she has them.

Creaking Door

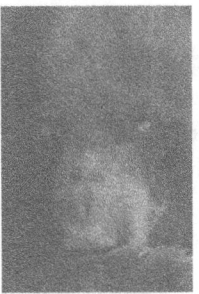

DNA

BECAUSE THE CASE will be tried in Alberta, the DNA samples are sent to Edmonton for processing. A priority rush is placed on it and in just about forty-eight hours they have their answer: Jimmy is Leinaala's biological father. The preliminary results show a match from Lei's Y-DNA, the paternal set, to Jimmy's sample. The test is signed by a Janet Rousseau, a name he does not recognize. But whoever she is he wants to give her a great big bear hug. She has made everyone's day.

Once this link is established, they move fast. Squad cars are immediately dispatched to Makaha once Jimmy's exact whereabouts are established; he is, as usual, in his office in the lobby of the Awaawa.

Jimmy is arrested, cuffed, and then escorted out to one of several black-and-whites on the scene. Hotel guests and employees are stunned. James, who was on the sixteenth hole of his hotel's championship golf course, receives the phone call from their concierge that his son has just been arrested. He jumps in his golf cart which, unfortunately like all golf carts, has a device called the governor that limits its maximum speed depending on terrain and grade. He cannot get there fast enough, literally. The police cars are driving away just as James gets to the hotel parking lot.

Alejo Melendez

He places a phone call to his longtime friend and sometime golfing and fishing buddy HPD Detective Pauly Magat. He asks if Pauly knows anything about this. Unbeknownst to James, Pauly has secretly been building the case against his good friend's son. He tells James his son is being arrested for the murder of Mark Tam.

James is flabbergasted. He was there to personally witness Mark's death and knows with one hundred percent indisputable certainty that his son is innocent, but of course he cannot tell Pauly that. He hangs up, speechless and in total shock. A million questions buzz in his mind; what evidence do they have? Where are they taking him? Waipahu, the nearest precinct, or Honolulu, the main jail with the most modern facilities. How soon until arraignment and how much will bail be?

Instead of letting himself become overwhelmed, he does the smart thing and calls Preston Akahana, the longtime family attorney and chief counsel of his own firm. Preston the administrator seldom litigates nowadays except in high profile priority cases that just so happen to have massive billable hours, and he is also a close personal friend of the Kanoho family. Preston has been James' close friend from before he was even married, Jimmy has called him Uncle Pres since the day he could first speak those words.

Creaking Door

Arrested

PRES AKAHANA IS put in touch with ADA Byron Abercrombie. They schedule a meeting the very afternoon Jimmy is arrested. When Preston arrives at the Honolulu Hall of Justice it is already a sweltering eighty-seven degrees in the adjacent top level parking lot. It is made from a special sand based concrete chosen for its reflective properties. On warm days, it is fully and minimally ten degrees hotter. This is where visiting defense attorneys park.

He takes the elevator with polished and burnished hazy stainless-steel doors up to the seventh floor. A lovely Asiatic receptionist tells him to be seated and buzzes her boss. She hangs up and tells Preston Mr. Abercrombie will be with him shortly, and three minutes later his door opens and he personally comes out to greet Akahana.

Byron points to a handsome rich brown leather wingback and tells his old friend Pres to sit. Abercrombie joins him across a mahogany coffee table on a matching dark chocolate leather sofa. He wants this to be a friendly encounter so he has steered Pres away from his large cherry wood desk.

Akahana has always thought Byron's office too small for a man of his stature and accomplishments; a local football legend turned second-top cop who has prosecuted far too many of Hawaii's most dangerous criminals. Despite the pedigree he was still a civil servant and this was still a government facility. His prosecutorial exploits have his path to the Governorship set in stone. He does however have an outstanding view southeastward of the ever-burgeoning Waikiki skyline and mighty Leahi, or Diamond Head as most people know it. Despite the urban sprawl, Leahi is still majestic enough and big enough to tower above the buildings trying to obscure it. The floor-to-ceiling windows are a nice touch.

Abercrombie details the information he is both required and allowed to give. Preston already knows about the warrant for DNA so he knows it has something to do with that. He is stunned to learn that Jimmy is the biological father of the daughter of Jimmy's best friend. Preston listens intently but already knows that so far, the evidence, though strong, is all circumstantial. That he fathered Mark Tam's child does not mean he also drugged the man and left him for dead.

Far more worrisome is that Jimmy will be extradited to Edmonton, Alberta soon and the US attorney will not oppose it. The two lawyers once battled on the high-school gridiron and have known each other for decades. They have a great mutual respect for one another.

Byron pours two glasses of Glenlivet and they discuss the facts further. Preston is told about the Nebraska connection and that Kelly too is presently incarcerated and as of yet uncharged for conspiracy to commit murder, but her extradition as a material witness is still pending. The main player they have been targeting has always been Jimmy, and now that they have him Pres can expect them to move with lightning quickness on the matter. Pres sips his scotch. Glenlivet is his drink of choice and he enjoys the rich, mellow aftertaste of peat. It is in a nice roundbottom amber tumbler but nothing like the Waterford crystal he sports back in his digs. He knows this is the classic rush to judgment and he is already thinking of ways to use that in his vigorous defense of the younger

Creaking Door

Kanoho. The love triangle, sexy in its prosecutorial allure, is always an irresistible and seductive motive for jurors. The defense will have its work cut out for them.

They are just about finished when Abercrombie's phone rings. His answers are terse and he looks at Preston once or twice while saying "uh huh" repeatedly. When he places the phone back in its cradle he lays a bombshell; Kelly Tam, originally brought in for interrogation, has just been charged as a conspirator. A bottle of Alanitrol had been mailed to her fourteen months ago.

When Abercrombie is through laying out the discoverable facts of the State's case and the investigation, Preston rises, shakes his friend's hand and thanks him for the drink and for his time, then exits quietly for the short drive to his office three long city blocks away. He must call James to update him then drive out to Makaha to confer rather than have the poor man drive out to Honolulu. He has been through a lot today and it is all going to get much worse before it gets better.

When Preston exits the steel-reinforced light-grey concrete building, he is hit with the typical reflected blast furnace tsunami of tropical heat he has become familiar with, having exited this building many times. This third floor's lobby exit has steel-edged tinted glass double doors that lead to the roof level of an open concrete parking structure designed for visitors with official business and requires a special decal authorizing access. The decal is for favored repeat customers like Pres. The rest place a huge tacky bulky license plate sized placard on their dashboard. This placard might as well have the word "loser" stamped on it.

Preston's car, like all the others on this level, has been baking in the direct Hawaiian sun and he knows it will burn when he gets into his Cadillac CTS-V. Both levels below are the conveniently covered and shaded reserved employee parking lot. Every visiting lawyer knows this is one of the DA's home field advantages coming into play. Pres removes his double-breasted jacket, loosens his tie, then clicks on his key fob. He's not had a big case in a while, and this one has all the trappings of an international scandal and may even be his biggest ever. He knows his firm is going to be overwhelmed so he will assemble his team the way all top-notch litigators do. He will begin by recruiting the very best specialists, both legal and technical. With a client that has a massive reserve and collateral, money will be no object. He thinks of the exposure and decides he will need a publicist.

    He is just about to call James when his phone goes off. It is James' ringtone. He answers and lets James begin; Pres wants to see if the man is hysterical yet. He is not. That is the James Kanoho Pres has come to admire, the level-headed warrior, the combat tested Marine. James tells him Kelly has also been picked up and Pres says he's already been told. He decides to end the call thirty short seconds later and opts to deliver all information in person, so he tells James to sit tight and wait for him. He places his phone on the center console and starts up his Caddy. The ignition is whisper quiet and the high quality British air conditioning mech kicks in almost instantaneously. When he puts it in drive the motor purrs as if the car is wafting on an ethereal cloud of coolness and comfort above and across the scorching hot concrete.

Creaking Door

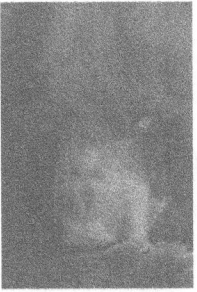

Squall

WHEN KELLY IS picked up at about the same time as Jimmy, she is peeling raw kukui nuts with her daughter Leinaala in their front yard so they can be polished, boiled, softened, and, when cooled but still penetrable, fashioned into leis and bracelets for the hula dancers of their local *halau*, the Hawaiian word for a hula dance troupe. They will be presented to them at the airport and worn by the dancers onstage when they fly off to the Big Island for a special annual hula competition. Kelly and Lei are wearing baggy surfing shorts and old faded cotton T-shirts and are sitting on woven grass mats under some towering kukui trees. The kukui nuts they are polishing were harvested from those same trees last month and allowed to harden and dry. Kelly sports a big floppy canvas garden hat to protect her fair skin and has her T-shirt knotted just above the waist, the way she did as a young girl on the farm, while Lei wears nothing on her head but a ponytail.

Lei has danced for this halau since she was five years old but will not be making the trip because of college. She has not practiced with her halau for over ten months, and although she knows the moves by heart she knows she is rusty and not competition ready, so she helps in the best way she can, with their stage garments and implements and the accompanying ornamentation.

Alejo Melendez

Hibiscus bushes, their blossoms bright with red petals and joyful yellow stamens, stand side by side under the taller plumeria trees with their yellowish-white fragrant flowers, both perfuming and lining the east and west sides of the yard. Towering mature coconut trees with trunks that have curved skyward surreptitiously like Arabian swords since before Kelly was born, have their long fencing foil-like leaves kiss and stab each other playfully in the ever-freshening trades. The ocean is their backyard and lies straightaway south and shimmers sapphire with pasty ivory foam gracing the sandy white shore line. The sea is not angry today and gentle waves lap at the shimmering jet black basalt lava rock formations jutting intermittently from the sand. These rock formations have been worn smooth by waves but were once as jagged as the rock croppings a mere thirty feet further up from the shoreline. There is a cooling breeze making this a soft day weather-wise, and the grass beneath their mats poke through some of the weaves and imparts its moist cooling touch on their bare legs. Gentle lapping surf and rustling palm fronds gracefully and lovingly touching each other are the only sounds until five police cruisers squeal to a stop in a most threatening manner on their three-car wide semicircular macadam driveway.

When the police arrive Lei and her mother are stunned. When Kelly is cuffed Lei begins sobbing hysterically. She'd lost her father to a gruesome hunting accident about a year ago and now suddenly and without warning or provocation her mom is being taken from her as well. Lei hears only the officer telling her mother she is being officially detained as a material witness in her husband's murder, followed by her Miranda rights. She asks for details from any of the officers who will listen but gets none. Instead, they all tell her forcefully to get back and nothing more. The cruisers pull away leaving her confounded and in tears. She immediately calls her Uncle James and he sends a car for her. The waves and the fronds are silent to her now, nor does Leinaala smell any of the sweetly scented flowers surrounding her. The police action was a

Creaking Door

fast-moving squall moving angrily through the area, unexpected, doing its damage, then exiting as rapidly as it had advanced. And now the swath of its destruction lies quiet again.

It was all a deception. The police's real intent is to have Kelly eventually arrested as a co-conspirator.

When she arrives at the Awaawa, James sits her down in his office, offers her a cup of tea, then briefs her on what he knows so far; that Jimmy has also been arrested in connection with her father's death and that her mother and her Uncle Jimmy both may end up being tried in Canada, a long way from Hawaii. James hands her a Kleenex as she continues to sob. He assures her it is all a big mistake. Lei is devastated and James knows she will remain inconsolable for a long while. He personally walks her to a private VIP elevator and leads her to a vacant unused luxury suite facing the ocean on the sixth floor. The suite's sound proof walls are so effective James can practically hear Lei's heart breaking. They are accompanied by his top hostess Judith Halawa who is instructed to stay with her and see to her every need. Lei wants to stay in the office with him but Uncle James insists there is much to do and he can get more done this way. He promises to update her as soon as he himself knows anything. Right now she needs very badly to decompress.

He says he will send something to her room and he orders her to take it. She is expecting valium or a sleeping pill but instead gets a seven-year-old bottle of Kendall Jackson white, an excellent vintage if she remembers correctly. There is also a warm Turkey club with melted cheese and avocadoes on toasted rye. The wine is excellent and the turkey club James Beard worthy. Uncle James is no dummy, the Chardonnay and the turkey's tryptophan combine to produce some much-needed sleep. He does not tell her that Preston Akahana and his team are on the way to strategize.

Soon after being processed at the main jail, Kelly is brought to HPD for questioning. She innocently and perhaps naively provides motive as she reveals the lurid tales of how Mark had become abusive and negligent of her needs. Affection had left the marriage a long time ago and it seemed they were just biding time until Lei was out of the house.

Bearing in mind the strong resemblances, Kelly is asked about any romantic ties to Jimmy. She is told to "start at the beginning." Taking Henri at his word she admits she had taken a trip to Hawaii when she was seventeen and had met Jimmy purely by chance at Waikiki. This long-ago history between the two was previously unknown to the detectives. She explained how they'd had a torrid three-day whirlwind romance and that Jimmy's integrity and the visit to Oahu had helped her decide to ultimately attend the University of Hawaii, but not to pursue Jimmy, she fully expected to never see him again. She didn't even know his name or where he lived. This was all the truth but naturally the detectives found that last part regarding their mutual anonymity hard to believe.

Henri told Kelly that they knew Jimmy was Leinaala's biological father and was about to further pursue that line of questioning to finalize their theory of Jimmy's motive to kill Mark when Glenn Kaneshiro walked into the room and proclaimed to the detectives that they were done. Kelly was stunned by that last revelation and about to refute it when Kaneshiro glared at Kelly and shushed her by putting his finger to his lips, then politely asked for the room.

Kaneshiro had been dispatched by Preston to save their damsel in distress. The cops left the room to afford the lawyer some privacy with his client. Kaneshiro instructed Kelly to say nothing further and to follow *to the letter* his instructions and his instructions only. Still in shock from everything that had transpired in the last hour, she nodded her head. Her maternal instincts kicked in and she asked about Lei. Kaneshiro told Kelly that her daughter was safe with James at the hotel, her every need being met while Preston, with his team of associates and James, were strategizing back at the hotel. He comforted her by saying not to worry and that some very skilled and powerful attorneys were working to clear this mess up.

Creaking Door

She felt a lot better knowing Leinaala was with James at the Awaawa, a veritable fortress fortified by modern technology and guarded by two mighty mountain ridges and a closed secure valley bringing up the rear. No better sentries existed than James Kanoho, his now not-so-merry band of loyal Hawaiians, and the powerful influence he exerted as a major player in the Hawaiian economy and community.

She was taken back to her cell with many dizzying thoughts but most prominent was how the police had discovered and come to believe that Jimmy was Lei's father. The story of Leinaala's father, which she had thought a well-guarded secret for over eighteen years now, has never been known to anyone but Lei's biological parents; not even to Leinaala herself. That they had been compelled to provide DNA samples had, with the entire present whirlwind of tumult, completely escaped her at the moment.

Alejo Melendez

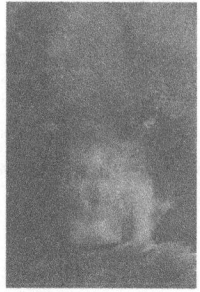

Mrs. Tam

WHEN LEINAALA WAS born, Kelly's entire life and world were turned upside down. The feeling that came with this life she had carried in her body and was now holding in her arms was beyond words and emotions, at least any she'd ever known or experienced. There were, of course, pre- and post-natal hormonally-based swings, which were probably harder on Mark than Kelly. But once Leinaala entered the world she was instantly and forever her mother's daughter. Maybe because Mark spent a good deal of time away, Lei had always been closer to her mom than her dad.

This bond grew stronger over time and was especially fun when little Lei began to walk and then talk. Her unsteady stumbly legs followed by the many flops on her rear as she attempted her first step was the most entertaining thing she and her husband Mark had ever seen. When Lei began speaking, first baby talk then semi-coherent gibberish phrases, that then became the most consuming thing in their lives. New parents want nothing more than to nurture and give. Their child wants nothing more than to tell them what. When that finally happens, verbally communicating with your infant child is the quantum leap parents seem to find the most rewarding. As happens with most new parents, they

Creaking Door

sometimes forget to take care of each other, focusing much or all of their attention on the baby, especially their first born, and, more exacting than any other circumstance, an only child.

Mark and Kelly were tempted to have another child when Lei was three. They even tried earnestly for about two years. Kelly suspected but never told Mark that it was most likely his fault. He most likely suffered from low counts or unhealthy swimmers. She could feel her potent fertility gushing through her veins. Kelly, at that time, wanted desperately to give Mark a son. It wasn't in the cards. Mark had a business to run and spent his free time hunting or surfing. He was also still working at the Awaawa part time, which for him wasn't so much a job as it was the opportunity to hang out with his best friend and his second family. The Kanoho family, as employers, inspired a tremendous amount of loyalty among their workers. Mark might've been seeing an old flame or two as well, after all he and Jimmy were quite the players back in the day. A leopard and his spots. Those employment barriers were his reasons when they discussed family planning. Kelly secretly went on birth control. She never bothered to give her reasons. Mark, the self-centered adventurous traveler, never bothered to ask.

In her spare time Kelly volunteered at the Waianae youth center. She taught science with an emphasis on her specialty, chemistry. She made it clear to her class of teenagers that she would not be revealing drug-making techniques and the kids laughed. She grew to love these economically disadvantaged children and saw the beauty and kindness of the Hawaiian heart. It made her feel awful that her ancestors probably saw the same naiveté and used it to swindle these generous innocent people into giving away their land. Despite her looks she was fully accepted as *kamaaina* and everyone also knew she was married to local surfing legend Mark Tam. She was still a beautiful woman and many of her adolescent male students had obvious crushes on her. Some of their fathers too, but she was Mrs. Tam and completely off limits. Mark was a known bad ass who could put a bullet between your eyes from five hundred yards in a stiff wind.

She knew the odds were long but if she could help one kid, just one, graduate from college purely on academics then it would have all been worthwhile. A lot of athletes were harvested from the Waianae Coast, skated through college, were handed a meaningless degree, then moved on to pro football where they made millions, were broke by their mid-thirties, physically debilitated by a sport that cared nothing for their life after, and possessed no useable skill set or higher education that would allow them a chance at a normal life and occupations other than something that required bashing your brains out.

Kelly made that her mission once she had decided not to have any more children. Not with a selfish, cruel, and absentee father traipsing across the globe in pursuit of pleasure. Either he had to break off his partnership with Jimmy or Jimmy had to get married and settle down, that was the only feasible way she saw to keeping Mark home full time and being a responsible husband and father. And even that drastic measure was probably no guarantee that leopard could or would ever change his spots.

She could not discuss this with her husband, he simply refused to give up chasing waves and the hunt, for either business *or* pleasure, wherever it was happening—Spain, Peru, Bosnia, Alaska. Kelly suspected he had other pursuits as well. She stopped accompanying him because all that happened would be her and Lei being left alone in some hotel room for days while daddy and Uncle Jimmy were out being a pair of twenty-year-olds.

So Leinaala was raised more or less in a single parent household, and both of her parents seemed fine with that. Thankfully Lei turned out completely normal despite the fact that a cyclonic soap opera was secretly frothing and building and taking place right there in her precious and serene Makaha Valley home.

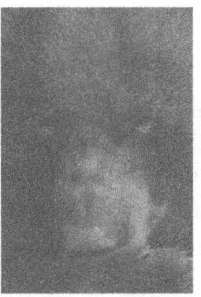

Redo

AS SOON AS Rohypnol was detected in Mark Tam's blood his gear was taken out of the Edmonton evidence storage lock-up and stringently retested. It was found that the delivery method was from his canteen, which was found to be lined with traces of the knockout drug. From the canteen remnants and the medical examiners autopsy report, it was forensically determined that only enough Rohypnol was used to cause a brief period of unconsciousness, roughly twenty minutes, a quick nap if you will. The ME concluded by the oxygen to blood ratio in what remained of the jugular vein that the victim, Mr. Tam, was still alive and conscious (as video evidence clearly displayed) but under the influence when the bear attacked. That same blood sample showed Rohypnol unequivocally in his system. They had to find out the significance of this low dosage and how it correlated with the killer's ultimate murder plan and exit strategy. More likely they thought the bear attack was unplanned somehow because of the discovery of Alanitrol. Laplatt's theory was that the killer had most likely used Rohypnol for phase one of the plan then would mask it in a second phase. But he or she never got the chance.

Enlightened, Magat expounded on that logic. The Alanitrol was lost in the woods. And why would someone lose a five-thousand-dollar bottle of damning evidence? Because they were sloppy. And when do criminals get sloppy? When they are under pressure or being rushed. Their killer for some reason was forced to bid a hasty retreat. Why was their man Jimmy rushing? Was Jimmy even their man? Video shows him arriving to shoot the bear about eight minutes after the attack started. By then the bear had been taking his sweet time chowing down on poor old Marky Mark. Of course, the canteen was most likely contaminated beforehand. So who could have done this? They still liked Jimmy because of the paternity angle as motive and his proximity to the victim as opportunity, but still they had no actual evidence to prove means. For this, they may have to pound harder on Kelly.

Henri was more closely linked to the initial crime of murder itself. It happened in his neck of the woods after all and he'd been on the case since day one. But all of the people being looked at were Hawaiians or in Kelly's case a transplanted citizen of Hawaii, and all from Pauly's neck of the woods. This offered him a unique perspective of their collective psychological profiles as persons of interest. People from Hawaii were absolutely different than their mainland counterparts. That "more laid back" reputation that precedes them exists for a very good reason. And for Pauly Boy, Jimmy was fading as far as prime suspects went.

They needed to dig further. This case was maddening with all of its twists and turns. Magat, like the Tams and Kanohos, was also a lifelong leeward Oahu *kamaaina*. He was born and raised in Waipahu with its large Filipino demographic. Pauly Boy was also a martial artist: a black belt in Aikido and an expert at Escrima. The most important lesson martial arts philosophy has imparted upon him is the one creed he lives by when investigating crimes: that the true sign of intelligence is an open mind, and it looked for all the world as if his partner Henri Laplatt was fixed on Jimmy Kanoho when it was starting to look for all the world like Jimmy had no viable chance or reason to do it, at least not in such an obvious manner. At least not to Pauly Boy Magat.

Creaking Door

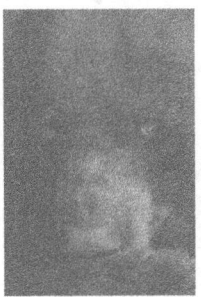

Ointment

KELLY WAS INSTRUCTED by James upon his visit to her in prison early the next day to provide Glenn Kaneshiro with complete and full disclosure. That included the very secret truth about Lei's father. She was to tell counsel every little thing, then let him take the lead during their next round of police questioning. When unsure, she was to look to counselor Glenn for approval on what to answer and when to clam up and let him do the talking.

It was hard but Kelly told Glenn the truth as she knew it, every painful detail. Most of it was surprising but Glenn maintained his trained look of neutrality during that most delicate of times; full client disclosure.

She disliked besmirching not only the dead but the man who also had raised their daughter. Mark Tam the icon was really Ivan the Terrible. What was amazing was that Mark had been able to keep the deception of being best friend to Jimmy and loving husband to Kelly going for years. It was for the same reasons as the split he was planning from Kelly; he'd wanted to wait until Lei was not only out of the house, but old enough to take care of herself. Kelly was given her most important directive from Kaneshiro: Say absolutely, positively **nothing** about Lei's real father. They were representing Kelly but only insomuch as their Kanoho ties allowed.

Protection and defense of all clients but fastidiously defending the Kanohos was the Akahana Firm's prime directive.

That afternoon, the day after her arrest, she was again brought in for questioning, this time armed with her attorney. Magat and Laplatt were there. They did the smart thing and just let her talk. Kaneshiro nodded and Kelly began her undoubtedly well-rehearsed and scripted monologue.

She claimed that soon after Lei entered adolescence, Mark began asking questions about why Leinaala looked so much like her Uncle Jimmy. It was the exact same thing that compelled the detectives to seek DNA samples.

Kelly managed to pacify Mark for a time, having him shrug it off at first, but it stuck in his craw and his curiosity and his questions persisted over the years as Lei's resemblance to Jimmy became more evident; slowly at first, like the trickle on the crack of a dam, then vehemently as the raging waters of his suspicions finally broke through and as Lei entered young adulthood.

The troublesome misgivings had been going on for years. Kelly said she knew it was all coming to a head, and that Mark was going to do something violent and extreme to exact justice on the matter, and before she and a decent man like Jimmy would be killed she knew she had to take action.

There was the motive.

They asked if she ever helped Mark pack for his hunting trips. She said of course, she was his wife and he was busy running charters, sometimes right up to the hour of departure for his scheduled hunting or surfing trips. She would often help pack clothing and small incidental items of gear like ropes, gloves, a very small first aid kit, energy bars, and his water bottles.

There was the means.

Jimmy and Mark were together the entire trip until the day they mounted, as usual, separate tree stands that were, in this case, half a mile apart. Mark then changed locations which shortened their distance to a quarter mile, a distance bristling with bushes, brambles, and thickets that Jimmy supposedly covered in eight minutes when the bear attacked.

There was the opportunity.

How could they tie all of this together? There seemed no cohesive final element to their Holy Trinity. The details of the investigation had never been revealed. No one but the cops and the perp knew about the contaminated canteen. But they weren't the only ones withholding information.

Throughout her second and more detailed interview, Kelly never once disclosed that she told James Sr. everything about her crumbling marriage or the extent of Mark's well-hidden anger. She did expound on the building resentment that was years in the making and ready to explode into murderous reality. More importantly, she never relayed that James had clearly stated his desire to stop the impending disaster. He was easily drawn in to the efforts to save his real son at the expense of his "adopted son".

When asked about the Alanitrol she had received from her brother Ken, Kelly looked surprised and asked what the hell Alanitrol was. She flatly denied having any knowledge of it. It was the kind of reaction the detectives knew was nearly impossible to fake. There was something genuine about her surprise and Magat instantly thought to pursue it further.

And so Laplatt put two and two together and realized he and the police force may have had it all wrong this whole time. Kelly the lying bitch just might be the mastermind. As usual, the story book fair maiden was overlooked because of a primitive instinct among the testosterone driven, the one that says women are weak, docile, and incapable of such evil.

It wasn't the first time a criminal mind had fooled Laplatt or police detectives in general. The criminal always has the advantage of knowing, while law enforcement performs the unenviable task of both anticipating and the solving of such deeds, always having to start with a blank slate, from in the dark so to speak. Guesswork, unfortunately, is often involved.

Pauly seemed happy that Henri was finally removing his blinders and climbing out of his "Jimmy Kanoho only" box, the one that was closed on all sides. But now all sorts of possibilities were springing up. Like any good mystery, one answered question brings to light a dozen more. If Kelly and Jimmy had somehow conspired to kill Mark, what was their end game? To be together as a family, so the real daddy could be the man of the house? Could it be a classic example of Occam's razor and the answer so obvious as to be right beneath their noses the whole time? Could it have been a love triangle gone badly?

The simple and obvious theory was that she poisoned Mark's canteen to allow Jimmy easier access to a compromised Mark. To somehow render Mark incapable of defending himself before a bear could eat him. Restraints would leave marks, but breaking bones would incapacitate him while he was still alive; breaking his legs so he couldn't run away for instance. And all the while they were describing the basic outline of James Kanoho's sinister plan.

According to the interview with Alanitrol inventor Dr. Susan Zao, once the antidote is administered to an unconscious patient, they regain consciousness within thirty seconds. But, she states firmly, it was meant to be used by conscious beings who first suspect they have been afflicted. Alanitrol's masking, converting, and resuscitory effect is directly proportional to the active heart rate of the victim and its ability to circulate the drug in time. That same active heart rate would be much lower in a comatose person.

Again many more possibilities arise. A plausible one is that their unconscious victim, Mark Tam, is prepared for death somehow, then awoken just before it to mask the Rohypnol, killed upon revival, and since the chosen scene of the crime was the bear-infested wilderness, the method to dispose of the body would be a seemingly natural one. Remaining flesh and/or blood would test clean of any toxins.

It seemed brilliant except the sealed, virgin vial of Alanitrol was never used and subsequently found a mile away, in a creek that could have carried it for ten miles for all they knew. Of course Jimmy could have dumped it there well beforehand, but why? Jimmy had also remained at the scene until the emergency responders that he himself called arrived, and then well afterward with the police to boot. Video from Mark's hunting cams and police confirms all of this. Perhaps it was a ploy to throw them off?

What interrupted the killer so much so that, alone in the woods with no witnesses and a chance to commit THE perfect crime, a bear was prematurely allowed to both kill and partially consume the body with Rohypnol still in it? That did not ring true as a well-thought-out planned crime of opportunity. It seemed more like an unexpected fly in the ointment.

Alejo Melendez

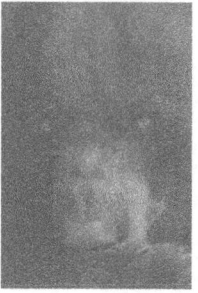

Dawn

MAGAT WENT TO the post office on Beretania Street, flashed his badge and asked to look at PO Box 669. The guy behind the counter could not have been over twenty-four and was probably stoned on some good *pakalolo*. His eyes widening at Pauly's tin revealed bloodshot veins and was a giveaway. But Pauly was here to check out the PO Box and he most certainly was not vice or some beat cop. Records showed it belonged to a Dawn Novak. A new player or Kelly's alias? He suspected the latter; Kelly would not be dumb enough to rent it in her own name, although the Alanitrol itself was mailed, according to Vernon Bosworth and her brother Ken, to Kelly Tam, not Dawn Novak. He also remembers his boyhood crush on the actress Kim Novak. She was the all-American girl every male in the world was in love with. Kelly had those same qualities, just not the international exposure, as least not yet.

He asked the kid to open it. It was empty. He then looked at the PO Box contract again and saw it had been closed two months earlier.

Magat asked the guy, "Whose authorizing employee signature is that on the paperwork closing out her rental agreement?"

The kid, Peter Gasper, said it was his.

Paul asked if he remembered this Dawn Novak and Peter said

Creaking Door

"yes" because she was a "majorly hot milf."

Seeing no video cameras anywhere in the facility he asked Peter to describe her. She was about 5'6, brown hair, killer body, definitely a mainland haole which meant fair skin and no pidgin. The description matched Kelly if she wore a brunette wig and avoided the sun for two weeks. Knowing that was all he was going to get for now, Paul steps out and immediately studies the surrounding shops. He hits pay dirt; there is a security camera mounted on a stoplight twenty yards away, surveying the street. It is facing the small satellite post office's entrance.

He gets the traffic video from the timeframe of the Alanitrol's known delivery. He reviews seven days-worth of surveillance just to be safe. On the video's third day of seven, a woman fitting the description is seen walking out of the joint carrying a shoebox sized package wrapped in plain brown paper. It matches the parcel's description as given by both Vernon Bosworth and Ken Herzog. She is wearing a baseball cap with most of her hair tucked under it and sunglasses that obscure some but not all of her face. There is enough nose and cheekbone to cast doubt on it being Kelly. The more he studies it the more he is convinced. There is a new player in the mix, and she goes by the name Dawn Novak and has been receiving mail in Kelly's name.

He reports his findings to Laplatt and everyone on the team. Keyboards fly as everyone begins their search for this Dawn Novak person. One hundred and sixty-five women go by that name in the US. Her vitals are entered and the search narrows it down to twenty-seven. The ones with criminal records are chosen; there are only three. Apparently Dawn Novak is the name of choice for goody two-shoes. Those three are then studied inside and out. It is exhausting work but the third and final report comes in from Athens, Georgia. That Dawn Novak, like the two others from their refined search parameters, had not left the state. The local LEOs had tracked down her alibi and it, like the other two, was airtight. There was no choice now but to run down the other twenty-four.

Those two-dozen were also a big fat *nada*.

So this Dawn they are looking for is either a ghost or using a fake name. Detectives know there is a kernel of truth to most every lie, and there is usually a reason a criminal chooses an alias. So what could the name Dawn Novak possibly mean?

Pauly, who believes wholeheartedly in this theory of a new player, sits at his desk and does an extensive and exhausting internet search for whatever tidbit or obscure factoid can help him.

He reviews the Kelly interview transcripts and starts at the beginning, when she visited Hawaii with her two best friends Zora and Willadean. He had to dig deeper and turn over two more jacket pages to discover their last names. Zora Vukovich and Willadean Janzen. With nothing to lose he punched both of their names into his computer; no records, both were clean. For kicks he decided to follow up on their history since Waikiki and their current whereabouts. Willa is married with five kids and living in Columbus Ohio after graduating from Ohio State, where she probably met her husband, who at present was of no concern to Magat. Zora had attended Stanford way over in Northern California but had not graduated. She never got her bachelor's degree in communications despite needing less than a year to complete her studies and obtain her lambskin. Whereabouts unknown. She was off the grid. Something to think about thought Magat. Last confirmed residence was Halsey about sixteen years ago.

Vukovich and Janzen, two interesting surnames. Vukovíć was Croatian and most of the Janzens in America had come from Denmark. A Dane and a Croat. Their photos on record showed two stunningly beautiful women. What destruction the three of them must have caused growing up in Nebraska! There was no current photo of Zora, only a Stanford student ID photo from about sixteen years ago, but if she was anything like her friends, her genes had insured she was still a knockout to this very day. He also

Creaking Door

knew most Slavic families had hard-to-pronounce names and "westernized" them after settling in America. He looked up Vukovich and saw its original spelling was Vuković, not much of a difference there. But the search also turned up a list of common Croatian surnames and one of them was Nowak. The common westernization of that name? Novak.

This got his hackles up. It was a stretch but they'd connected details more obscure than this, and they were at the stage of the investigation where grasping at straws was now perfectly acceptable. Hell, it might have even been official Department protocol for all he knew.

He then looked up common Croatian first names. What popped on his computer screen hit him like a Smokin' Joe Frazier left hook. He practically ran out of his office trying to get a hold of Laplatt.

Alejo Melendez

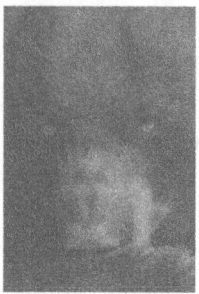

Cobblestones

WHAT A BRILLIANT day this was in Paradise. Zora couldn't believe that she was here at the famous Waikiki beach sunning herself into what she hoped would be a sexy light-brown tan to show off back in Nebraska. Her best friend Kelly was out trying to surf with a dreamy surfer she'd just met. The girls knew there were golden-skinned handsome local surfer boys with perfect teeth and perfect bodies waiting to be smiled at and spoken to. Like any smart gal, they also knew if you played them right, you could get a free meal and maybe more, like the surfing lessons Kelly was getting. If the boy was right they wouldn't even mind giving away the milk. They were in full vacation mode and wanted to experience life and get away with things they could never pull off in Nebraska, then be able to leave them here, far away from home and small-town gossip.

    They'd also agreed to lounge as solo players today so they seemed more approachable, but not too far apart so they could keep an eye out for each other. They even had fake wedding rings they could quickly don in case an undesirable dared to approach these Midwest beauty queens. Kelly with her flaxen gold locks drew not only the first boy of the day, but the best looking one as well, which was saying something because they were *ALL* magnificent. But it wasn't long before Zora was also approached. He was dressed only in his beach shorts and his abdomen muscles looked solid enough to make any cobblestone street in the south of France jealous. He had perfect teeth and sun-bleached golden-brown surfer hair. She declined his invitation to swim or surf, so he invited her for some ice cream, and with that the two got their conversational ball rolling.

    The proof of the inherent goodness of man lies in beginnings. We are always eager to undertake them because they are exciting and hold promise. A great void and mystery await us. We never think that meeting the right guy or girl could ultimately end in heartache, tears, hateful divorces, and bitter property settlements. No one thinks about those kinds of things or that kind of promise when a pretty girl or a handsome guy smiles their interest at you. One is swept off one's feet and the blinders of oblivion that are rooted in optimism from man's inherent goodness are suddenly thrust upon you gleefully like the last winning number drawn in the lottery while unseen and unnoticed golf ball sized hail, like that in a lower Midwestern trailer park, plummet upon you and your winning ticket during a summertime F-3. Fascinating, joy filled even, but sure to bring the future pain that seems to always accompany those upsides.

Alejo Melendez

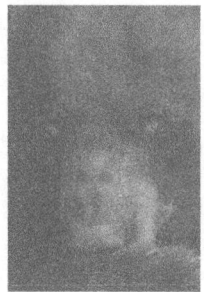

Breezeway

MARK TAM HAD just watched his best friend Jimmy Kanoho disappear into the beach throngs on this sunny Saturday in Waikiki Beach. It was not only the weekend, but they were in the middle of peak tourism season, and the pickings were good. He and a bunch of the local boys liked to come here and hit on the haole chicks, who were looser than most of the local girls. They got their share of Kamaaina wahines as well but picking up tourists was like shooting fish in a barrel. The haole chicks were here to have a good time, lose their puritanical inhibitions, and Jimmy and Mark were happy to oblige.

Mark zeroed in on a lovely dark-haired gal with creamy fair skin that was just starting to turn. It was also burnishing red, the tell-tale sign of pain to come, so he used that as his opening line.

"You're starting to burn."

Zora pretended she had not seen Adonis approaching from her left and managed to act a little startled by his voice.

"Excuse me?" she replied.

"You're turning red and if you don't do something about it you're going to have a painful night. Maybe even a painful remainder of your vacation."

"I suppose you're going to offer to rub me down with lotion?"

Creaking Door

She was playing hard to get but the thought *did* excite her.

"I suppose I could offer that up but I was thinking more along the lines of you getting into some shade, and quickly. I used to be a lifeguard here and I've seen it too many times to count." That was smooth but a total lie.

"Well what would you have me do Mr. Former lifeguard?"

"You could jump in the water then roll around in the sand. It would act as a natural sun block, literally. Or I could teach you to surf. That way we'll be in the cooling water but at least doing something constructive."

"I'm gonna pass on that cowboy, salt water doesn't agree with my hair."

Mark saw he had engaged her and she was loosening up to his subtle advances.

"Well then for starters, why don't we get you up and off of this very reflective sand and head for that breezeway near the bus stop?"

There were a lot of people, including bike-riding beach patrol police officers in regulation shorts, so she saw no harm. Besides, she truly was starting to burn and it was becoming painful.

"And then what?"

"And then you could let me buy you an ice cream cone. Two scoops if you're nice to me."

She smiled. He had her hooked. Fish in a barrel.

Alejo Melendez

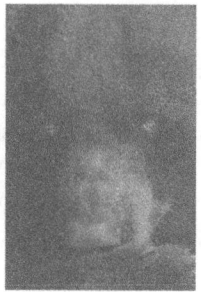

Zoo

SHE GOT SOMETHING she had never tried, one scoop of pineapple ice cream. It was beyond delicious. The creamy tropical flavor was sinful and positively decadent. They didn't have anything so wickedly exquisite back in Halsey.

The ice cream turned into laughter, then fully engaged loose banter, then some hinting at romance, certainly a flirtatious milieu was ventured into, and then a hand-in-hand stroll down the boulevard and into a Surfing Museum. He pointed out and explained all kinds of artifacts and wild things completely foreign to a Nebraskan. Things she didn't know existed. There were photos of local watermen riding HUGE waves at powerful breaks like Waimea, and legends like how Captain Cook, the first European to lay eyes on Hawaii, described the way the dark-skinned locals used long wooden planks to ride the kind of thunderous surf his seafaring ways had taught him to avoid. But here were these aboriginal types who'd completely mastered this force of nature. People back in England thought he was delusional when his crew brought back drawings and described such things. On the same four-foot by four-foot plaque, in much smaller print and strictly as an afterthought, was the tale of Cook's demise; how he had been skewered onto a spit and roasted over an open flame, then *joined*

Creaking Door

the Hawaiians as their guest of honor and main course for dinner.

They laughed and frolicked and came dangerously close to each other's lips several times when conversing in close quarters about the fun they were having. The humorous banter turned to hushed tones of intimacy and eventually whispered desires of sin and lasciviousness between kisses. Unlike Jimmy, he drove her to a deserted section of Kapiolani Park, near the Honolulu Zoo and just off the main drag at Waikiki. Surrounded by various animal nocturnal cries and the acrid smells of misery and captivity, they themselves became animalistic in their own overly excited way. They started in the front seat and finished in the roomier backseat of his father's SS Chevy Nova.

When he first approached Zora, he'd become so immersed in captivating her that he failed to notice Jimmy teaching some other haole chick how to surf just off the shore in front of him. Offering surfing lessons was one of their tactics when prowling for tourist chicks. He was not as smooth as Jimmy, who did not disclose his real name to any of his new female friends. He also occasionally would get a room to fulfill his romantic desires. They had different approaches, Mark's being a bit crude, but as long as their objectives were met, the boys would go home happy and swap tales back in Makaha the next day.

Jimmy and Mark spent the next three days romancing and engaging their new friends. They would absorb themselves fully with these gals and, except for football practice, not see each other for a week. They had no way to know these two girls were best friends and had vacationed together. Jimmy and Mark were both dedicated first year students at the University of Hawaii by day, but for those three magnificent nights they were Lotharios to their heartland Juliets.

The day came for the girls to fly back home. Kelly fell in love with the climate but accepted her detachment from the boy she'd met on vacation. Zora, on the other hand, had fallen in love with the boy she knew as Mark Tam. Neither boy had come to the airport to see them off, Jimmy by mutual agreement and Mark because he was ready to move on to the next filly. Zora was missing her guy before they'd even boarded the plane. And she would not soon forget him.

Creaking Door

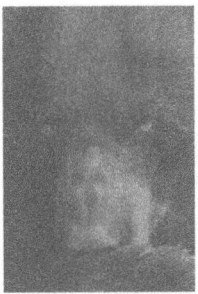

Crumble

IT'S BEEN TWO years since their escapades on Oahu but all three girls have moved on with their lives and their education. Zora and Willa are enrolled at Collins junior college south of Lincoln while Kelly attends a better one near Omaha. Kelly's family farm has been more prosperous than their neighbors the last couple of years.

The girls are happy for each other and still get together. It is apparent that Zora is still heartsick over her Hawaiian fling. She'd been a virgin up to that point. She felt tossed aside like yesterday's trash and her friends kept telling her to forget about it, that they went there to have a good time and not hang on to whatever they experienced in Hawaii. But it was not so easy for Zora to let go. Still, she seemed OK and emotionally stable. They all got good grades and planned to move forward to bigger schools to earn at the very least their Bachelors, then become gorgeous independent wealthy heartbreakers extraordinaire in that big wide beautiful world that awaited their grand entrance into its loving arms.

Zora was not sure what she wanted to do but when Kelly announced plans to try and get into the University of Hawaii some emotional wall she'd built for herself began to crumble. Kelly had the smarts for University. Zora's longings came back to the fore.

Alejo Melendez

After Kelly's announcement she felt depressed and that in all likelihood she would remain a farm girl for the rest of her foreseeable miserable life.

Creaking Door

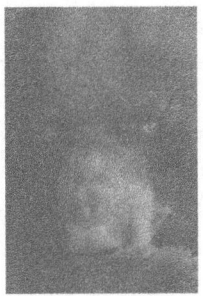

Stanford

WHEN KELLY HAD been accepted to the University of Hawaii on a chemistry scholarship, a kind of fire was lit under Zora. Her grades improved and she wanted desperately to leave the farm and experience life other than crops and combines. She'd won awards for her reporting at the Collins Press, the newspaper publication at her Junior College. She decided that journalism was as good a means as any to make her way into city life. She declared herself a communications major and actually had the grades to apply to some of the bigger and better institutes of higher learning, like THE Stanford University. Through government aid programs and grants allocated to farmers and their dependents, she was able to gain admission there, the most prestigious school in the west.

She had turned her mediocre life around and things were sailing along. She'd made a conscious decision to let go of the pain Mark Tam had inflicted upon her when he selfishly swindled her out of her virginity. She had given herself freely but under the belief that it would become so much more and that they would keep in touch. But once she left Oahu no contact was ever made between them. He never answered her letters. He'd hurt her but now her life was blossoming and bright with promise as a future award-winning journalist.

Then something happened during the very first week of her junior year that would dramatically alter her life forever. Some underclassman flunky was passing out fliers for a "Welcome back to School" shindig that was open to all students. While attending her very first fraternity party, with her college best friend and fellow junior Alanis Zao, they became ill, fell unconscious, and then woke up in the Stanford Hospital's emergency room.

Zora regained consciousness first, about two hours before Alanis. She watched and prayed from the next bed over that her friend, who had come from money back East, would awaken and be all right. Once Alanis did regain consciousness, she was whisked away to a private room upstairs to recover. As Zora watched her friend being wheeled away, she remained in an out-care wing of the ER. There were nine beds separated by thin hospital curtains. She was so close to the patient next to her that she could hear his unlabored breathing. He'd been admitted for a broken foot and his lungs were clear as a bell. Alanis was upstairs, above the ER madness and riff-raff, receiving premium treatment and care while Zora was being discharged two and a half hours after she woke up. She was sore all over. There was nobody to pick her up or meet her, so she walked back to her dorm room three miles away. Classes would start in two hours at 8 a.m. The pain lasted for three excruciating weeks.

She felt ashamed that she had passed out in front of so many classmates and students.

She didn't leave her room for a week due to migraine headaches and muscle soreness throughout her entire body. She knew she had fallen dangerously behind academically so she soldiered on despite any lingering pain. Her return to campus was accompanied by sideway glances, suppressed laughter, snickering, and whispers. She couldn't understand why it was happening, why it was such a big deal to these clowns that someone couldn't hold her liquor, but it all made her feel humiliated and only about six inches tall. She could not possibly have been the first student to get drunk and pass out at a frat party, could she?

She'd finally been contacted two weeks later by Alanis, who was back home in Connecticut, and finally told the truth. Alanis had been drugged, so she suspected that Zora had been too. But there was more; Alanis had been administered a rape kit which turned up positive. She told Zora to get tested for STD's as soon as possible. But the worst was yet to come. Alanis then tearfully informed Zora that a video of Zora passing out then being "abused" by several boys whose faces never once appeared on camera had gone viral over the internet.

Alejo Melendez

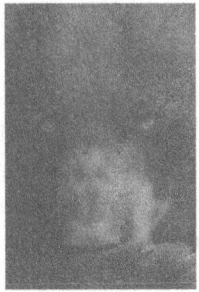

Return

ZORA MOVED QUIETLY back to her parent's home in Nebraska and put up a brave face. She never told anyone about the horror that had happened at Stanford. When asked, she just said big-city life wasn't for her anymore and that she could finish up her degree any old time. Thankfully her neck of the woods was not internet savvy so her viral video had never been seen in these parts. Folks around here didn't much care for that morbid shit on the "web" anyways, so there was no real danger of anyone finding it through a search for similar items.

She could never bring herself to watch or even look up the wrenching video but Alanis told her the camera was jostling around so much you couldn't really tell it was Zora. No comfort was given by that. When asked, Alanis said her lawyers and police were viewing it for evidentiary purposes and that it would be available to Zora's legal team if she wanted. Zora thanked Alanis and promised to get back to her, then cried over her inability to pursue the matter both financially and emotionally. She would speak to Alanis once more a few years later. After that, Zora never spoke to Alanis Zao again.

She still kept in touch with Willa and Kelly. Willa lived in Ohio while Kelly was still in Hawaii. Sporadic reports from Kells

Creaking Door

told of tropical life, days at the beach, chemistry classes, and her dating then marrying a football player from the University. Her latest letter finally contained photographs. One was of her new family. It showed her holding her infant child with a Hawaiian name Zora could not ever hope to pronounce. Her other arm was around her husband, a man, it read, whose name was Mark Tam.

She struggled to finish the letter. It read how Kelly detailed the most bizarre coincidence; that her husband's lifelong best friend was Daniel, the boy she'd hooked up with when they were vacationing. His real name was Jimmy Kanoho and they owned a famous hotel called the Awaawa. Of course she would never tell her husband Mark about it despite the fact that they live in the same town about a mile apart. The Tam and the Kanoho families are very close. In fact her daughter calls "Daniel" Uncle Jimmy. It was all very bizarre but that secret was part of normal life for them now. There were other secrets Kelly failed to disclose.

The freshly arrived stage of anger, which had been lying in wait blanketed by the stigma and trauma of her being secretly drugged then publicly raped, had now officially ballooned into a biblically epic rage accompanied with a very confusing torrent of sadness and regret. Always introverted and the quiet type, Zora knew that once again forces beyond her control were taking her to dark and disturbing places she never envisioned herself being in.

Three or four years, she wasn't sure which, have gone by since Zora walked off the Stanford University campus never to return. She'd lost track. Time stood still for her. She eschewed and forfeited all monies and grants provided her by government subsidies. It was a golden goose that had been buckshotted down by some rich frat boys in a swamp blind of privilege and cruelty. She was technically still alive and working at a drug store in Halsey, the town she grew up in and a light year from Stanford. She found it ironic that, because it had been built on one, Stanford's nickname was "The Farm" when all she'd ever wanted to do was leave hers. But now she meandered in a life devoid of purpose. It had taken a good long time for the five stages of grief to progress onto anger, but here it finally arrived. Three or four years later. She'd lost track.

In the vast open space of the Nebraska plains and the rolling fields of corn and soy that seemed to spread out forever, the occasional straw-filled scarecrow twisted in the warm summer wind with lifeless black button eyes that stared vacantly and uncomprehendingly over his sphere of influence; while a woman scorned was awakening to a long-dormant dispossessed anger she was finally ready to own.

Creaking Door

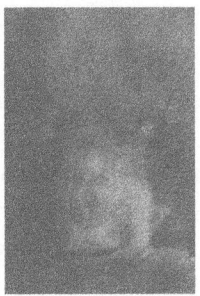

Transplant

FAST FORWARD FIFTEEN YEARS

FIFTEEN LONG YEARS have gone by since Zora had received that fateful photograph depicting Mark Tam as Kelly's husband. Zora had never gotten over it. She'd never really gotten over her first encounter with Mark back on Oahu. When she was finally ready to expunge him from her life she'd suffered that unspeakably horrible and devastating setback of being drugged then raped while attending Stanford.

    Continuing her meandering haze all of these years, she wanted to do something, anything, to make the hurt go away. Whatever it was she needed to do would have to involve Mark Tam and be done in Hawaii. Alanis had caught one of her rapists. Her mother was a rich and powerful and now famous Doctor on the board of some big pharma out in New Jersey, so they'd had the means to pursue at least one of her attackers all the way to prosecution. But Zora was a farm girl from a humble family in a modest middle-of-nowhere town. She needed grants and loans to attend school. She was the archetypal cliché little fish that always got eaten by the bigger fish. She was mad as hell and not going to take it anymore. She'd finally had enough of this undeserved and interminable pain. She was a smart gal. She'd made it into Stanford against all odds. Stagnant and apathetic no more, a plan, at long last, was being formulated in her mind.

Zora scrimped for a year to get enough money for her mission and a one-way ticket to Oahu. She'd saved Kelly's letters so knew her current address. She still wasn't sure what she wanted to do but she figured, even after all of these years, locating Mark then possibly speaking to him was a start. Good or bad start had yet to be determined.

She didn't know what she was going to say should she ever confront him, but she was sure it would contain elements of how badly he'd hurt her. She knew there was a chance he'd completely forgotten her. At best, he would apologize and be genuinely contrite. At worst, he could classify her as a stalker, take out a restraining order, then have her imprisoned when she violated it. And violate it she would, she was that screwed up in the head from all of this.

Kelly was actually family through marriage. Zora's first cousin Eunice was married to Kelly's brother Kerry. She'd been in touch with Eunice over the years but certainly not regularly. You couldn't really say they were close. In fact, Zora knew if she ever asked Eunice for a favor the stuck-up bitch probably wouldn't give her the time of day. She even kept her maiden name, Paxton; unthinkable there in conservative old-fashioned Nebraska farm country.

During the year it took to save for Hawaii, she kept her nose to the grindstone and spent that time wisely by cultivating a friendship with the least desirable of the Herzog boys, Kenny. She spent time plying and manipulating him, even gave him hand jobs on occasion. Necessity being the mother of invention, touching any man's phallus after Stanford seemed impossible until her necessity to go to Hawaii and invent a way to kick Mark Tam's ass took hold. Intercourse was out of the question. Ken was getting off, he didn't

Creaking Door

care.

Zora also told him she could get in touch with Kelly if he so desired and that she could put her in touch with him, something Kelly hadn't done in eons. He eagerly agreed. She then told him she had acquired wanderlust again and needed to get away from the farm. Ken agreed to loan her money for the trip. She never said where and he never asked. He got a handy thrice a week and the possibility of contact with Kelly, and Zora got her hooks into him for not just future use but also the financial help she needed to escape from home. Ken Herzog cared little for anything or anyone outside of his own immediate needs, but he *did* care about his baby sister. He was unaware that his use as a pawn in Zora's game had already begun, and the designated damage was just over the horizon.

It was not quite a full calendar year when Zora discovered she had accumulated enough money to leave. She'd used the internet and some phony documents to secure employment once she was physically there on the island. She would continue life with an assumed name and a phony Master's Degree in what else but communications. She might as well pursue an occupation she had plenty of training and education in. She was sure she could pass any interviews or tests imposed on her by potential employers.

She did, however, take a planned detour on her way to Hawaii. She'd had a secret stash of money for two express interconnected purposes, to make her assimilation into Hawaiian society much easier and to alter her appearance in furtherance of her impending crime. She'd stopped in Los Angeles and had her eyes narrowed, slanted, made to look more Asian. It took a month and a half but once she had healed and the bruising had vanished, she continued her flight into a kind of twisted providence she foresaw as her preordained right as a disparaged woman. And although the surgery was thoroughly professional and a top-notch job, Zora would never quite grow accustomed to her newly formed Asiatic eyes.

Alejo Melendez

It took a few months for her to settle down on busy Oahu. She'd found a job right away thanks to her impressive phony resumé. And of course she still had her looks to fall back on when seeking employment; that attractive people were hired exponentially more than the rest of the mere mortals was an established fact.

She wanted to remain incognito so rather than use her looks to procure some kind of television journalism gig she took a job as a cub reporter for Oahu's biggest newspaper, The Star Bulletin Advertiser, which once upon a time was two separate competing entities; The Star Bulletin, the afternoon paper, and the Advertiser, the newspaper you found on your porch when you woke up and had your morning joe with. Her mediocre but accurate reporting was, however, noticed by the paper's star reporter Hoaloha Ao-Smith and she was given the tough but prime assignment of being a fact-finder and corroborator for Miss Ao-Smith. All the while she was secretly keeping tabs on the Tams. She even drove way out to Makaha a few times and stole glimpses. She seethed and put all of that energy into her work. She gained a reputation as a dedicated worker and tough but fair investigator. No one really knew or suspected what really motivated Zora or her semi meteoric rise on the coattails of and alongside Hoaloha Ao-Smith.

She called Alanis Zao once more with a phone which was purchased in Halsey and smartly retained a Nebraska area code. They spoke for half an hour, catching up, strolling down memory lane, commiserating over that tragically interrupted junior year in Palo Alto. Zora eventually learned that it was indeed Rohypnol that was specifically confirmed in Alanis' blood. There could be no question that the same was used on Zora.

She'd also remembered hearing all over the news about some miracle antidote to combat date rape drugs that was still flying off the shelf. To no one's surprise, women married *and* single were buying it in droves and keeping it in their purses with the other modern woman's marketing handbag standbys: tampons and pepper spray.

She'd planned on something vile against Mark, perhaps tarring and feathering him, maybe shove splintery broomsticks up his rectum while gagged and bound. But he was a big strong man. Her only hope was to render him powerless somehow. How fitting that Rohypnol, the drug once used to render her helpless, fit nicely into that category. And now there was another drug that could mask all traces of the Rohypnol ever being used. It could be the perfect crime.

The first phase would be to re-establish communication with that lowlife Ken. She would ply him into doing her bidding by sending letters he would think were from his baby sister Kelly. Zora also knew for quite some time that Eunice worked at a medical supply facility. Claiming she wanted a steady bargain-priced source of the antidote, Alanis was kind enough to text her Bannon Industries Midwest distribution list and Zora found that Eunice's company, Husker Medical, was receiving shipments of it for resale to clinics, hospitals, and pharmacies across the Midwest.

It took a few letters to set him up, but in less than two months and with six heartfelt letters, Ken was ready to help his baby sister with a problem she was having. It didn't hurt that Zora threw in a bribe she knew he would accept then pass on down the line in pursuit of what it was Zora really wanted: a vial of Alanitrol. Date rape drugs were easy; they were sold on the streets like Quaaludes back in the seventies.

Under the guise of Kelly, Zora wrote to Ken and offered him a thousand dollars for a tiny bottle of something called Alanitrol. Knowing the lazy dickhead wouldn't care what it was used for, she claimed it was a cancer treatment medicine for a close friend of hers. The poor man's insurance wouldn't cover it and he might die without it. She told him where the drug could be found and even suggested he pay that dumb cow Eunice a couple of hundred bucks to get it for him. Further completing the ruse, she reminded Ken her birthday was coming up and it would be a wonderful gift if he could get that medicine for her. She asked Ken to write her back when all of this had been done and to NOT mail the vial until she gave the go ahead.

    Zora got her reply two weeks later. In his letter Ken asked why he was sending all of his mail to a PO Box. She replied simply she was constantly between addresses because of fluctuating rents on the island. She then detailed how to carefully pack then send *ONLY* the vial in an unmarked package with no return address, no letter, no birthday card, and that she would be busy for the next several months with some big Hawaiian festival that she needed to help out with. She placed these explicit instructions and a cashier's check for one thousand dollars in the envelope. Once he'd gotten his money he would not give a damn if that cancer-stricken friend of Kelly's lived or died. But he *was* happy to oblige his sister.

    Zora had cut off all ties and communications with Kelly years ago with the idea of her husband and the pain he wrought being out of sight and therefore out of mind. She didn't want to take the chance of Kelly ever mentioning her to Mark accidentally or in passing. And if she did, hopefully the self-centered prick would not remember her name. It was a long time ago and a horn dog scumbag like Mark had probably gone through dozens of women by the time he'd met Kelly. Football players like Mark Tam were just that: players.

Creaking Door

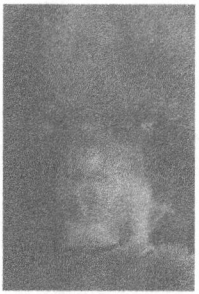

Baggage

BECAUSE SHE WAS now working for the star investigative reporter on Hawaii's leading news publication, Zora had the kind of unfettered access to information most normal journalists could only hope for. She had built up a network of sources and informants and established unmitigated trust because she had always protected them. Her vigilance on Mark's very public charter business gave her very little of what she sought: intimate information on the man personally. But through this she had determined a few things that may prove useful. He loved to hunt and still loved to surf. This was gleaned from his use of advertising in her newspaper and from client testimonial when she posed as a surveyor of local businesses. She decided to recruit from the Kanoho side of the valley. She did a little digging and found two Awaawa employees who were willing to covertly give her inside information about the hotel and its owners. Zora openly disclosed her position as a journalist. The Awaawa sources were told to tell no one about this future as of yet unwritten story in the making or the money would dry up.

Awaawa employees were all loyal and treated like family so she trod lightly at first. As trust developed and the quality of the information improved, their payoffs increased, Zora was able to get more and more intimate details. One source was all but useless.

The other, a mother of three, proved very reliable. Over time Zora had learned about some very heavy baggage the Tam and Kanoho families were carrying.

The biggest dirt was how Leinaala Tam looked a lot like Jimmy Kanoho. The rumor mill was in full swing over that tidbit. Despite that, Jimmy and Mark remained joined at the hip and still did almost everything together, at least outwardly. They traveled the world on exotic hunting and surfing safaris. Jimmy was still single and playing the field while Mark's marriage was said to be unstable due to the stagnancy brought on by the natural course of time, Mark's wandering eye, and doubts about his biological tie to his only child.

That the Tam marriage had become rocky was no surprise. Mark had always been shallow and somewhat misogynistic. Zora confirmed with her main Awaawa source, a woman named Judith Halawa, that Mark had indeed become abusive toward his wife because of his suspicions. The same suspicion was a strong source of grist for the rumor mill that Mark very privately harbored a grudge against Jimmy and was planning to do something. When? The most prudent juncture would be when Lei was old enough to become independent.

From this Zora deduced that Mark was carrying on a kind of deception and that something like this had to be driving a massive wedge between him and Jimmy. But to what end? Something was keeping them together. His business did well so the tie could not be financial. Was it out of loyalty?

Knowing they traveled together often, she would form a plan using this as a vital component.

Judith also confirmed that Jimmy's father, the very well-known and dashing James Sr. was mindful of the rift and determined to protect everyone involved, especially his only son.

Zora started pumping more money into Judith Halawa, a high-school dropout. She was going to require her help to tie all of the components of her devious plan together. Judith was still kept

Creaking Door

in the dark about Zora's true purpose in seeking revenge and made to gather intelligence thinking an exposé benefitting the hotel was in the offing. Her loyalty to the Kanohos would wisely never be tested by Zora.

First she wanted Judith to slowly and steadily feed James controlled information. To put it into his mind that Mark was up to something, and now that Leinaala had gone off to University the danger to Jimmy was imminent. They had a bear hunt in a remote part of Canada coming up. It would be a perfect opportunity for James to believe that Mark would act upon it.

Zora then used her sources at the airport to retrieve flight manifests to Canada. Never using the Tam and Kanoho names for her request, the information she sought was easily found without raising any suspicion. Now she had times and dates. Learning from the manifest reservations list, she quickly learned which travel agency the boys used, then subsequently was able to gather information on their accommodations.

Through Jimmy, James was already abreast of the travel info so Zora put the main parts of her plan into effect. Through Zora's manufactured intelligence, James had been led to believe that his son would be in grave danger in Canada. Judith then told him she knew some powerful people that could help him for a price. The payoff was necessary to maintain the integrity of the deception and was also a nice bonus and motivating tool for Judith. It was a great insurance policy towards the plan's success. Smartly, all money from James was given to Judith and deposited in her account as her unexplained income. Judith protested not a lick, and none of it could be traced back to Zora.

In some very clandestine meetings with Judith in James' office, Zora's plan was masterfully instituted.

James was no dummy and he'd already used his influence and money to obtain a false passport, a false identity, and the accompanying documents to complete the illusion. Those actions could be traced and ultimately prove disastrous.

With Zora's guidance, Judith would instruct James to discard the identity and documents he'd obtained through his sources. She would get James another, more secure fake passport and identity. Judith assured him hers were untraceable and better suited for his covert operation. She would also give him a special drug that would revive Mark when the time came. Next came the delivery system. James would somehow gift Mark with an expensive top-of-the-line hunting canteen in which packets of flavored electrolyte mixes would be inserted to look like complimentary additions. One of which would be doctored with Rohypnol, then carefully placed back in its packaging and resealed to look brand new and untouched. He would give it to Kelly with the instruction to pack it with Mark's gear *AND* to remove his other canteens so he would have to use the new one. Kelly believed Mark would appreciate the gift as a loving touch from his still caring wife.

Then came the most difficult element. Knowing the boys would operate from different locations, James would have to do the unthinkable. He would have to somehow find a way to kill Mark. It was actually not that difficult a decision for him. He would do anything to protect his son. And he knew Mark could be a cruel manipulative son-of-a-bitch and was verbally and sometimes physically abusing his beautiful wife and daughter. He would use his military training to this end. The trick would be to do the harm AND keep Mark alive long enough to administer the second drug which would eliminate and mask all traces of the first drug, thereby taking any foul play completely out of the picture. Zora even thought of using the bears to dispose of the body. That the bears would be emerging from hibernation and ready to eat anything would be a major help. The end result would be a hunting accident. The real reason for James' lack of reticence would be revealed later.

Creaking Door

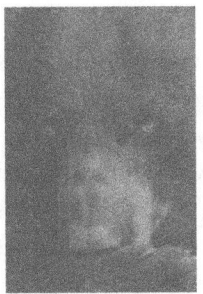

Mistaken

FOOTSTEPS ECHO DOWN the cold gray concrete walls as Jimmy listens while sitting quietly in his fourth-floor jail cell waiting to see who will walk by. He is seated on a flat metal grate that serves as his bench. It is affixed to the cinderblock wall with two-inch diameter masonry bolts, is exactly three feet long and just wide enough to house a human posterior. Everything is painted cheap gunmetal gray. A small window at head height with a view to the world below is his only diversion. It contains two-inch thick Plexiglas fitted into a slat three feet long but only six inches high, not enough room for even a Filipino contortionist to squeeze through.

Loneliness forces a man's mind to wander in bizarre directions. So what *do* you call a Filipino contortionist? A Manila folder. He tells these kinds of jokes to himself to occupy his thoughts, to keep them from wandering into negative territory. Did you hear about the skinny scrawny pervert who moved to Alaska? He came back a husky fucker. His imprisonment, his circumstances; they are ALL negative territory. So these little jokes bring a smile to his lips. Anything to keep the isolation from driving him insane.

At forty feet up, his window has never been cleaned by human hands, relying instead on Mother Nature's cleansing rains to rinse away any annual encrusted buildup. Dried spotty water marks left by the same rains tend to negate the effect.

Jimmy's only view of the outside is an obstructed one. It shows a backstreet strewn with trash and various low-level shops, like two run-down rot-gut cheap liquor stores, a convenience mart that hardly looks convenient, and a laundromat with a busted window and, judging by the amount of people it services daily, has only two or three working machines in what looks like two rows of five. Each business has some form of steel or iron to protect its front. Some use a corrugated steel alloy roll-down from above; others have side-to-side iron bars that fold back like an accordion when not in use.

This section of town is mostly deserted, even at high noon. Two old sodium street lights reveal a few drunks and hookers at the witching hours, and he is sure violence occurs regularly though he has never seen any in the three months he has been incarcerated.

The footsteps reveal a guard, Fenton, who has always been a prick to Jimmy. He signals the control desk with a walkie-talkie and Jimmy's door clicks. Fenton takes one step through the threshold and tells Jimmy, "roll'er up, we're going downstairs."

Jimmy is wary but like any prisoner who sits around all day doing nothing, and especially doing nothing new, he is anxious and curious about the change in routine. He rises up off of the flat metal slab and feels the blood circulating back into the crosshatched hollow ridges imprinted on his ass from the grated metal. He grabs his one possession—a dog-eared paperback version of a novel by some writer so painfully obscure that Fenton and the rest of the prison guards view the reading of the threadbare pocket-sized book as another form of punishment.

"Still reading that stupid book?"

"Yup, and it ain't so stupid Fenton, you would actually like this author. His stuff should be right up your alley."

"Oh yeah? What kinda shit does he write about?"

Creaking Door

"Oh, you know, the good guys versus the bad guys. He is all about the struggle, the pain."

"I get enough of that crap in this shithole from assholes like you."

"Seriously Fenton, you should check this writer out."

"Is he famous? What's his name?"

"He's not famous yet. His name is Hugh."

"Hugh? Hugh what?"

"Jarekshun."

"Jarekshun? What the hell kinda name is that?"

"I think it's German."

"Hmm, Hugh Jarekshun huh?"

"That's right Fenton, and Hugh Jarekshun fits right up your alley. You should check him out. You'd like the way he gets into guys like you. It's raw and will make you uncomfortable, but for a guy like you, totally rewarding."

Fenton has not read a book since he was forced to back in the ninth grade.

"Ain't a reader but maybe I'll come across some of his work."

"More than you know buddy, more than you know."

"OK, enough chit chat, get a move on it!"

Jimmy does as he is told and takes three steps toward the Correctional Officer and stops. He is about to pivot but decides to wait for Fenton to initiate it. It is but another small capitulation designed to keep Jimmy in whatever good graces can be refined from the vein of this destitute and fragile unlit mine shaft.

Fenton never finds out that Jimmy's paperback is a Patterson.

It is cloudy outside and the dampened light from the window confirms it. Jimmy stands in his thick cotton prison jumper, which is really a pair of elastic waisted pants and a slip-on V-neck long sleeved shirt. Both are prison issue orange but designed for the harshness of the cooler northern climes. Jimmy takes advantage of the momentary pause to stare at Fenton. He is in his usual crisp, beige khakis. A cloth emblem star indicating law enforcement is stitched on to his shirt just above where the heart would be if correctional officers actually had one. It was decided some time ago that a metal star pinned onto the CO's would and could constitute a weapon if ever taken off the CO's shirt. It in fact happened twice before and was therefore banned. That it took two occurrences is a source of humor among the inmates and is in fact one of the first stories told to the newbies. "Turn around, hands behind your back," orders Fenton gruffly. They both know the routine.

    Jimmy complies and is cuffed. The steel is cold and it feels unpleasant against his skin. Thankfully Fenton has not clamped them tightly enough to pinch. Once restrained, Jimmy is led down the hall past two other cells and a drinking fountain he has never seen used. They board an elevator which they then ride down to the first floor. They arrive somewhere deep in the bowels of the prison's lobby, a drab and gloomy-looking area devoid of any kind of joy or decoration, just more cinderblock walls with color-coded, two-inch-wide striped lines painted onto the cold, unforgiving cement floor to assist people to specific sections. Jimmy and his escort stroll through the frigid halls of a place that was never meant for the public to see. It is well away from the reception area which by comparison is brightly carpeted, well lit, has portraits of past decorated police officers mounted throughout its cherry wood panel walls, has its waiting room furnished with clean, bright blue-cushioned and upholstered chairs and matching sectional sofas with two teak coffee tables laden with various books, magazines, and other periodicals for visitors to pass the time with as they wait to conduct their official business. Fenton grasps Jimmy's elbow firmly and leads him into a small room with a small desk and, at present, two chairs. Inspector Henri Laplatt is seated in one of them.

    "Have a seat Jimmy," he says without rancor. The room is cold and a south-facing window offers some bleak northern winter light, but even that has the dreary effect it was probably intended to give. Laplatt nods at Fenton, who then uncuffs Jimmy. A singular motion of his head sideways, the universal signal for "scram", tells Fenton, who was expecting the gesture, to leave, which he does obediently.

Jimmy eyes the plain wooden chair, varnished with ribbed backing and no armrests, lays his right hand on it to gauge its temperature and comfort. As expected it is cold to the touch. He then rubs his wrists to warm them and sits slowly to ease the joints that have stiffened from his limited exercise and the pervasive and permeating Canadian winter chill. The chair's seat is slightly double concaved to conform to the derriere. Though cold like the room, Jimmy knows it will warm quickly from his body heat. Although it offers no consolation at the moment, Laplatt's chair is the exact same model.

"Do you know why you're here?" asks the jetlagged Laplatt, who sits facing the window, probably to offer better lighting for the documents he has before him. They are all undoubtedly pages from Jimmy's jacket.

A bird, unseen, flies past the window and casts a quick flickering shadow across the inspector's face. For a second Jimmy wishes the seating arrangement were switched so he would have something besides Laplatt's ugly mug and the drab cinderblock wall to stare at.

Once he is seated, he notices the light is bright enough to show a weary counterpart across the table, bags drooping under his tired eyes and stubble indicating the man had not shaved in at least three days nor slept well in perhaps two. He has the look of a well-travelled, well-worn weary man. A man who has been on a tough pressure-filled case for months.

"Nope," replies Jimmy.

"Things have changed and our investigation has taken a turn, a good turn for you. We have some pretty strong and compelling evidence now that may prove your innocence."

Laplatt, despite his apparent fatigue, has been careful to formulate his words in a manner that does not guarantee anything or provide false hope. For all the cops know, Jimmy may still have had a hand in this heinous crime.

Stunned by this turn of events, Jimmy replies, "I knew it. The evidence was all circumstantial and the DNA tests had to be wrong. I've been telling you guys all along I am not the baby daddy," he says using jailhouse vernacular.

Laplatt's thoughts turn to the forensic lab newbie Janet Rousseau. His volcanic, over pressurized, pus-filled abscess of anger has not yet subsided, "No Jimmy, we thought they were conclusive but we may very well be wrong."

"MAY?" Jimmy thinks to himself. He knows he will not be getting an apology and he doesn't waste his time waiting for one. Instead he is eager to hear more about this unexpected turn of events. He anxiously waits for Laplatt to continue.

During the investigation Jimmy, Kelly, and especially Leinaala were asked to give DNA samples. That is when the biggest surprise of the entire investigation turned up. Jimmy's DNA was seen as a match to Leinaala's; he was indelibly identified to be the girl's biological father. This was enough overwhelming motive, albeit circumstantial, to cast Jimmy into a most negative spotlight as the man responsible for Mark Tam's death and therefore enough to get a warrant for his arrest.

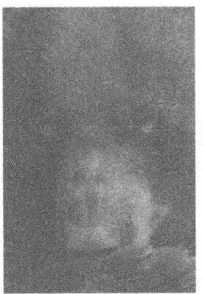

Diligence

FOLLOWING EDMONTON'S TEST results, Preston Akahana, Jimmy's dutiful lawyer, had obtained the DNA samples during pretrial discovery and had them forwarded to two US labs for independent testing, one of which was the FBI. An officer from the Judge Advocate General's office of the D.O.D. ensured they were processed quickly. Jimmy's small yet secret employment with the Pentagon had come to the fore much to Jimmy's benefit and the Akahana firm's surprise. Falling under the protection of the United States Military was not an entirely bad thing. His continued affiliation with these top cops, Jimmy knew, would prove very beneficial down the road of his life one day.

The mitochondrial DNA link to Kelly was clear, but the Canadian authorities had jumped the gun on the rest of Lei's sample. A much closer and thorough look revealed only a quarter of the DNA sample matched Jimmy and Lei exactly, and this exposed the premature call to action by Canadian police to arrest Jimmy. After all, during the murder Jimmy was only a short distance away, a quarter of a mile, and was at the same lodge with Mark the previous two days, ample time to slip the drug into Mark's canister.

A child will have fully half of its DNA from each parent, and the quarter amount shown from Jimmy's sample led investigators directly to his father James. It was an unintended consequence of Preston's diligence.

When asked to submit his own sample, James Sr. eventually did so under protest. He stalled for as long as he could, claiming everything from a civil rights violation to his protection under the fourth amendment. James continued filing motions through his attorney, Pres, and exhausting every legal means to prevent him from complying. Eventually the courts had ruled in favor of the prosecution. Finally, a warrant compelling him to comply forced his DNA into the better qualified hands of the United States federal authorities. James, caught in a classic catch 22, hated the stall tactic knowing it would keep his son behind bars that much longer to await trial. This time the testing was done by HPD and the FBI. The tests were conclusive. James Sr. and not his son Jimmy was the actual father of Leinaala Tam. This "aftershock" stunned everyone yet again, most of all Jimmy and his mother Kui. It was a secret Kelly and James had lived with for almost two decades. It was a secret Mark Tam would now never realize. And it bothered Jimmy immensely that his best friend believed he had betrayed him, then had taken that to his grave.

Yet another bombshell had been dropped. This gave the case more of its Hollywood drama and an international tabloid veneer. How many more bombs were in the offing? So far this was beginning to rival Nixon's Cambodian Carpet Bombing Campaign.

James was first brought in for questioning, and he did not deny having a brief three-year affair with Mark's much younger wife, and he had been well aware of the possible consequences. As for Kelly she said she could not help herself. Mark was gone a lot on hunting trips, then absent even more on overnight charters, and when he was home he paid little attention to her, especially after her pregnancy. She found James Sr. a very attractive and attentive man, and not just in his looks. He had charm, poise, and enough regal bearing and confidence born of a man who owns his own multi-million-dollar hotel.

He reminded her a lot of Jimmy, who was also always gone with Mark and for whom she still harbored vestiges of those three, romantic, lust-filled nights so long ago now. The affair with James just happened, she was not strong enough to resist and overcome the loneliness.

James was also quite guilty by his own admission. He told authorities they needn't search hard for his reasons. He loved his wife but Kelly was a woman still with an almost perfect, hard, athletic body, and a face that could launch a thousand ships let alone what she was like eighteen years ago. How could any middle-aged man say no to that kind of candy? The relationship between James and Kelly was of course far more complex than just sex and lust and primal urges. There was also a strong emotional element that brought them together, but that was a byproduct of loneliness, non-trial related, and nobody else's business.

They'd been intimate for about a year before Kelly became pregnant. Within three days and without any science or confirmable testing she had known instinctively that she was pregnant. Luckily Mark had just come home from a two-day fishing charter. She knew how to arouse him and made passionate love to him that night despite his fatigue. They'd spoken of having children but not until they owned their own home, about two years from then at the rate Mark and Kelly were earning. Two months later when their doctor confirmed her pregnancy Mark was overjoyed. Kelly was relieved. Life was blissful for the family of three to be.

Alejo Melendez

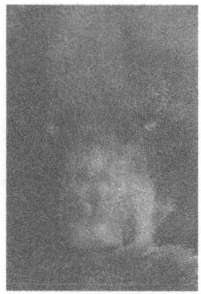

Tangible

PAUL MAGAT WAS home in Waipahu enjoying a freshly brewed cup of Blue Mountain Coffee. It had been a gift from his friends at airport customs who had confiscated it from a Jamaican national. This clown had been on a watch list for drugs and was denied entry into Hawaii on a direct flight from Mexico. His belongings had been confiscated and placed in lockup for the required year before they were either properly disposed of or auctioned off.

It was a cool morning so he sat on his lanai reading this morning's paper, the Star Bulletin Advertiser, the "SBA". He'd been following a story about some Hawaiian homesteaders on the windward side fighting over their sovereignty in a small sleepy town called Waipio. They practiced ancient ways by growing taro and raising pigs. They fished and harvested whatever they could from the surrounding mountains: wild guava, mountain apples, lilikoi (passion fruit), oopu (freshwater gobies from mountain streams) and various fruit tree orchards they maintained—mango, lychee, tangerines. It had been proven through carbon dated hieroglyphics that pigs had in fact been brought to Hawaii by the ancient Polynesian maritime travelers who'd first arrived here an estimated ten thousand years ago. And now some mainland

Creaking Door

developers had hardballed the local property owners into selling their plots thus leaving the heritage farmers out to dry. Those heritage farmers were claiming ancient ancestral rights to the land, and they were probably correct. But of course, granting them that right would open the can of worms that ALL of Hawaii would in fact fall under that umbrella. Yet another impossibly complex native Hawaiian story being covered and explained by Hawaii's premiere newspaper journalist Hoaloha Ao-Smith.

He was impressed with this reporter's matter-of-fact style and the way she chronicled Native struggles. It was now automatic for Pauly to seek out Hoaloha Ao-Smith's weekly column in the home section.

The air was calm, the morning chill bidding a slow farewell to make way for her ugly stepsisters: the afternoon heat and humidity. There was a mango tree in Paul's front yard that he had seen grow from six-inch sapling to forty-foot skyscraper. He'd planted it when he was twelve at his then grandmother's house. He would need to rake the yard and inspect the fallen fruit to see which were usable. The single tree bore so much fruit that he'd learned to make both pickled and dried Chinese style mangoes. They were popular gifts among friends and coworkers. It was just another reason the affable detective was a favorite son in the station house and his neighborhood.

But for now he was enjoying this fine Hawaiian morning. There was good coffee in hand and the company of a beautiful island gal, Hoaloha Ao-Smith and her conspicuous hard-hitting prose.

The front pages held their usual bad news; the second or third pages sometimes had pieces of their investigation. Hoaloha Ao-Smith was an investigative journalist for business and social corruption, particularly those perpetrated against Hawaiians. She did not do current events or breaking news so there was little to any chance she would walk into HPD one day and interview him. He harbored a secret fantasy of meeting her one day.

Alejo Melendez

The back-story on Hoaloha was that she was born on Maui but raised on Oahu. Her mother *and* father were both Hawaiian Chinese in various percentages. She did indeed very much reflect both of those bloodlines. She went to Stanford and married young, a local haole boy named Smith. The marriage failed but she kept the name, hyphenated as a show of strength and independence. She'd had a few modeling jobs during her college days, nothing explicit or pornographic, and was always known as ambitious and a go-getter.

Her parents were both retired and living on Maui, near Kaanapali in the affluent areas surrounding Lahaina. Her father had made his bones in real estate on the mainland specializing in that crazy Silicon Valley housing bubble from once upon a time. He'd done well and gotten out. Golfing and fishing are the only things he speculates on nowadays. Her mother stays busy campaigning and volunteering for local Republicans, perennial underdogs in the liberal Aloha State and a perennial source of embarrassment for her Democrat Hawaiian activist daughter.

She loved going back to Maui during breaks and holidays. There, family and friends knew her as Ming, short for 黎明 Límíng, her Chinese name. She went strictly by her professional and Hawaiian name on Oahu, it was good for business.

When Hoaloha first started at the SBA, she was assigned, relegated really, a story about a man on the windward side of Oahu who made poi pounders, ancient pestle and mortars carved and chiseled out of lava rock. This was used to pound the Taro root into the starchy paste known as poi. Pretty much all haoles find it inedible. It remains an island staple to this very day, made by machines now and sold in plastic pouch bags at the local chain supermarkets but to a dwindling degree of customers with each passing year. The practice of poi pounding, like most of Hawaii's proud culture and ancestry, was in danger of being lost forever. It profoundly moved the young reporter and ever since then she has made it her cause to elevate the culture, her culture, back into

Creaking Door

societal consciousness.

She gathered what little equipment a rookie reporter was given—a tape recorder, some pens and notepads—stuffed them into her handbag, then walked into the bathroom. After peeing out her two large coffees, she stood at the mirror to touch up her lipstick. Standing next to her was a pretty young woman who looked nervous.

"Hi," said the woman, "I'm Dawn Novak."

"Hello Dawn, I'm Hoaloha. I'm new but I don't believe I've seen you around. Are you also new here Dawn?"

Dawn confirmed she was. That was the end of their very first conversation, because Hoaloha then had to run. But they kept bumping into each other and got to know each other better with each passing encounter. It turns out they had something significant in common besides being hired at about the same time. They had both attended Stanford. Hoaloha had gone on her parent's dime and was a business major. Hawaii's employment landscape was festooned with nepotism and finding gainful and meaningful jobs were beyond her semi-affluent family's scope.

She'd heard there was an opening at the paper for a research assistant, it paid fairly well, and she applied for and got the job. Two very short months later a story broke on a fire in downtown Moiliili, a subsection of Honolulu, and, in a pinch, she was asked to cover and report on it. She did it with such acumen that her bosses elevated her responsibilities with a few more stories. She aced enough of them that she soon became a full-time reporter, and when her popularity over ongoing coverage of Hawaiian heritage was lauded, she was given a pay raise and a column. She would handle Hawaiian affairs and her anti-establishment op-ed pieces struck a nerve with the locals and circulation increased accordingly. Her rise was somewhat meteoric. She had filled a need that for some reason had never been filled before. There was a massive amount of scuttlebutt regarding unfair treatment of the locals but no one had bothered to articulate then publicize it. Thus Hoaloha's star was born. She became the "star" in the Star Bulletin Advertiser.

She'd run into Dawn continuously in the claustrophobic halls of the SBA. Their paths were entirely different yet somehow Hoaloha and Dawn had hit it off and became close over time. When busy Hoaloha could spare it, they'd have lunches together. As the pressures on Hoaloha grew, Dawn became a confidante as well, and the pair found themselves leaning on each other when it was called for.

What Hoaloha immediately noticed about Dawn was the very obvious plastic surgery eye job she'd had. Hoaloha believed it to be a botched surgical attempt of some kind but dared never mention it to the shy wallflower for fear of devastating her, which in fact it would have. Dawn had always hated that surgery and was never comfortable with its outcome. When Hoaloha asked other coworkers if they noticed it they all said either "no" or had no idea what she was talking about. Hoaloha supposed she had a much keener eye than the rest of the building. Maybe that's why she was being asked to cover more and more stories as a first-year reporter; her observational skills were unparalleled.

It turns out Dawn had excellent journalistic skills but for some strange reason avoided any kind of spotlight. It was almost as if she were allergic to it. Knowing this and wanting to help out her little buddy, Hoaloha enlisted Dawn as her official lead fact-finder and girl Friday. The two became inseparable and did award-winning work together. Dawn only asked that she be kept in the shadows and that Hoaloha, when on one of her public speaking engagements and thanking her team, never utter her name publicly. Dawn claimed extreme shyness and that true power lay behind the throne, where she resided by choice and somewhat uncomfortably. Hoaloha, now Hawaii's top investigative journalist, knew there was more to it than Dawn obviously let on. But she loved her little farm girl and more importantly loved the behind-the-scenes work that she did. So Hoaloha was happy to take all of the credit and readily agreed to keep Dawn as anonymous as was possible in the world of

Creaking Door

journalism.

They grew to fancy and trust each other, spoke daily and incessantly now that Dawn was on staff, gossiped, shopped, had beach outings alone, and, on one fine summer evening as they gazed into each other's eyes, fell deeply and unexpectedly in love with each other in Hoaloha's downtown thirtieth floor high-rise condo. It happened so innocently, neither realizing their closeness was really a physical attraction as well. Hoaloha, like Dawn, was considered highly attractive and desirable by members of the opposite sex, and they both followed this path biologically and religiously right up until the night of their first kiss. An unseen force drew their lips together in the midst of an innocent hug which became a deep, longing, and tightly locked embrace that could not be broken. Soft Hawaiian music played in the background. Uncle Gabby Pahinui crooned a fable in his native tongue, the lyrics sad and mournful as all dying languages seemingly sound when condemned and reduced to their vestigial selves and their final declarations and protestations. The large sliding screen door to her balcony let in the cooling trade winds easily at that great, towering height, and the moment was right for the two girls to be caught totally unaware by the self-revelation of their deep subconscious ache. Now Hoaloha and Dawn had *two* secrets to keep.

The entire state was buzzing as the notorious Mark Tam investigative noose tightened. You could feel it especially within the walls of the SBA. The place was practically humming with phone calls and internet searches trying to ensnare the latest developments.

One day, Hoaloha returned to Oahu from covering a story in the Big Island. She went straight to the SBA building and was walking through the lobby when she spotted the two lead investigators of the Tam case, Pauly Boy Magat and Henri Laplatt. Hoaloha, an exceptionally beautiful woman, turned male heads whenever she entered any room and this was no different. She wanted to get right to her office on the top floor and begin her latest byline that would have her typing fingers, as usual, banging away with fury on some hard-hitting testimonials.

She and Dawn stepped into the elevator when Magat's hand interrupted the door from closing. He looked right at Hoaloha and wanted to shake her hand. He gave her praise, the kind she got all the time, then quickly left them alone.

On the way up Hoaloha noticed Dawn had turned a whiter shade of pale and was visibly shaking. That is when her worst fears were confirmed. Dawn was involved somehow in the biggest story to hit the island since Statehood. On the seventh floor they exited the elevators and walked in silence to their respective offices four doors apart.

After a few vodkas to decompress from the Big Island to Oahu flight, Hoaloha sat at her desk and began hammering out the story. She began to worry about Dawn and called her office. When she didn't answer Hoaloha felt great concern. She'd always relied on her very strong sense of presence in her day-to-day life and work, and she couldn't shake this very strong and ominously foreign feeling that something bad was about to happen. She took the short walk over. She knocked gently, turned the steely cold knob, then opened the door to an empty office. Dawn's tormented weeping ghosts could actually be felt, and the fear, sadness and despair left behind were tangible. Magat's close elevator encounter had shaken her beyond the obvious claustrophobia. She knew right then she would never see Dawn again.

With a heavy heart she closed the equally heavy door. It creaked. Her parents travelled the country extensively when Hoaloha was little. A long-forgotten memory of a long-ago camping trip with her parents in Chadron, tucked way up in the northwest corner of Nebraska, has unconsciously surfaced. What they were doing way out there and in that part of the country she cannot recall. But she remembers seeing and hearing elk for the first and only time in her life. She was only five years old but she never forgot that inimitable and irreplaceable sound. It was a

Creaking Door

mournful wail, like a sad, heartbroken, and lonely being calling out to its forlorn mate. Like the vacant spirit of a long-suffering lover crying out for help and receiving none. Like the now sorrowful creaking door of Dawn's barren office. It was the sound of anguish and abandonment.

Alejo Melendez

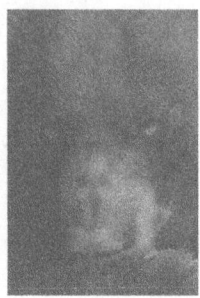

Bounced

FORTY-EIGHT HOURS BEFORE DAWN LEAVES HOALOHA

A NATIONAL MANHUNT was put into place for the capture of Zora Vukovich a.k.a. Dawn Novak. Federal, state, and local resources were being pooled to bring an end to the yearlong mystery that involved a wealthy and famous hotel owner, his son and his son's lifelong best friend, a love triangle, two states, two countries, two Midwestern female beauties, two aliases, and a massive man-eating black bear that was limping and still roaming the wide open woods of upper North America.

In Nebraska, they had to dig very deep and go back fourteen long years to find the first known sign of Dawn Novak. She had paid cash for a one-way ticket to Los Angeles. Two mysterious months later, she purchased a one-way ticket to Oahu, then went underground and dropped off the radar. Thank goodness for flight manifests.

Not only could she now be anywhere but she could also look like anyone. With advances in corrective surgery she could even be a full-fledged man. But logic and need dictated that they stick with

Creaking Door

what they had, and that was her student id photo. They ran a software program that digitally advanced her appearance to what it would most likely look like at present. It was not perfect but they put the composite out for a woman of about forty with gray streaks in her black hair and her rounded Slavic almond eyes surrounded by crow's feet from living in Hawaii.

Zora the journalistically devout researcher was naturally constantly abreast of any breaking news. The latest leads in the hunt for a female killer was a big one. Scandalous, compelling, sexually charged, and local, it had the Fiftieth State abuzz with excitement.

The quiet town and valley of Makaha was the center of the national universe right now, and Oahu was bursting at the seams with the expectancy of an all-out gunfight between a desperate modern-day Ma Barker and the coppers and G-men that were hunting her down. One almost expected to romantically and nostalgically see and hear Tommy guns rattling off around the island at any given time.

Knowing the authorities were closing in, Zora smartly had some more cosmetic surgery done two months prior. Her crow's feet were removed, her nose narrowed, her cheekbones uplifted, and, just to boost her ego, she had her breasts augmented to eliminate the sagging brought about by age.

As soon as her face healed, a makeover was done; her eyebrows plucked, some Botox here and there, and voila, not only did she look ten years younger, but her appearance was altered enough so she no longer resembled the composite Zora that was digitally constructed and bandied about electronically and virally. It was a well-timed anticipatory strike on her part and it kept her two steps ahead of her pursuers yet again. And big money bought her the kind of private, subtle, undetectable, and effective change only the most discreet Beverly Hills specialist was capable of.

She continued on with her work. She was currently helping with a report on some beef local fisherman had with the government about closing down some coastal areas on the Big

Island. That kind of stuff was ongoing here in Hawaii. Hawaiians had never gotten over how their land had been stolen from them when they were forced into a system of government that allowed people, foreigners no less, to take ownership of their land, the sacred *Aina* that belonged to no one and everyone. They were the confederate south and the rest of the western world was the Yankee north. And like the rebels of Dixie, the wounds ran too deep to ever heal in this or ten lifetimes.

She came back from the Big Island energized and ready to work. She felt she had compiled a good story and was anxious to get it ready for Hoaloha and the editors, then quickly on to print where locals would continue to read and worship the local reporter who always sided with the Hawaiians.

From the airport she went straight to the news building where her office was situated on the seventh floor. The top floor. The penthouse level. Only the paper's very best occupied that floor.

The building's exterior was dark because it was specially made from the black sands of Kalapana. Every load taken from that beach had to be blessed by a Kahuna. Milton Kaahinui would at first make a spectacle of it and chant over the dull yellow front loaders before they would scoop the tonnage needed to fill the massive beds of the dump trucks parked next to it.

Milton was decked out in formal aloha wear with, around his neck, a five-foot long open-ended lei made from the traditional Maile vine. Ti leaves were tied in bands around his biceps and a pikaki headband adorned his noggin and nicely covered his widening forehead and some of his balding pate. He was being paid a pretty penny for his services after a Hawaiian Rights activist group that he was a member of lobbied and convinced local legislators that the blood of their ancestors ran through that beach and the black volcanic sands were the tears shed by the deity Madame Pele knowing she would one day have to bow to progress and have her "children" pilfered. The mainland contractors were pissed. Eventually, so many loads were taken that Milton, also an avid golfer, found the chanting and praying cumbersome, tedious, and entirely interfering with his tee times. Soon the showy twenty-minute ceremony was whittled down to ten, then five, then, as the weather grew warmer and the tee times harder to secure, those same chants became one minute quickies, sometimes lasting less than thirty seconds. A wave of some ti leaves and a line or two, then poof, Milton was paid his usual five hundred per session and was on the first tee just as the sun was peeking over Mauna Kea. Once or twice he even showed up in his Ashworth pullover sweater and Greg Norman shark-logoed hat. It was truly laughable when he started wearing his two-toned metal spiked Footjoy saddle shoes to the beach. You could hear them crunching while he ran to his car once he reached the asphalt parking lot.

On the Big Island, Zora had helped Hoaloha detail the disappearing subsistence hunters and fishermen and the government regulations that were strangling them into not only oblivion but poverty as well. She had pulled into her reserved parking space and entered the lobby when she was startled by the appearance of Inspector Henri Laplatt and detective Paul Magat, the lead investigators in the Mark Tam murder, the one that had everyone buzzing and a little frightened as well. She looked away quickly when the pair of detectives noticed her somewhat grand entrance into the building and her heading quickly toward the elevator.

The ornate koa wood elevator doors with carved, inlaid depictions of natural Hawaiian flora and fauna were two inches from closing and preventing her dangerous interaction with the pair when a large dark male hand reached in between the crevice. Her heart stopped. The elevator's safety mechanism kicked in and the double doors bounced back open. It was Paul Magat. He didn't get in but rather held the door open and reached his hand out to her.

"I know you're very busy but I just wanted to say I'm a big fan and I wanted to personally shake your hand. I admire the work you do."

Her stomach had leaped up into her throat and she was momentarily speechless. She managed to suppress her stunned look, watched Hoaloha return his handshake, and then calmly say, "That's very kind of you Detective."

With that, he stepped back, the elevator doors closed, and she exhaled and just about fainted right there in the elevator. She backed into the polished steel handrail that enveloped the three fixed sides for safety, leaned against it and grabbed it hard for maximum support from her failing and flailing knees. She made it to her office where she poured herself a vodka rocks and downed it in one gulp. After another drink and about ten minutes, she was able to sit at her computer and finally get to work.

Creaking Door

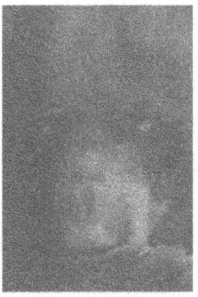

Glossy

BACK AT HPD, Magat was glowing over having met Hawaii's foremost journalist and being impressed at just how beautiful she was. They were at the newspaper office because of a hunch that Zora might be there. They knew she was a failed communications major and that she might actually fall back on that to earn a living. It was a long shot but they wanted to be thorough. They passed Zora's old pic and the composite around but none of the newspaper employees knew of such a woman.

At his desk he couldn't shake the feeling he had known Hoaloha from somewhere. His spider sense was tingling and it would not seem to recede. He found her very attractive and wondered if she was married. Of course she was. Her hyphenated last name was a dead giveaway. And he loved her three-word modern woman moniker, kind of like Hillary Rodham Clinton, but younger, hotter, with a hyphen, and just as ambitious. He found that modern woman stuff sexy. In that fashion, he could not stop thinking about her. He was a boy again and she was Kim Novak.

He perused over the investigation files once more knowing they had Zora cornered if not close by. Where would a killer like that hide? Natural good looks like that could easily snare an unsuspecting man and surely weaken his will into doing whatever it was she needed from him. He kept staring at that student ID and the video footage still frame. His head began to hurt.

One desk over, on Robert Fernandez's usually cluttered desk, was a copy of yesterday's paper. He grabbed it and turned to the middle of the Home section. He wanted to reread his favorite reporter's article. He'd been reading her devotedly for a few years now. Only in the last year or so had her picture adorned her regular column's headline. It was a small square, in USA Today fashioned color, and she showed off a million-dollar smile. She was a typical tanned sun-bleached mixed-race melting pot resident of Hawaii Nei. Her hair had turned golden from days on the surf, her skin bronzed and her dainty nose perfectly sharp. That dainty nose was the only dead giveaway to any work being done because Hawaiian noses were never that angular. Maybe it was her Chinese side.

His fascination, born of typical male lust and desire, caused him to punch up an internet search on her under the keyword "images". Dozens of pictures appeared. They all looked recent like her newspaper byline profile. They all showed a beautiful hapa woman at, best guess, forty years old but passable for thirty. Most likely she was part haole, part Hawaiian, and part Chinese, a typical local mix.

He put a sheet of HP super high glossy photo paper in the inkjet and sent the image he liked best to the printer. It would emerge as an 8x10 and he would have her autograph it when they cracked the case. She was sure to come around wanting an interview when the big day arrived, and he knew it would because his spider sense was tingling. Or was that lust from staring at Hoaloha Ao-Smith, Hawaii's best reporter and best-looking celebrity older than thirty-five, his ideal range for the perfect woman.

He placed the photo in a wooden frame he kept in his bottom drawer. It used to contain a picture of him and James Kanoho posing with their ocean fishing rods. James was holding a seventy-pound ono (wahoo) and Pauly a forty-pound opakapaka

Creaking Door

(red snapper). Both fish were trophy-huge for their species and beyond delicious when they devoured them that night with friends and family. They were cooked on a big koa wood fire and the beers were icy cold. That was a decade ago and the last time he'd been on board the Kuialoha, the fishing boat named after James' lovely wife. His fantasy was to marry a beautiful country girl like they raised them in Makaha. He would settle for a hot career city girl like Hoaloha Ao-Smith.

He placed the newly framed photo on the right side of his desk, just behind the ugly black, department issued, twenty-year-old PBX phone. The picture immediately brightened his landscape.

The days droned on and no new leads turned up. Zora was in the wind. The trail had gone cold. No citations from the Mayor or personal interviews with Hoaloha Ao-Smith for this cop. The thing that helped him through his days was looking at Hoaloha Ao-Smith's photo. It had a meditative effect. It was juxtaposed with Zora's criminalistic photo on the murder board.

He looked back and forth between the two. He did it again, then another time, but slower. "Oh no," he thought. Could it be? The resemblances were faint but noticeable with enough skill and a sharp eye. The sharp discerning eye and observational skill of a first-rate homicide detective. He asked for their computer expert to run that morphing software to see how easily Zora could be turned into Hoaloha Ao-Smith.

Alejo Melendez

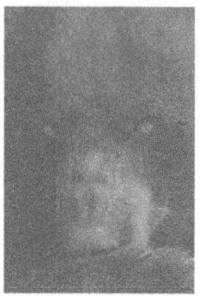

Ming

PAULY CALLED HOALOHA Ao-Smith's parents on Maui. He got a recording. No surprise, he'd heard they were still vital and active retirees. Unbeknownst to him they did not exist.

A few of her friends were listed in her dossier, so Pauly tried that. He managed to get a hold of one associate, a gal pal named Cindy Liu. They'd met when Hoaloha Ao-Smith was in Lahaina to research the historical whaling trade of yesteryear and the unfair practices committed on the locals, this included Chinese immigrants lured away from the cane fields for the higher paying and more exciting life at sea. It was neither. They were treated horribly by the mostly Puritan New Englanders who considered their dominance the divine providence of God over whales and brown skinned people alike. Cindy was contacted by Hoaloha because she was a direct descendant of one those abused at sea.

She mentioned something odd to Magat about Hoaloha's purported Chinese heritage. When Cindy brought up a few of the customs and idioms, Hoaloha Ao-Smith looked ignorant and was quick to change the subject, as if she knew nothing of Chinese culture. Cindy figured it was her "Haolified" upbringing. But what also stood out was Hoaloha Ao-Smith's insistence that Cindy and her friends call her by her familial nickname Ming, which was short for 黎明 Límíng. It was in all likelihood her way to engender her Chinese self to them and pump them for information for her newspaper article.

When Paul asked her what 黎明 Límíng meant, Cindy said it meant sunrise, or dawn.

Alejo Melendez

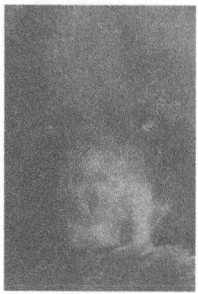

Amassing

IT WAS THREE in the afternoon when half the force descended upon the Star Bulletin Advertiser News building. The seven-story, light black monolith stood erect and distinct from the surrounding shorter white and grey buildings. The beaches of Kalapana could be seen shimmering off her western abutment. Two SWAT vehicles crawled noiselessly into the parking lot. The editor-in-chief was covertly called and asked to quietly and systematically evacuate the top floor. To evacuate all seven floors would not only take too long but the amassing crowd would draw their target's suspicion. Her huge picture window faced south and looked down directly onto one side of the four-sided parking lots surrounding her rectangular high rise and the lobby's main entrance and exit.

    Blueprints of the building had been obtained and studied and a rock-solid plan of attack was put in place. They were seconds away from executing it.

Creaking Door

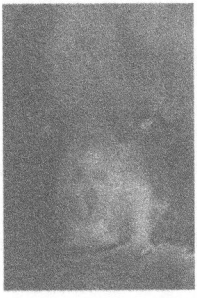

Taken

ZORA VUKOVICH WAS taken without a fight. She'd actually been surprised when the cops knocked on her office door. She had no idea it was coming. It was actually anti-climactic, especially for the two detectives who had spent so much time and energy solving it. They had no problem with that.

Meeting Paul Magat a few days ago had shaken her but all seemed quiet on the western front so, for her, life resumed as normal. There was no hint of recognition in his eyes. To her, the man, like everyone else, was totally fooled and bought the manufactured persona wholesale.

She was banging out another check sheet for her next big story when a soft knock was heard. "Come in," she quipped thinking it was an associate coming to cross reference a story. A SWAT commander simply walked in with weapon drawn and his red dot pointed straight between Zora's tits. Two more SWAT team members followed and Magat and Laplatt brought up the rear.

So engrossed in her byline, Zora did not look up until three heart stopping seconds later.

"Hands where I can see them!" was the only thing yelled during the entire arrest.

Zora had a calm accepting look when she obeyed, and this told the cops there would be no trouble. They were still careful but spoke in normal, even hushed, tones when declaring her under arrest and giving her Mirandas.

She was surrounded. She made eye contact with the detectives only briefly. She mostly hung her head throughout the ordeal.

Mark Tam stealing her virtue, drugged and raped by callous anonymous boys in college, then watching her best friend marry the man she never forgot or forgave; all of this insanity immediately came flooding back and became the albatross around her neck. The physical weight of that huge metaphorical bird forcing her head to droop could almost be felt as well as seen. She had operated unknown and unchallenged with ruthless and unswerving power over her dominion, imposing and manipulating others to do her bidding, and now her head sagged in shame, acceptance, and defeat.

Heavy lies the head that wears the crown for it is but an albatross around the neck. Sullen and morose echoes arose from an empty office four doors down: All hail, the Queen is dead, long live the Queen.

This was the same empty office that had her bosses and coworkers stumped. They believed it an eccentricity, but Hoaloha's work and results allowed them to indulge her. She never gave a reason but all believed it was for extra storage, although it was never cluttered. Some thought it a meditative sanctuary because of the farming artifacts, paintings of crop fields, miniature farm equipment like combines, threshers, and silos, some of them bronze but most plastic. A framed reproduction of American Gothic and a Nebraska Cornhusker football pennant adorned the wall behind an empty organized desk. It was all very enigmatic but for the most part left unquestioned. Star power had its privileges.

Hours later, after processing, after giving her a meal, and after giving Zora her new prison issue clothes in her holding cell, she was brought to a cold, dark, starkly painted off-white colored room with an old fashioned two strip fluorescent tube light fixture mounted on the ceiling. The lighting tubes were old and yellowing at the ends, but at least they were not flickering. The two detectives were already in place. She declined legal representation, which was surprising. She said it was all kind of a big relief and would be willing to make a statement in writing. But first she had some questions.

Laplatt held up his palm, the universal "halt" signal. They were first going to tell her what they knew, what they could prove. This was designed to serve as a template to help ensure her statement would be accurate, truthful, and consistent with what they now knew as the facts of the case.

In no ordered sequence, Magat and Laplatt took turns spilling the long sordid tale of the destruction Zora had caused and how they painstakingly put the many pieces together that led them to her.

They named all of the players and all of the motives and all of the methods. First was the spurned love from Mark when she was newly-turned eighteen, then the rape at Stanford which furthered her mental instability. Next, from Kelly's disclosure, came the mailed family photo and discovery that Kelly had married Mark and that Mark, to Zora's knowledge, had fathered a daughter with Kelly. Then an unexplained fifteen-year gap back in Halsey where they figured, correctly, she laid low in a perpetual state of trauma. Then one day she was inexplicably motivated to take action, booked a flight to LAX, got a new identity sometime in that interim, made her way to Hawaii and then used her incomplete communications degree to get a job at the newspaper.

They knew being a reporter gave her sources, and she used them to gather intelligence. She recruited Ken and Kerry Herzog, Eunice Paxton, and Judith Halawa, who then used manufactured information from Zora to ultimately manipulate James Kanoho into attempting murder.

They knew she used Ken to pay off Eunice who had access to Alanitrol. James knew Mark's new canteen was drugged but did not do it himself, so that was another charge on Zora. There were a few odds and ends but the detectives seemed to have tied it all nicely together.

There was something they needed to ask her.

"One thing Zora.. how did you get the drug into the canteen?"

"Easy," she boasted, "I gave Judith Halawa a modified package to give to James.."

She explained her method while savoring the memory and daydreaming the most likely scenario...

One glorious warm sunshiny day before their impending trip to Alberta, Mark's brand spanking new field canteen was presented to him by his wife Kelly. It had been given to *her* by James along with some rudimentary instructions.

Mark took hold of the canteen, still pristine in its tight stretched plastic wrapping and bright, open faced cardboard encasing. He used a knife to breach the impossibly tough packaging, caught a whiff of the newness of it, then handed it back to his wife.

Kelly picked up some of the carboard that it came with.

"Look Honey, it says it's already pre-sterilized and ready to use. And it even comes with a few of those flavor packets designed to replace electrolytes. I'm gonna rinse this out anyway and fill it with some of that electrolyte stuff OK? I'll just put it in with your camo like we always do."

They were sitting at the kitchen table, so Mark watched as Kelly performed this innocuous wifely routine and favor, just like she did before each hunt which required check-in luggage. He liked having it prefilled with good, clean Hawaiian mountain water instead of whatever might be awaiting him in places like Bosnia. The residents of the Makaha Valley had prehistoric mountain dikes as their reservoirs, and the rain water that kept them filled and filtrated through them was famous for its purity. After she had filled the canteen and added one of the packets—the grape flavored one like James had instructed—Mark took it from her.

"I'll put it in my bag hon, I'm gonna add a few more things

Creaking Door

before I close it down."

Once Zora had relayed this likely scenario, she snapped out of her reverie and told the detectives that "the final piece of the puzzle was for James to remove the canteen and dispose of it."

But of course he never got the chance to clean the site by using the Alanitrol or taking hold of the canteen.

What was once convoluted was now crystal clear. What was once a total mystery has now had every avenue solved. Her trail and her crimes were brilliant albeit sick and perverse. The cops were thrown at every turn. It was bizarre, it was cruel and abhorrent, it was brilliant, and it was probably going to allow her to plead not guilty by reason of mental defect. The genius contained in her crimes showed no lacking in her confession. You can say many things about the heinous and horrible nature of her crimes, but it is hard to dispute it was all born from a bona fide lunacy, the legal kind.

Zora sat there and began her series of questions, all of which pertained to how the detectives were able to find her after she'd taken such painstaking measures to disappear then hide in plain sight.

Henri took this one. He said he'd caught a lucky break when by chance he researched her Croatian heritage. Zora means Dawn in her ancestral tongue. And the Croatian name Nowak translates to Novak, thus Dawn Novak was correctly connected to Zora and searched for high and low but to no avail.

Then Magat says he placed a picture of her Hoaloha persona on his desk because he truly admired her work as a journalist and also because he was developing a boyhood crush on her, like he did with Kim Novak. Novak made him think of Nowak and back to the Croation name conversion link. He juxtaposed the surveillance photo of her and the framed photo on his desk. The resemblance was almost nonexistent. So some deep digging showed Hoaloha Ao-Smith had received plastic surgery twice, an eye procedure two years ago as Dawn Novak, and two and half months ago as Hoaloha in Beverly Hills. They even procured a list of the exact procedures. Zora said she paid a ton of money for that surgeon's discretion. Pauly smiled and said she wasn't the only one with sources.

The final straw was her latest identity. While Hoaloha means friend, Ao means dawn. The added Smith was a nice touch to compensate via association her inescapable haole looks. Even the spray tan she applied every day and the streaked hair dye job were no match for the keen eye of Pauly Boy Magat.

Zora smiled. They had outsmarted her when she believed herself infallible. She asked for some cold bottled water. When it came three minutes later, she calmly took a sip and grabbed the generic blue bic pen, was handed a standard yellow legal notepad and began detailing the horrors and pathways of her very sordid adult life.

It would take Zora three hours to submit her final draft, all seventeen pages. It was beautiful yet distasteful, articulate yet venomous, with every word and sentence grammatically correct and professionally written. It is said that people suffering multiple personality disorders will often have beautiful penmanship belonging to at least one of the personalities. Her stunning and striking handwritten script was like staring at calligraphy. Furthermore, like Lincoln's eloquence, her statement was in uncomplicated Midwestern prose.

Unforgettable to the two detectives who sat there witnessing its execution were the haunting physical and emotional words of a madwoman.

Creaking Door

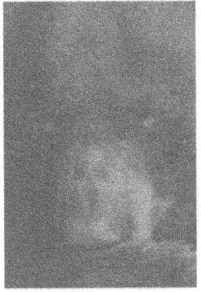

Part

PAULY AND HENRI, both non-huggers, grasped each other's mitts in a handshake so firm it could turn charcoal briquettes into diamonds.

They'd been through a lot and that bond and those feelings were coming to the fore. They weren't touchy-feely types who expressed their feelings openly, but today they each came damned close.

Henri refused the lei Magat's department made for him. Pauly Boy insisted. It was a Hawaiian tradition, a big part of the culture, and everyone would be offended if Pauly didn't bring back proof Henri had worn it. So the phone camera was utilized, the bedecked Inspector bearing a genuine maple syrupy Canuck style grin. Then Paul had a stranger take one of them together. And then it was time to part ways.

They'd done good works and effected real change on a national and even international level with the Rohypnol ring bust and the crossing of borders between Magat's neighbors to the north. A lot of hard work was done by some very good and dedicated people, spearheaded by these two knuckleheads.

Henri was on the next flight out, and just when he was starting to like the warmth. An online check revealed a twenty-seven degree morning in Edmonton with an afternoon high of thirty-eight. Home sweet home. He walked through the departure terminal alone. He told Pauly to get on back and keep Hawaii safe.

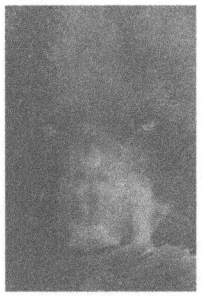

Ward

ZORA'S MENTAL ILLNESS was verified by the best doctors and defense attorneys her grief-stricken family could buy. She'd finally cracked, it was believed, at about the time she received that family photo of Kelly and her husband and daughter. Mark taking her innocence, Stanford and the humiliation, there was simply too much weight on her back to withstand whatever final straw was being placed upon it; in this case that fateful photo Kelly had innocently sent so long ago now.

The descent into madness was a slow and inevitable one culminating in a not so rare form of stress induced multiple personality disorder. She truly believed she was a local island girl, the ultra-confident Hoaloha Ao-Smith, being followed around by her farm girl best friend, the painfully shy Dawn Novak who preferred to hover in the darkened and unlit background of secrecy and criminal brilliance. They were perfect complimentary alter egos. They were one in the same person.

Zora, who appeared at various intervals, had all but surrendered her existence to those two dominant personas. So complete was Dawn's separate existence and reality to Hoaloha that she actually fell in love with her and believed they were in a deep committed relationship. That kind of self-absorbed self-infatuation was extremely rare medically and was THE extenuating and mitigating factor in Zora's otherwise standard and lucid insanity defense.

All Zora has left now are her daydreams, which not surprisingly become more vivid as she settles deeper into the isolation and deprivation of a prison mental ward. In one of her rare moments of clarity she has recollections, and one of them harkens back to when she was sixteen. Willa's cat Hera often visited neighboring farms, travelling great distances at times. But Zora and Willa's houses were separated, as the crow flies, by a mere two miles, and Hera made this nightly round easily. The Vukovich barn was teeming with mice, and they welcomed the feline visitor, fed her and treated her as one of their own animals.

Zora loved her. But one night, in a depressed and psychotic state, she committed her first murder when she zoned out and beheaded the beloved cat. She did not recall it the next morning, nor the next. This memory surfaced years later as her illness progressed, and she was still not apologetic about it, though she really couldn't tell anybody why. For weeks Willa had asked about Hera and Zora answered truthfully that she did not know.

Another memory is from the age of eighteen. A month after Zora's return from vacation she noticed she had not gotten her period, which was due the week before. She paid it no mind, farm life kept her busy and college considerations needed to be organized.

When it did not arrive the next month she thought she was sick. The only one she could turn to was Willa, who was worldlier on such matters and on boys in general because Zora suspected it had something to do with a boy.

Willa took her to a doctor in Brewster two towns over to the east, well away from small town Halsey gossip. Two days later Zora received the dreaded news that she was indeed pregnant. She clung to the phone but failed to hear the rest of the doctor's words; her world was now effectively over as she knew it. Willa advised her to get an abortion. At her age and in her situation, there were really no other options and therefore no other real discussions of such.

Zora had only heard of such farfetched alien things, and now she was going to have this unnatural act performed on her. There was only one possible father, and he was thirty-five hundred miles away and ignoring her.

When it was over Zora became zombie-like in her numb and auto-piloted performance of her chores. She plodded on courageously to avoid suspicion from her parents, who never suspected a thing. This led to the complete absence of any familial support and also the resulting opposite effect of a void of shame, and it also led to the kind of combustible internal pressure dark secrets like that can often have.

When the fog lifted and the physical soreness had healed, two very crucial things remained; guilt and confusion. Following that abortion Zora now saw herself as a murderer, and the proverbial clock was now ticking.

The prison compound was located on a lava field that had once flowed into the ocean seven miles away. You could smell the ocean, and at night you could actually hear it. Only the guards roosting in the watch towers high above the walls could see it. The waters were restricted ten miles out and ten miles wide, and the prison was equipped with maritime sensors. Any incoming boats hoping to affect any kind of escape would have been detected immediately by both the corrections officers and the coast guard.

Because of her elaborate planning and the malice driving it all, Zora was convicted of murder and given life rather than the court's allowing the marauding bear to minimize it to manslaughter. She pleaded insanity and is being custodially treated in a state correctional psychiatric ward and will eventually be transferred to a minimum-security state prison built on the same remote lava field on the Big Island. She writes an activities column for the psychiatric ward's in-house newsletter, which is published once a month. Her current deadline is quite leisurely and offers no pressure whatsoever. She is allowed to write for the prison paper as Hoaloha Ao-Smith, no longer as a function of her delusions but as a professional pseudonym from which she no longer associates. The nom de plume still carries great weight and increases readership. There are still loyal fans, even in prison, of the famous and now notorious "*Hawaiian*" newspaper reporter.

Creaking Door

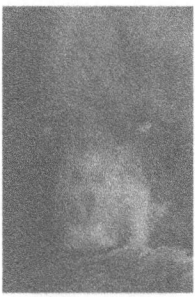

Full Circle

FAST FORWARD ONE YEAR

DR. SUSAN ZAO is all smiles as she attends commencement ceremonies and watches her daughter Alanis receive her MS in Biology. She has graduated pre-med and will go on to Johns Hopkins next year to begin the slow process of becoming a board-certified physician so she can mend the injured, something she is all too familiar with. With counseling, therapy, and most importantly time, Alanis has not only healed but thrived upon her return to school. She was even well enough to volunteer in a mentorship program.

Among her class load was an elective Asian American Studies Class. Alanis wanted to know more about her Chinese heritage as it pertained to their presence and influence in this country. The edification was interesting, surprising, and depressing all at the same time. That people like her mother and father had overcome the unspeakable abuses her Chinese ancestors endured in this country was beyond noble.

Through that same class Alanis met the perfect underclassman protégé. A beautiful young woman who also bore a Chinese surname and stood out among the other students because of her diligence, grades, and her quiet determined demeanor.

An hour after the ceremonies Alanis finds her mother and approaches her with this younger friend.

"Mom," says Alanis enthusiastically and with pride, "This is my mentee Leinaala Tam. The bright girl I was telling you about."

Susan extends her hand warmly. Leinaala is as lovely as her name and obviously a native Hawaiian. They walk and speak about her future plans here at Columbia. Leinaala, like Alanis, was experiencing an arrested development and also had her studies interrupted by a family crisis. When they both found that out about each other, the bond was forged even stronger and tempered by the common thread of devastation and heritage. Leinaala would not find out about the Zao's connection to Alanitrol until several years later. Ironic in that it was so vital in the investigation of her father's death. It did not change her deep abiding affection for the Zao family. She and Alanis would remain close friends for life.

Susan, who was now on the Board, offered Lei a summer job at the new Bannon Industries Hawaiian facility which manufactured meds for distribution throughout Asia, the advantage being cheaper shipping costs than those loading docks in New Jersey. It would be a perfect opportunity for her to be home and earn good money and most of all keep busy moving forward with her shattered life. Uncle Jimmy became a major shareholder a few years ago before Alanitrol became a household name, his interest fostered by and mostly due to the infamous trial. His grander vision of Hawaii being a technological bridge to Asia has become a reality in the manifestation of Bannon Industries erecting, at Jimmy's insistence and influence, a complete manufacturing plant on the leeward side of Oahu, in the town of Aiea where he attended grade school. Many of his lifelong friends and their families received preferential treatment for the highly sought-after employment the new facility provided.

A joint task force spent the last thirty months investigating a

Creaking Door

huge Rohypnol drug ring initiated by a lead uncovered unintentionally by Laplatt and Magat. It immediately became the Fed's problem and they gladly took the ball and rolled with it. Two and a half years later a press conference was being held to announce they'd finally cracked it.

At the end of his nickel stint in State Prison for the rape of Alanis Zao, David Mackin had done something surprisingly complicated and successful with his life; unfortunately that something was to build a large illegal drug corporation from a rich, white neighborhood no one would have ever suspected as the hub of a criminal enterprise by so young an evil entrepreneur.

The ring was being run out of an affluent Northern California suburb called Los Gatos, and the ringleader was that same now freed convicted rapist David Mackin. He was a Stanford graduate with enough brains and organizational skills to pull off something that massive. It was also discovered his tendrils extended throughout North America, to Canada and Mexico. He was in bed with the Sinaloa cartel and using their distribution network to pawn his poison as far south as Nicaragua.

Federal prosecutors convicted Mackin with overwhelming evidence. Two consecutive ninety year sentences without the possibility of parole were what the court imposed based on his previous heinous rape conviction, the massive scope of the drug operation, and the direct connection between both.

He was taken back to State Prison for a quick one day hold while the Feds made arrangements. There he renewed a few acquaintances, took a farewell punch in his gut from a guard he had mouthed off to, then was transferred to Federal prison to serve the remainder of his sentences. He will come to be known as Duncan in his new cell block not because he is Scottish, which he is not (Mackin is Irish), but because he will have his doughnut glazed every week. Mackin was destined to die of old age in Federal prison but for the cartel's enormous reach. When it is rumored that Mackin will turn songbird in hopes of an early release and witness protection enrollment, the only thing he will get early is a fatal shank to his jugular, courtesy of the Sinaloa cartel.

Kelly was exonerated and lives alone in the same house on the beach. She has remodeled it, added extensions, had it painted Kelly green and Cornhusker red with maize yellow trim, and surfs when the waves are just right; not too big and not too small. Along with her blonde hair, surfers in the valley call her Goldilocks. She will sometimes think of her brothers, especially poor Ken and Kerry, in prison now more for their stupidity than anything else. Every one of her siblings, through a peculiarity of her late parents, had first names that started with the letter "K."

A distant memory puts a smile on her lips. A young swashbuckling Jimmy Kanoho is teaching her to surf at Waikiki. She cannot stand up and is frustrated by the endeavor. She knows she will never be able to master this impossible aquatic skill that bears a powerful prejudice against land lubbers, Nebraskans in particular.

She has never been happier and awaits her daughter's imminent annual summer return from her Ivy League schooling in the very Big Apple. Kelly never falls off her surfboard anymore.

James Kanoho pleaded down to five years for attempted murder with some very unusual mitigating circumstances. He is getting out in three for good behavior. It did not hurt his cause that the prosecutor and the judge had all been guests at the Awaawa during its annual charity golf tournament in past years, though this was never discussed at allocution. He was also shown consideration for his avoiding a lengthy trial at taxpayer expense. He is scheduled to be released from his reduced sentence in two months. Jimmy has run the family business so well that James will finally retire and give up virtually all control.

Despite the horrendous turmoil she has been put through, Kuialoha Kanoho still loves her husband and is willing to forgive him and, like Alanis Zao, has allowed time to heal most but not all of her wounds. She has never once visited James at Halawa State

Creaking Door

Prison, ironically where Judith Halawa is also incarcerated for her part in the conspiracy. Judith is serving her time in the women's facility.

Kui has, however, written to her husband exactly three times, once a year on their anniversary, and finds she rather enjoys the solitude his imprisonment has afforded. Like Kelly, she too has made changes to the household, though not as drastic, just enough to put her touch on the place knowing her contrite husband will soon be ponying up to whatever future changes she will demand.

Ken, Kerry, and Eunice were all given hard time at Leavenworth when the federal government chose to make examples out of them for mail fraud. It was their misfortune that a string of terroristic crimes was being perpetrated using the US Mail at the time of their trials. White powdery substances were being sent in the guise of biological warfare, nasty stuff like anthrax. Once in a while those powders were the real thing. And so it went for what prosecutors and the press had dubbed the three postal felons: the phony express. It was hard time for some white trash who allowed their small feeble minds and their petty greed to let a criminal mastermind manipulate them. Vernon Bosworth was not charged.

Kimo and Francine did indeed have their day in court and were prosecuted in near record time. Kimo is doing a dime in Federal prison for his part in the Mackin connection, perhaps unfairly so. His third week in the joint he cold cocked a black inmate twice his size and broke his jaw. Kimo was given two weeks in the hole and emerged as the king of the Polynesian brotherhood.

Francine's sentence is the Federal female equivalent. She has a television in her private cell and all the cigarettes North Carolina can produce annually. Francine does not smoke but the cigs are as good as gold in the pen. She has become the runaway favorite consort of the guards, male and female alike. She continues to slide on her exceptional good looks.

Jimmy and Kelly have once again resumed their long dormant

love affair and, like the first time eons ago, they do not overtly move about town with public displays of affection like their arms around each other or even hand holding. It is not exactly a secret in the Makaha Valley but everyone appreciates their discretion. Marriage is out of the question, at least for now. With Leinaala being his half-sister it would be too weird. Again like the first go 'round, they are content to enjoy the strictly physical pleasures two healthy adults with vigorous athletic bodies and appetites can pleasure and bestow upon each other. Discreetly.

In death, Jimmy has forgiven Mark. He did not know until after the fact how angry Mark actually had been, not just at him but at everything and everybody, so complete was Mark's deception. But it was all a misunderstanding. Despite the rumors and what Mark personally came to believe, Jimmy never once rekindled his romance with Kelly while the pair was married. He loved Mark that much then and enough to forgive him now. They were the brothers neither one had.

The Awaawa runs like a well-oiled machine. They operate at full capacity ninety-nine percent of the time. With such untold success, Jimmy is often asked why he doesn't expand and open up more hotels, acquire more property. James once taught Jimmy a valuable lesson, one he imparted when Jimmy was very young, perhaps seven years old, and again reminded on the day he relinquished control. He told Jimmy that wealth is a bonfire. You can feed it, fan it, and make it bigger. Stand back and admire its largesse and brilliance. But you will use up all of your fuel faster. Big fires will warm you but at a greater distance. You can only use what is on the edges; the center of a big fire is unreachable, therefore unusable. They are harder to control, can become unsafe very quickly, and they will consume anything they can touch. Rather than make your bonfire bigger than you will actually need, keep it manageable; one should enjoy it knowing it is safe, use its light to read by, its fire to slow cook by, and its heat to warm you when you stand comfortably close to it. You will have to feed it

Creaking Door

regularly, but you should only do so to maintain it, never to exceed your actual needs. Your fuel will last longer. Too much wealth is a good way to get burned.

Willadean Janzen came home summers from Ohio State University to work in her parent's diner. When Kelly's parents were killed by those repulsive Stinson boys years ago in a horrible head-on collision just up the highway, many peace officers responded to such an unusual occurrence in that part of Halsey. One of those officers was a handsome young man who had a commanding presence, helped control the chaos, directed traffic late into the night, took diligent investigative notes from the numerous interviews he conducted the rest of that week, and ended up catching the Janzen family's fancy. He became a regular at the diner and would stop in with his family for lunch every Sunday after Mass. Officer Ogden Jessup sat in the same booth with his wife and three sons. The one closest in age to young Willa was Arlen, and he would continue his patronage to the Janzen diner for years to come.

Eventually twenty-four-year-old newly deputized Sherriff Arlen Jessup worked up the nerve to ask twenty-one-year-old Willa out. They saw each other for an entire summer, the one between Willa's junior and senior year.

Willadean went on to meet and fall in love with a pre-law student from the University early in her sophomore year and married him at the start of senior year. Like Kelly, Willa had every intention of breaking away from farm life. She cared deeply for Arlen but knew he would be an anchor to the shallow waters of Halsey. There was a big wide world out there and she wanted to spread her own mainsail and cast it onto the winds of fate and explore the geography beyond the prairie oceans of Nebraska; Willa's ship needed to sail. Arlen was handsome, spry, and very good in bed. His second big flaw that Willa simply could not overlook was his disgusting and distasteful use of chewing tobacco.

Willa went through senior year with an unplanned pregnancy.

Alejo Melendez

She gave birth two months before graduation. Her husband finished law school two and a half years later with honors and landed at a big firm outside of Columbus. He eventually made partner. Life and family have both turned out exceptionally well for Willadean.

Without telling her husband as of yet, she has finally unburdened a two decades old secret. Sherriff Arlen Jessup has recently learned he has an adult daughter. She is twenty-one now and looks just like her mother, Willa. For now, only Arlen and Willa know. Plans on just how to break this to her family, especially their secret daughter, are still in the works. Into Willa's perfect life a little rain must fall.

Winter had arrived in The Great White North. It was twenty-two degrees outside with a wind-chill of four. Everyone was hunkered down inside of the fortified Edmonton Police Department. Janet Rousseau has been forgiven her egregious error in the infamous Mark Tam murder case. She has, in fact, thrived and is now assistant supervisory director of skin tissue and blood, via a made-up promotion to a position designed to console a completely distraught rookie forensic scientist who had a major priority unfairly thrust into her lap.

Henri Laplatt sits comfortably in his office thankful for the eighty-five degrees he maintains year round. The truth is the maintenance people are hard to get a hold of, and they can never get to his work order request inside of two weeks. They are backlogged and everything they do has to be approved by the entire fuckin' Canadian Parliament figuratively speaking. And when the thermostat *IS* tweaked it takes another two weeks for the mechanical adjustments to kick in and regulate. So he just leaves it and wears short sleeves in the summer. He'd wear shorts if it were allowed.

He is looking out of his icily framed and snow encrusted window watching the snow fall sideways in the God-forsaken arctic wind that has the whole of Alberta in its frozen grip. It is pretty to look at but deadly to be in. He is thinking of that Ruben he'd had

Creaking Door

for lunch his first day in Hawaii and the clean streets of Waikiki. There were uniformed cops on bicycle patrol wearing shorts. He thinks of that life and smiles, then thinks of the starting salary those guys make and frowns. The phone rings. This weather is a natural crime deterrent and he is almost thankful for the phone's startling clang.

"Laplatt." It is the way he always answers, even at home.

He listens and stares at the miserable snow piling up in what is now ten-foot drifts and sure to double by the end of his shift. A big smile creases his lips. It is Pauly Boy Magat. After pleasantries Henri is told there is an opening in HPD Homicide, they are looking for someone with at least six years of experience, and Pauly Boy, its lead detective, has recommended his favorite Canadian for the job.

Alejo Melendez

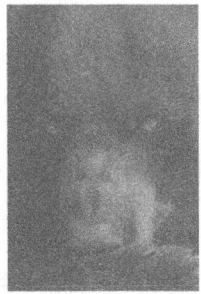

Limpy

JIMMY HAS NOT returned to Alberta since he was released from Edmonton's custody. That he harbors lingering resentment is quite natural. If he ever saw Laplatt or the correction officer Fenton out in the woods he would shoot them on sight.

But here he sits on a plane bound for Edmonton International. An attractive flight attendant has brought him a cup of dark roasted coffee with cream and two Splendas. It is piping hot and in a cardboard cup with an old-fashioned pair of flimsy handles that need to be unfolded off of the sides of the cup. They do their level best to impersonate cup handles, have hollowed centers for your fingers to grasp, and have always reminded Jimmy of Chimpanzee ears. The attendant is blonde and in her upper forties but still sports a sexy figure and youthful facial skin; she must avoid the sun like deer smelling one of his old football game jerseys. It would not be a mistaken assumption that these are unspoken requirements of the airline industry. She smiles at Jimmy and he feels aroused. But, he notices, she is smiling at everybody. Yet he knows her smile towards him has a distinctly different tick and upturn to it. He's still got it.

He has kept in touch with his good friend JSP over the years. He has flown him out to Hawaii a few times to hunt. JSP is in awe of the grandeur of the Awaawa. He thinks it makes his mighty log cabin lodge look like a hobo's lean-to by comparison. Jimmy jokingly tells JSP his pile of campfire wood can only *aspire* to be a hobo's lean to. Their back and forth has grown lovingly more acerbic over the years.

One day last week JSP places a call to Jimmy and tells him *THE* bear has been shot. That is all that needed to be said. In less than thirty-six hours Jimmy is booked and on a plane taking a flight he has refused to make in two decades.

The bear will not be kept in cold storage but rather processed immediately whereby Jimmy will offer to purchase its fur from its rightful owner whom, he is told, is willing to part with it. The grand old age is a rarity but not entirely unheard of. There have been bears, especially black bears, known to reach upwards of thirty years.

He is unsure where he will place that bearskin rug but a gathering area in the hotel lobby with a large, crescent-shaped moss rock fireplace would be ideal. The light colorings of the furniture and the ivory white walls will contrast nicely with the dark lava tones and the blackness of the bear. It will surely make a great conversation piece for years to come, but Jimmy will never tell the delicate and morbid tale of its origin. Rather he will demur and tell folks the "other" truth; that it was a generous gift from some very thoughtful Canadian friends.

It lays in the Awaawa for a mere three months when Jimmy realizes he cannot abide its presence. JSP is invited to a Maui buck hunt with Ray Espinoza and Uncle Kaimana. At the end of his weeklong visit he is asked to allow the bearskin to accompany him back to Mount Becker. His grand lodge would be a far more fitting home for the bear and the powerful and sorrowful memories it evokes upon the Kanoho and Tam families.

About two months before Jimmy returned to Edmonton, a man named Randall Whitaker and his dad Chet were on their annual spring hunt for bear. They were both up in the same tree stand with a platform big enough for three people. Chet was holding a video camera. Randall, the fourteen-year-old boy who found James Kanoho's bottle of Alanitrol, is now a grown man with his own small first-grader and sports tattoos and a soul patch. He held fast to his new, more powerful rifle, the .338 Winchester Magnum mounted with a Vortex Optics Strike Eagle Scope, 30mm 1-6x24mm with a .5 MOA Adjustment. It is serious equipment for a serious hunter. His original boyhood rifle is being held for his now six-year-old boy for when he is a bit older and ready to join them. Randall figures about three more years ought to do it. Avid hunters, the Whitakers have taken excellent care of their guns over the years and none of them have ever misfired or malfunctioned.

The biggest bear they had ever seen wandered into their peripheral vision. It was a little over a hundred yards away but with this gun, it was well within range. Its size and its labored movement was clear evidence this was a very old bear. It needed to be put down.

Randall lined it up and did not hesitate. The bear was on all fours and in profile. His previous kills had polished his sighting abilities and this huge monster, its distance, and its innate animal caution were no match. The blast echoed throughout the forest. Birds and chipmunks alike scattered with the quickness of a mountain lion on the chase. The bear jumped, sprinted away, and then went down. Chet and son whooped it up. Ten short minutes later they were on the ground practically running toward the blood trail. Chet reminded his son it would be best to slow down "just in case." The bear's final resting place was in a clearing thirty yards from where Randall's bullet first penetrated its lungs. Its head was as big as a medicine ball, its paws as large as catcher's mitts.

When game wardens processed the Whitaker's tag and their kill, confirmation as well as relief was had. The notorious man-eater had at long last been killed. Word spread quickly. The necropsy turned up Jimmy's bullet still buried in its left hind quarter. Jimmy also wanted that as a memento.

Creaking Door

The Whitakers would not accept any payment from Jimmy. The history of heartache and the injustice appropriated by their local government to Jimmy was well known and they offered its pelt as a gift of contrition not on behalf of their appointed officials but as decent citizens and fellow hunters. That abnormally large bearskin could have fetched thousands on any open market. Its symbolic notoriety and direct connection to the infamous trial morbidly elevated it to "priceless" in the collector's market. The Whitakers could have surely used that kind of supplement but steadfastly refused. The history and symbolism was too odious for any hunter to do anything but hand it over to the mistreated Jimmy Kanoho, not as a charitable gesture, rather a moral one.

For obvious reasons, the meat from the bear affectionately but notoriously dubbed "Limpy" was never eaten. For one thing the grand old man was just that; too old. Jimmy asked that it be buried in the forest so part of Mark could join his spilled blood and lay eternally with the wilderness he so dearly loved. The rest of him was of course circumnavigating the earth via the ocean currents he rode and piloted his entire life.

Limpy was the very best his species had to offer. He was bigger, faster, and stronger than the other bears. Even when injured and disadvantaged, he found a way to feed himself and stay alive. He was wily enough to avoid the fate of dozens of his brothers every hunting season during May through June.

It almost seemed that when he was finally put down by a hunter, Randall and Chet noticed he veritably sauntered out into the open like a defeated warrior, battered and ready for his foes to take him. He walked with a haggard and defeated gait, had filmy eyes that squinted with struggle, and sniffed at the air desperately as if he had sponges stuffed in both nostrils. It was as if he himself knew it was time, and rather than die a naturally slow and torturous death from his old age, he gave himself up to the species he had once taken one of, as if paying it all back, leaving this world with a clean, even slate. It was almost as if he left with a clear conscience and on his own inimitable terms.

He WAS able to pass on his genes and those glorious qualities that made him stand alone. He was a magnificent fellow, a survivalist, a king, a worthy adversary, and perhaps the most noble creature the Alberta wilderness has ever produced.

Creaking Door

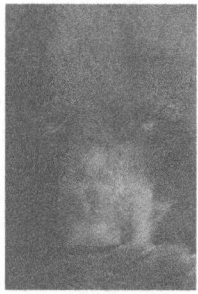

Closing

WARM SUNSHINE CASCADES down upon the Makaha Valley. Its beauty timeless, its rhythms still whimsical, its greeneries still opulent. Jimmy sees all of this as he is transported from an ambulance into his parent's house, a house he himself has lived in with his beautiful wife of thirty-seven years, Kelly. This will be the last time eighty-year old Jimmy Kanoho will feast his eyes upon his longtime coastal home and valley. Jimmy has come home for the final time. He is in the concluding stage of prostate cancer and there is nothing more the doctors and the hospital can do. It is his wish to return to Makaha for his absolution.

He has lived a good life and raised a wonderful, loving family; two children and seven grandchildren. Three people are in the room with him; his wife and their two children. Many more remain outside; friends, relatives, politicians, dignitaries, and hotel guests past and present; it is but a small country bedroom and there is a spatial and oxygenation issue preventing more people from paying their respects up close and personally. Hotel staff have placed a multitude of tables and chairs on the Kanoho's massive yard in anticipation of this. Jimmy has accomplished much, seen much, and loved much. He has treated everyone who deserved it fairly, and he will die happy knowing all of this.

Alejo Melendez

As his gathered family talk amongst themselves in whispers and murmurs, Jimmy lets out a low wistful moan. He is in and out of consciousness. His closed eyelids flicker with the movements of dream, of recollections of a life full and fulfilled. He seems to will something he has longed to see for a very long time now. There is a flash, a brilliant speeding light, a feeling of transport, a sudden stop, then a whiteness that is not exactly like the color but totally encompassing and ethereal. He sees his best friend Mark Tam, he is young. So too is Jimmy now. Mark stands holding the cut crystal knob of a fifteen-foot arched white door. Jimmy feels he is about to enter Heaven beyond this threshold and Mark is some kind of guiding Angel to lead him through this portal of eternity. But instead Mark simply opens the door, and it creaks. It is a wailing elk, a Tyson, and soon Jimmy and Mark are on the aether floor laughing their Heavenly asses off.

Silence follows. Jimmy closes his eyes and without flourish breathes his last. There are respectful and loving tears, no overly dramatic banshee wailings from the classy Kanoho clan. The portable home monitor flatlines its monotonous and continuous beep.

Some men die in fear amid chaos and violence, like soldiers on the battlefield with whistling projectiles in ballistic flight all about them as blasted clods upheave and cast themselves outward into bodily crevices that were thought impenetrable. Some die coldly, unhonored, and undistinguished, like victims of a senseless violent crime, especially the ones who never get identified and are buried in the anonymous Potter's Fields of the world. Some thrill-seeking men, like rogue mountain climbers who tackle their challenges solo, will die in remote, desolate places and will be lucky to have their bodies eventually found. And some men die to the laud of cheering masses, like a hated dictator who has long ago stopped caring that his people suffer while he continues to live off the fat of the land gathered on the broken backs of those he was sworn to serve.

Creaking Door

Makaha is beautiful today, radiant with its verdant and russet sharp valley ridges and the deep cyan of a gentle rolling beach break; frightfully erect black basalt formations with volcanically sharp edges stand at attention like sculptured sentries and contrast eternally with the ubiquitous white sands at their base that patiently seek to dominate the land and obscure the rock soldiers one centimeter at a time, one big-wave winter at a time.

It is Kelly, nearest to Jimmy and a healthy seventy-eight years young, who finally, lovingly, turns off the toggle switch. It begins a peaceful transition and gift not every man is granted nor deserves in death—a blanket of comfort and love as well as a welcoming darkness, an old friend from our humble beginnings in the womb where we were nestled within the sound of a loving, protective silence.

Alejo Melendez

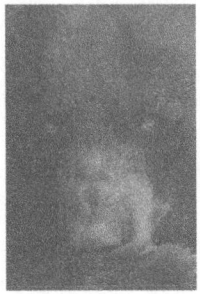

Appendix

Author's Personal Views on Hunting

IN THE FOLLOWING notes I have used my fictional characters Jimmy and Mark as representatives of the responsible hunting community.

Not all, but MOST hunters will try to use all of the animal; the meat, the fur, and the hide. Jimmy doesn't know any purely trophy hunters himself. Most of the hunters in Jimmy and Mark's orbit are harvesters of a natural resource, not trophy seekers; they both find that form of killing understandable but somewhat despicable. They both think that killing a lion just to say you killed one, then mount its head in your home to show it off, is a sin and abominable. The meat of flesh-eating predators is generally horrible, too acidic and "gamey" for consumption, even by other animals. Of course there are exceptions to any predicament. Like if the lion/animal is terrorizing a village and has killed humans, or, something far less likely—if there are too many lions in one area and they, unfortunately, need to be managed. Lions, however, seldom overcrowd. Their aggressive territorial instincts make this a self-correcting problem, so the killing of one under this guise is usually a lie and a blanket statement.

Now Jimmy himself does not need the meat per se. He is a strong, well-fed adult male. He *prefers* the game meat. Eating supermarket meat, the kind in Styrofoam and wrapped in cellophane, now THAT he considers cruel. Those poor animals are kept in pens or cages, fed chemicals like hormones and steroids, or genetically modified plant feed, like GMO soy or corn, then slaughtered without once ever having been allowed to roam and graze or even mate out in the open. The trend now is the phrase "grass fed", and this terminology is used to make consumers pay more for the "purity" of this flesh. It is a huge irony for Jimmy and Mark. When the duo kill a buck or a stag, or even most bears, they are harvesting a source of meat that IS grass/vegetation fed and has lived a quality of life that allows for the animal's soul to be happy, therefore every part of its body is happy and healthy and in tune with its environment. In other words, better tasting, better karma too.

Most people will never know this because hunters will always be in the minority. With most of the post-industrial age population migrating to the big cities for work and living in the outlying suburbs, this is just a fact of modern life and has been for over a century now. It is far easier to grab big corporations' processed foods at the local national chain supermarket then it is to brave the weather and wait patiently for a wild animal to present itself and come within range of your gun or bow—let alone having to skin and butcher it. And most folks could never imagine doing the things Jimmy and Mark and all hunters do to mask their scent from those ultra-sensitive noses of their prey, like spraying themselves with deer urine extracts or pheromones.

There is a code that hunters live by, and it is something they call the ethical shot. Jimmy and Mark do not take the shot unless it is virtually guaranteed to be a kill shot. Hunters do not intentionally maim, injure, or wound an animal only to kill it later.

Jimmy and Mark only take a shot to kill the animal humanely, instantly if possible. Hunters don't want the creature to suffer any longer than necessary. Also, an animal not fatally wounded excretes adrenaline, which generally makes the meat bitter. Ideally, hunters call it the double lung shot for obvious reasons. So conditions have to be perfect; a perfect shooting alley in which the animal reveals its flank to the shooter, is at a standstill, and there are no obstacles impeding the bullet's or arrow's path, like branches or herd females or does.

Ideally extraneous conditions like weather should not affect the shot—things like wind, rain, even elevation differences. Some hunters are so highly skilled they can overcome these, but again, ideally, most shooters would prefer the perfect conditions of sunny and windless weather, and not just for their sake or comfort, but so the shot fired will be true and therefore merciful in the harvesting of the game. Also the hunter him or herself should not be nervous, sick, hyperventilating, or worse, ill prepared therefore rushing the shot. Jimmy and Mark will sit there patiently, weapon loaded and at the ready, usually looking to take down a male of the species, but knowing sometimes females have to be managed as well.

There is another thing most people do not consider when it comes to hunters and hunting. They are by and large conservationists and wildlife managers. Take deer for example. Jimmy and Mark only shoot bucks, and they never shoot bucks in their prime. Those are left for breeding and to offer better protection for the herd. Jimmy and Mark always try to take older bucks, males past their prime. Bucks who will likely suffer at the tines of the younger stronger males. Older bucks who have had their chance to pass on their own genes and who will now languish as a weaker member of the herd. This buck no longer serves a natural purpose to its herd, it is now just "hanging around", eating and wandering; the younger bucks will no longer permit it to mate, and so, before it is so old its meat becomes unusable, Jimmy and Mark "manage" it by harvesting it for food, fur, and sometimes

Creaking Door

even the horns are useful as well. Both boys have buckskin apparel from animals they have harvested. And yes, hunters including Jimmy and Mark can tell the older buck by such indicators as its rack, the spacing and condition of the tines, the facial markings, and the size and shape of its body. And most of them hunt seasonally with dedication, and so Jimmy and Mark and especially their outfitters actually get to know the herd, especially the bucks, and so it is with great respect that they watch these animals year after year and follow their paths, their cycles, their journeys as wild, free, and natural beings in their respective environments. Managing bears is no exception. Ursine, like porcine, are terrific breeders and since they are apex predators, their cubs have a fantastic rate of success. We've all heard the expression don't mess with a mama bear.

 Another ridiculous and misinformed phrase whispered amongst the naïve and outdoor challenged is that hunting is not really a sport since "the other participant doesn't know it's playing." Nothing could be further from the truth. These wild animals are BORN knowing there are things in their world that are constantly trying to kill them. They KNOW danger is ubiquitous and are suspicious of EVERY little thing. You can see it in their normal behavior: they are always nervous, wary; twitching ears listening for the faintest sounds, noses constantly sniffing at the wind to try and detect smells of predators, tails twitching in nervous anticipation in what is believed to be an unending flashing of communication with the herd, and, of course, the God-given speed and agility they are blessed with to escape predators and attempted attacks. Their senses are far more acute than any of mankind's, and in this, they have the distinct advantage. There is a well heeded axiom among woodsmen regarding creatures of the wilderness; they see you well before you see them. It is why hunters take long, circuitous routes to their chosen spots then wait hours for the animals to wander into range.

—Alejo Melendez

www.ingramcontent.com/pod-product-compliance
Lightning Source LLC
LaVergne TN
LVHW041331080426
835512LV00006B/397